Loose of Earth

Loose of Earth

A Memoir

Kathleen Dorothy Blackburn

University of Texas Press ✦ Austin

The publication of this book was made possible by the support of the Meyer Levy Fund at the Dallas Foundation.

Requests for permission to reproduce material from this work should be sent to:
    Permissions
    University of Texas Press
    P.O. Box 7819
    Austin, TX 78713-7819
    utpress.utexas.edu

♾ The paper used in this book meets the minimum requirements of ANSI/NISO Z39.48-1992 (R1997) (Permanence of Paper).

Library of Congress Cataloging-in-Publication Data

Names: Blackburn, Kathleen Dorothy, author.
Title: Loose of earth : a memoir / Kathleen Dorothy Blackburn.
Description: First edition. | Austin : University of Texas Press, 2024.
Identifiers: LCCN 2023038207 (print) | LCCN 2023038208 (ebook)
    ISBN 978-1-4773-2962-7 (hardcover)
    ISBN 978-1-4773-2963-4 (adobe pdf)
    ISBN 978-1-4773-2964-1 (epub)
Subjects: LCSH: Blackburn, Kathleen Dorothy. | Children of cancer patients—Biography. | Fundamentalists—Biography. | Evangelicalism—Health aspects. | Groundwater—Pollution—Health aspects—Ogallala Aquifer. | Cancer—Patients—Family relationships. | Spiritual healing—Christianity. | Cancer—Environmental aspects.
Classification: LCC RC262 .B485 2024 (print) | LCC RC262 (ebook) | DDC 618.92/994—dc23/eng/20231129
LC record available at https://lccn.loc.gov/2023038207
LC ebook record available at https://lccn.loc.gov/2023038208

doi:10.7560/329627

FOR M & J

Truly I say to you, whatever you bind on earth shall have been bound in heaven; and whatever you loose on earth shall have been loosed in heaven.

MATTHEW 18:18

AUTHOR'S NOTE

THIS MEMOIR WAS BASED ON many sources. Research and interviews helped to broaden and deepen much of the context for what is, at heart, a personal story born of memory. Where possible, I have sought documentation to verify what, at this time, can be fact-checked. Many conversations and scenes have been implied. I believe I have indicated to the reader clearly where I have taken creative license in reimagining moments that I did not witness; in seizing that creative license, I have drawn from interviews and memory in an attempt to honor the integrity of the characters depicted, especially of my father. Almost all of the dialogue in the book is an approximation unless I was able to directly quote articles or interviews. Many names, including all of my living relatives, friends, and acquaintances, have been changed unless official correspondence or documentation was involved or unless I was granted consent otherwise.

PROLOGUE

AN EVANGELIST PITCHES A TENT off the only dead-end interstate in West Texas. Two nights and he'll fly bullet-fire straight up I-27, the same direction water once filled the irrigation ditches of one cotton field to another, stitching the southern high plains together with a shimmering thread. People say a man paddled a canoe from Lubbock to Amarillo in the 1930s, back when farmers believed a bottomless ocean lay beneath all the upturned dirt and the government gave them enough money to pump ancient rock and flood their fields. It is now 1998, and my family and I live in Lubbock above the southern edge of that once-vast aquifer. I am thirteen, with little idea that the Ogallala, the country's largest aquifer, is draining beneath my feet. I do not yet know the Sioux word *Ogallala*, meaning "to scatter one's own." Another kind of desperation has brought me to the revival.

Mom heard about the evangelist on the radio, heard the word "healing" in his billing, and her heart stirred. She announced to our family of seven that we would attend revival at Lubbock's empty fairgrounds, and absolutely no one was surprised. When I will recall later, as an adult, how often the Holy Spirit nudged Mom, I'll remember her brunette hair, hot-rollered and swept full at her shoulders. Lit red in the dawn, sailor take warning. She heard so much from God in the late '90s, her hair curled with it.

Stockyard air, thick with manure and chemical, wicks the tent walls. My eyes fix on the evangelist. He stands at the grassy front, a blur of beige suit and skin. A microphone pops with his breath. Dad says, "Tonight's the night." Mom closes her eyes and mouths the words to a prayer. I peel my legs up from the seat of a metal folding chair and tuck my hands underneath them. An invisible string cinches my shoulder blades together. I don't cuss, so I whisper, "Please."

The state fair usually comes in June and sugar-powders the air for a week of pig races between contestants with names like Rush Limhog. But it's early April, and we never go to the fair anyway. Mom says the rides are slapdash, the food heart-attack. Still, I picture a Ferris wheel in place of the tent. A gigantic sparkling bangle with a cotton silo for backdrop. I imagine riding up the Ferris wheel and pausing at its apex: I see Lubbock glittering to the edge of Caprock Canyon, a drop to nothing by night. I see the Lubbock Metro Tower, the tallest building in town, historic for being one of the last dominos standing after the tornado of 1970 wiped half of Lubbock flat again. Skyline of First Baptist Church, of Wells Fargo Bank, of shining red double-T on the university football stadium, of Loop 289 enclosing the city in convenience. At Lubbock's border, pump-jacks in buck and bow. Due west, streetlights mapping the asphalt grid past the dollar theater to the stoplight by my flat-roofed white brick house. I long to hazard my life at the top of the Ferris wheel, breathing air so dry you think it's light. To forget the prayer service and its prophecies. But the night closes overhead like an eyelid.

Each stranger in the tent could be a storyteller, so thick are their faces with living. My mother stands out in such a place. She is muscular, her skin dewy and smooth. Limbs clenched like a cage. One wonders what turn in life brings this woman to a gathering of the hard-up. But no one approaches Mom to ask. She looks like a dare, and most people choose truth. Besides, it doesn't take long to find the answer. My father is a young man growing old so fast it seems you can watch it happening if you stare. Eyes shift to take in signs of my father's bad fortune. His skin is tinted yellow. His shoulder bones peak under his polo.

But nothing establishes the gravitas of our situation like the sight of me and my four younger siblings. Here are the five children of a woman with a dying husband. Have mercy. Eyes fill with watery hope, as though the very thought of fatherless children harkens God's intervention. No adult has heard the news of my father without a shuddered heave and dial to the internist. Even the mailman dropped his blue canvas bag and cried. But here in the slipshod dwelling of the sanctified, people smile with satisfaction, like they've been cast briefly into the years to come and beheld there, if not Christ's return, the amazing fact of Dad's recovery. One woman braces herself over the chairs in front of us and speaks.

"God will restore the years the locusts have eaten."

I smile weakly. Mom nods. "Amen," she says. "Thank you."

The microphone overloads, and the keyboardist and drummer ready. The evangelist booms. "Turn to somebody and say, 'I believe you're going to get a miracle tonight.'" A woman taps my shoulder and takes my hands. Her fingers are cold, her squeeze hard. She draws me in and shouts that God has a word for me tonight. Just what I feared. I feel responsibility for the future of my family, who believe God physically heals, just as he did in the time when Jesus walked the earth. His miraculous touch—a touch that can bring health and wealth and long life in this fallen world—can be prevented by only one thing: a lack of faith. Each day that Dad wakes ill, I wonder if there is more I've yet to do, more faith to build up and to show. I wonder if the woman holding my hands is about to condemn me. She barks something I can't make out and bounces away, waving her arms. The aisle fills with fancy footwork. Some dance a spirited jig. A lady with a blond hive rattles a tambourine. The evangelist's hand shimmies. His body moves with every phrase, each word a kick, each cry a lunge. He raises a fist and throws a bellow to the ground. He points. "The Lord spoke to me, saying he's going to bless everyone here tonight. Believe it and you shall receive."

I've heard this language before, when preachers prophesy over Dad and when Mom prays at night, weaving scriptures from all parts of the Bible together. The words come piecemeal from the epistle of Mark. Forever I will remember them: "Whatever you ask in prayer, believe that you have received it, and it will be yours."

"For the power of the Kingdom," the woman in front of me cries. A chorus of *hallelujahs!* rises, and I feel my voice join them, my throat promising rasp come morning. Our excitement rouses the preacher. He pumps his arms and shuffle-ball steps across the ground. Then something jars him, a vision. He halts and holds up a hand. His voice growls. "Brothers and sisters, some of you are worried. Some of you are anxious. Some of you have come here tonight with hearts full of fear." He charges the aisle and shouts. "God says be anxious for *nothing*." I feel the heat coming off Dad's body next to me, a sign of life. *He is healed*, I say to myself. *He is healed*. My fists are clenched in determination. Or anxiety. I can't tell.

The evangelist lowers the microphone and pulls a handkerchief from his pocket, dabs his forehead, and returns it. Sweat darkens the back of his vest. Tonight is a warm one, like day won't let go. The air is pestilent, as if every particle buzzes around the light with the flies. Maybe God will come to this very place.

"I love a camp meeting," the preacher says. "God's flock doesn't need brick and mortar. We don't need a steeple and stained glass. Let me tell you something, when God touches you, you cannot sit quietly. You've got to dance, you've got to shout. Tonight, we're going to fill this tent with praise. This ground here, this is holy ground."

Dad judders a leg. The round silhouette of a Carmex jar bounces in his pocket. He closes his eyes and tugs at the crease in his Levi's. He will walk the cut-rate aisle between rows of the zealous, hands bird-winging like they're pushing him on or reaching out to catch him. He shakes with anticipation or pain. How does one get comfortable asking not to die?

"I believe," I shout, loud enough for my parents to hear, "he will be healed."

The chair in front of us rattles with the body of the woman. The spirit has arrived. Dad claps and cheers like he's back at college at an Aggie football game. The woman hovers her legs in the air and the foot of one leg reaches only to the ankle of the other. The evangelist sweats his way to her and nearly swallows the microphone whole as he draws it to his mouth and bawls.

"By his wounds."

The congregation shouts back, "We are healed."

The evangelist kneels in front of the woman. She lifts her face, and he speaks as if only to her. "By his wounds."

The woman trembles and whimpers and then nods in acceptance of the miracle unfurling. The evangelist raises his voice.

"By his wounds."

"I am healed," she cries.

The microphone thumps against the woman's calf as the evangelist grasps her shorter leg. A vein bulges in his forehead as he pulls one leg to meet the other. He holds the woman's feet together. The tops of her yellowed white tennis shoes align in a neat pair. The crowd wails.

"Praise God!" He settles her feet on the ground and stands, and she leaps from her seat and kicks in time to the music. A man in the front row hollers and holds his legs aloft. His right leg extends past his left. "In the name of Jesus," the evangelist calls out and grabs the stunted leg and stretches it flush with the other.

Briefly, my fear gives way to the calm that comes with engrossed observation. I feel I am watching humans grow tails—is it an illusion or God's work? Already, a basket is beginning to make its rounds, filling with dollar bills in support of the traveler's ministry. The timing feels pointed. *Appointed*, the evangelist might say. But I want to believe God is working through him. Can God not work through anyone? My feet bounce. Hope brightens in my chest, and its warmth spreads down my limbs. I claim it: this will be the night my family has been waiting for. I can't stop the sweat of relief gathering at my hairline and, with it, a feeling of triumph. Yes, I am filled with faith—enough, I hope, to save Dad's life. But then I turn to him. He is still hunched. His shoulders, pain flowing off them like water, do not roll back. His skin doesn't pink.

Why does God seem to touch everyone in this tent but him? As quickly as I felt excitement, my gut fills with dread. Am I not embarrassed by myself? Don't I know why God stays his hand? A catalog of recent transgressions opens in my mind: I've shaved my legs; I've imagined kissing a boy. On this very night, anxious that my dad would remain sick, I wished to flee the presence of God. Afraid that God would reveal that I am the reason, my doubt and skepticism a deadly poison that I might as well be spoon-feeding my father. I tuck my hands beneath my legs and bow my head in shame, not in prayer.

Years will pass before I sit with this memory. So many years, in fact, that I will sometimes wonder if I imagined the traveling evangelist and his tent. Was he a fiction? His revival an amalgam of things I'd heard on the radio and seen broadcasted by the Christian network? I'll admit that these questions bring relief. If I am making up the healing service, perhaps I'm also imagining the girl seated in the tent, her hope swinging violently into despair, her courage into shame. Maybe I was actually some other girl, one in a house across town, tucked between her parents on the living room couch, watching *Star Trek: The Next Generation* and dozing off to sleep. Perhaps, too, the man I picture seated beside the girl in the tent is not my father, and I will look up from this memory to see I've missed a call from the man who is. But my phone's screen is dark, and I am confronted with the sheer fact of my father's absence—a fact that leads my memory down a chain of images to a camp meeting tent. It glows in the dusk, ensconced in the darkening green of the South Plains Fairgrounds. I don't want to reenter the tent, but inside sit the only father I have known and the only child I ever was.

The evangelist, like a carnival barker, raises his finger and points at my younger self. My eyes sting as I watch her. Even at the distance of twenty-five years, I feel again the dread I felt at the revival, and I am desperate, once more, to save my family, whether by prayer or by dragging us from the tent. But I cannot collapse the years between us. There is my past self, here is my present, and somewhere between us lies the truth of what happened, how it happened, and perhaps why.

If I hoped to save my father's life then, I hope now to understand our history.

At the time, in 1998, I think I already understand. The evangelist raises his finger in the air, and I await my excruciating conviction.

Dad will die because of me.

CHAPTER 1

BEFORE THE NOISE OF TENT revivals and prayer circles, there were quieter days. I remember the mornings in West Texas. A crease of light widening on the horizon. Dried rivulets of soil hemming a flat and empty road. I close my eyes and see a child pedaling her bike. A man runs next to her—my father. Our Australian shepherd, Andy, keeps pace at his heel. The image occurs outside a concrete time line. I am five, and six, and seven years old, keeping stride with my father, not in the tent of a traveling preacher but on a highway at dawn the four days a week he's home from work. I join him, riding the pink Schwinn my mother scored at a garage sale. A plate hanging from the handlebars says, "SWEET THUNDER." As I remember this, my chest tightens, like I am once again striving for air. My throat thickens, and something rams the space between my ribs—a desire for nothing more than to hear traces of voice in my father's exhale.

The steeple of a white clapboard church rises before us, its aged foundation sagging into sandy loam. Not our church. Too old. Too Baptist. My parents are Christian evangelicals who hop from one newly planted congregation to another. They listen to recorded sermons of preachers who warn that America has lost her way. Are we prepared for the return of Christ? Already my mother is hard at work homeschooling her children with Bible verse and the science of a young and corrupted earth. We are in the Last Days, she believes. As a family we are, but I don't know that yet.

Dad is a pilot for American Airlines, commuting from the municipal airport in Lubbock to the company's hub at Dallas–Fort Worth by way of small passenger planes he calls "puddle jumpers." He is gone three days, back in Lubbock for four. I am eager to be near Dad when he is home. A first officer on his way to captain, he returns from trips with his pockets full of small gifts. My two younger sisters and I reach for the bags of in-flight peanuts he passes out. *One at a time*, he says. Each time his aging Toyota pickup creaks into the driveway after a trip, I elbow my way through my clamoring siblings to hug him first.

One afternoon, Dad picks up his truck keys from the blue kitchen counter, says he's going to get his hair cut at the Air Force base, and asks if I would like to go along. His barber's name is Yolanda, and Dad prefers to have her cut his hair if she is available.

"But," he says, "you don't ever really know who you're going to get." The windows are down, and he spreads his fingers in the wind. As a young Air Force officer in 1980, he trained on fighter jets at Reese Air Force Base in Lubbock, then shipped off to Guam to track Pacific typhoons in the C-130, a cargo aircraft. "Commanders sent us up there when they were bored," he'd told me. "School buses of the sky, Kate." We pass the hangar that houses T-Bird fighter jets. The words "REESE AFB" gleam across the hanger's roof like a bill-board aimed at the sky. After two years in Guam, Dad was again stationed at Reese, this time as an instructor, teaching flight above the endless endless to novice pilots. He liked training in fighter jets in West Texas, where he'd learned to love the flatness of the plains for affording more of the sky's real estate. He taught for six years before he went commercial and flew planes in the McDonnell Douglas MD-80 series for American Airlines. But he was third-generation Air Force, and the base was in his blood. The landscape of his childhood included a vast range of places—Colorado Springs, Turkey Hill, Baumholder, and Universal City—yet he also grew up in the same place: an Air Force station, planes crossing in a shackle maneuver, their contrails forming a white "X" overhead.

Stalwart behind the jet hangar is the base water tower, bearing Air Force insignia. The tower would be unremarkable anywhere with hills or skyscrapers, but here on the flatlands it portends great height, its girth bolstered by eight legs of steel, like the military fantasy of an octopus. Beneath it, every building is square, official, brown.

In the base barbershop, a bubble-gum machine takes my coins in exchange for a sore jaw. Yolanda has long black hair, thick glasses, and a voice full of gravel, as though the day proceeds from a late night of karaoke. She is a slim-cut woman of 1992. She grabs a spray bottle and wets Dad's coarse hair and trims it. She folds his ear down and shaves behind it with an electric razor. He looks young, like a boy, and the thought that he was once my age offers its vertigo. Loose hair from his shoulder falls to the floor like sawdust. In six years, he'll be gone.

Yolanda turns to me.

"You want a trim too?"

I climb onto the chrome chair. She has a time untangling my hair, which is waist-length and a mess of dust-blown knots from my morning runs with Dad. She tightens it in handfuls to spare my scalp while brushing the ends. Dad sits in a chair behind us, picks up a copy of *Texas Monthly*, and heaves a sigh. On the cover, Ann Richards straddles a Harley-Davidson, the fringe of her white leather jacket dangling like the pinions of an angel. The caption reads: "White Hot Mama." Dad flips the magazine open and says to give him a break. Says that Richards's chance at governor had a snowball's in you-know-where till the liberals gave it to her, go figure. Recovery from alcoholism and divorce and raising children as a single mother is all well and good. "But more power to the woman with nothing to recover from," Dad says.

I don't yet know how these words will sink with permanence into my memory. How almost every event to come could be augured to this phrase like the heavy-duty spiral anchors Dad used to ground the A-frame of the backyard swing set while saying, as he twisted each one, that not even an F-5 tornado could tear them from the earth.

"You know I don't like to get political," Yolanda says, "but I work hard for my money."

"Exactly," Dad says.

The barber next to Yolanda has two cents. "Nobody else paying my bills."

"That's the truth."

"Captain Allen in here yesterday saying they going to shut down more bases. You tell me that makes sense."

"War ain't over."

"It ain't ever over."

"Well," Dad says. He sets the magazine aside and shakes open the *Lubbock Avalanche-Journal*, the local paper. After a while, he looks up and cracks a joke that makes everyone laugh. Yolanda hands me a mirror and spins me around to see every angle of my trim. The ends of my hair are blunt and neat. Its discards mix with all the rest on the floor, and Yolanda sweeps the hair into a nest.

Later Mom will say that my haircut isn't really that good. "Too blunt," she'll say. But Dad pays Yolanda cash and touches the back of my head as we walk out.

We drive across the base, past the control tower that looms over headquarters. Past the Catholic church where, just before moving to Guam, my parents were married in 1981, their wedding small. Mom wore her sister's wedding dress. It swallowed her whole in satin, lace, and puff sleeves as she and Dad kissed under the arch of the groomsmen's swords. The Temptations are playing on the car radio and I ask Dad, "What's a rolling stone?" I watch the wind undo Yolanda's good work.

"It's a man who is not a very good family man," Dad says.

"Oh," I say and nod seriously like I know exactly what that means. I realize listening to a story of a rolling stone doesn't make you one, despite my mother's suspicion otherwise. She would prefer I listen to tapes of Christian children's choirs. But I feel as old as iniquity itself, sitting passenger side of my father, chewing bubble gum, listening to rock 'n' roll, planes climbing overhead, their contrails brilliant white comets, Dad and I racing dust and sky down Highway 114 with the West Texas fields rolling out in a flat forever, the dusk blue.

CHAPTER 2

ON THE AFTERNOON MY FATHER evoked a mythic woman with nothing to recover from, he must have imagined my mother, a woman who strove to be just that. But in my mind, the memory of my father running sits next to an image of my mother's hands gloved in white latex and blood. They reach into the chest of an orange tabby split neck to hind. I'm perched on a chrome stool across the surgery table from Mom, the cat's abdomen a cavern between us. My hands are also gloved. I swivel. If the key to keeping up with my father is movement, the rule for accompanying my mother at her veterinary practice is stasis, quietude, compliance. Mom tells me to be still. The powder lining of the latex gloves is almost numbing, and I disobey her, gliding my thumbs across my fingers as Mom peels the incision open wider. I am now to peer into the cavity. Blood pools dark. The acrid smell signals decay.

Mom nods at a tray of surgical instruments. "You want to grab that hook?"

The snook hook weighs in my grasp, its touch tingles up my arm like power. I've seen the slender cane fetch a wet, purple uterus from a dog's abdomen. Mom refuses to perform a hysterectomy on a dog carrying pups unless the carried are dead already, and this I have seen too: fallopian tubes swollen with the beads of defunct fetuses collected into a white plastic bag. Today Mom teaches me the anatomy of a gut.

She cranes under the surgery light and snares a rope of large intestine and drapes it over the cat's side. She sets the snook hook aside and requests the hemostats. "We got a bleeder," she says and fastens the hemostats around a leaking artery. The blood is viscous and dark. There is a sound like a spoon stirring broth as Mom's fingers swim. They pluck out the liver as though the organ hadn't been attached to anything. My hands turn to receive. The meat is room temperature and gelatinous, the color of beet, the length of my palm. The cat has not been dead long—Mom euthanized it this morning. She was a stray, a sweet one, by account of the man who found her and brought her directly to the clinic. Come right up to him, he'd said, but wouldn't eat.

"Probably feline leukemia," Mom says. In walks the office manager, Dierdre. Dierdre is the senior-most vet tech and institutional memory of High Plains Pet Clinic. She wears scrubs printed with happy-looking pigs. She caresses the cat's head. Orange fur sheds between her fingers and onto the table. The cat's eyes are open: an unforgiving gray.

A row of feline viscera gleams before me like severed tongues; I am supposed to understand the coherence of biology—how the stomach deposits food in the liver and the liver sends waste to the intestine. But each organ rounds like a creature all its own. A slurp sounds from the cat's chest as Mom turns a scalpel and cuts away the heart. My hands cup the pink, slick muscle with the futile tenderness of holding a baby bird. The ventricles splay easily from one another, and I am careful not to tear the tissue. I taste metal. Only hours ago, the muscle pulsed.

"Well," Mom says. "Time to close her up." I ask if I can return the heart. She widens the crevasse, and I lower it between rows of perfect white bones.

When I am not riding my bike next to Dad or sitting in his blue truck on an errand, my world, condensed by homeschooling, expands with the cranky hinges of the back door to the clinic. It opens to a cinder-block pantry, shelves stocked with cat and dog canned food and columns of clean, threadbare towels. Next bunks a dryer, a washing machine, a metal trash can, and then another door.

Following her into the clinic, I have learned there is more than one version of my mother. At home, she wears a wooden spoon in her back pocket, a chilly reminder to me and my siblings of the quick and calm strike evoked by our transgressions. At the clinic, she buttons up a pristine white coat with her title—Dr.

Blackburn—stitched above the left pocket. A speculum replaces her wooden spoon, and her kitchen surveillance gives way to the study of X-rays. Four days a week, Mom homeschools me and my two younger sisters at the kitchen table, where I've learned to observe Mom's movements for signs of her mood: how quickly she darts from the sink to the kitchen table, the changes in her tone when she says to let the phone ring, the hardening of her jaw when my chair's feet scrape the tile floor. Each gesture is a countdown to the finish line of her patience. But in the clinic's surgery room, I witness the rewards of her method. A curved needle engages her right hand, and with her left she clamps hemostats to one side of the cat's incision and pulls the skin taut. The cat's abdomen closes in a seam with each pass of the needle, each click, knot, and snip. Mom bends closely over her work, her desire for control bestowing one perfect stitch after another.

Once she finishes, I volunteer to clean the surgical instruments. A nearby sink holds a metal bin filled with a green sterilizing agent. In the treated water, the tools shimmer aquamarine. Each instrument must be scrubbed with an apparatus that looks like a toothbrush with steel bristles. I obsess. Leaves of blood fall from the snook hook, the hemostats, the speculum. The flecks turn purple in the bin. Pride brims in my chest as I set the pack without oversight. Mom's trust feels like delicate jewelry I am rarely allowed to wear. I arrange the hemostats in a row of descending size. The hooks I settle parallel to the hemostats, the speculum I align at the side of the tray.

The surgery room has emptied but for the cat lying on her side. I deglove and rest my hand on her and wait in the habit of waiting for an animal to breathe. When she doesn't, I withdraw. Dierdre returns, shakes open a plastic bag, scruffs the cat, and lifts her body. The cat's head does not droop.

"You learning?" Dierdre asks.

Inside the clinic, dogs bay so constantly you don't hear them anymore. *How do you stand it?* clients are likely to say. And, *Is the lady vet in?* Mom works Thursdays and every other Saturday, a schedule set in 1988, when she was hired by her associate, Dr. Bieri. *Thursdays and every other Saturday* is a phrase I've heard so much it might as well be prayer.

After the dissection, Mom sits in the office in an enormous leather chair and writes on a pink sheet of paper. Pink for cats, yellow for dogs. These pastel papers fill end-tab folders that line shelves behind the reception desk. Atop the receptionist's counter lies the clinic cat: a silver tabby named Gandalf. He is every bit of twenty-two pounds. *A bad example*, Mom calls him. Gandalf is also unflappable. I hug the corner of the hallway as a hound bounces up to nuzzle the cat before his owner yanks his leash. Gandalf yawns.

"That is one relaxed cat," the man says.

Dierdre leads the dog and his owner into a small room with a table scale and closes the door and drops the dog's record folder into a door tray with a click—Mom's cue. She rises, walks out of the office, takes hold of the record, nods to Dierdre, and turns to me.

"You want to come?"

The small exam room is heated with dog breath.

"How are we doing today?" Mom says.

The man says that he is fine, but his dog is not. "Started coughing about a day ago. 'Course, he's not made a peep since we walked in."

"They'll do that," Mom says.

Dierdre lifts the dog onto the exam room table. His nails clatter on the metal. "We can take care of those nails for you too," Mom says and hooks the handles of her stethoscope into her ears.

"You want to be a vet also?"

"Think so," I say.

"Where you go to school?"

I dread the question. The answer often ends conversation as nobody quite knows what to say to a homeschooler. Children my age get confused. They rattle off questions about doing school in pajamas, and I disappoint them by saying that I have never once done school in my pajamas.

"I'm homeschooled," I say.

"Well. Your mom must like having you around."

This guy doesn't know the half of it.

Mom replaces the stethoscope around her neck. "Heart and lungs sound good," she says. She sweeps her hands across the dog's flanks.

"Moment of truth," the client says.

"His weight's good." Mom strokes the dog's throat.

"You're so much gentler than Dr. Bieri," the man says. Clients often declare this. Someday I'll understand the gendered nature of the comment. But it is also true—my mother possesses a tender bedside manner. As I watch her nuzzle the dog, the muscles in the back of my neck tighten with the memory of her grip. How are these the same hands?

The hound refuses to cough. Mom steps back. "When you say a cough, what kind of cough are we talking?" The man hesitates. Mom makes a well-practiced impression of a dog's deep cough: a baritone rumble from the sternum.

"Or is it more breathy, like she's trying to cough something up?" The hacking sound Mom performs is equally impressive. Her throat tightens and there's a sound like releasing phlegm. The man ponders his options.

"It's the second one."

Mom says it is likely kennel cough, and the man curses his brother's disreputable dachshund. Dierdre lifts the hound to the floor, and we proceed to the back of the clinic, where the dog is once more hefted onto a table upon which his feet struggle to find purchase. Mom soothes in her clinic voice—a soft voice. Dierdre hugs the hound to her chest, and Mom tightens a tourniquet, pops the cap from a syringe, and strikes the vein.

My mother was around the age I am now when she found a stray cat panting in the Houston heat, with kittens that had not yet opened their eyes. She grifted a box and carried the feline and her progeny home. She planned to keep the cats secret from her father. Her mother was unlikely to notice them. She peered through her bedroom window. Smoke rose from her mother's cigarette and curled above the back fence. My mother fashioned one of her bureau drawers into a crib, replacing her clothes with a blanket and padding the wooden frame with dish towels. There the cat cleaned her young and coaxed them to her nipples.

In the afternoons that followed, Beverly Jacobs sprang through the school bus doors and ran to reach the brood. The Houston of my mother's childhood was not highways throbbing from the center of a city creased with bayous and flanked by oil tankers and shoreline, with a bustling art scene and cuisine from every part of the world. Her childhood's Houston was an ex-Navy businessman with road rage and a fierce hand. It was two sisters, Mom in the forgettable middle, where she learned to take care of herself. It was a mother, Rosanna, forty and wanting a do-over, a college degree, a Prozac, or at least a cigarette before Jack busted in asking, *Where's dinner?* My mother's Houston was a long day in the classroom. A sweltering brown bungalow on Braeswood Avenue, three miles from a downtown she never went to. A dirty white cat hidden in a drawer. After she arrived home, hushed her steps, and shut her bedroom door, Beverly Jacobs tucked a kitten no larger than her hand under her chin. But then one day she came home to an empty drawer, and her older sister said their father had dumped the litter off on some roadside.

Mom always says this is when she became a veterinarian. But to me, it is also the story of when my mother learned the value of vigilance. If only she hadn't been forced to go to school. If only she could have kept watch over the kittens every hour, protected them from her father, seen to their rearing and care. Perhaps even trained them to be still whenever they heard the sound of her father's Thunderbird in the driveway.

It is the story of when she became a mother.

I stand by, watching as my mother treats the dog with kennel cough, her hands moving with the confidence of one who might have created the canine and knows its innermost being.

When I join my mother at the clinic, my father watches my younger siblings at home. Eventually, my parents will have five children total, but in 1992 Dad has to watch only my two younger sisters until Mom and I return to them, my sisters' unwiped mouths smiling wildly when we walk in, my father boiling pasta at the stove to make Thursday de Jour, his signature and only dish, beef Stroganoff. Tonight we clear our plates, I wash the CorningWare, Karson, my younger sister, towels it off, and then Dad says we all ought to take a drive. Outside our neighborhood, he turns the van up the same highway where I tag along beside him in the mornings. Our van passes the white church, the one-mile mark. Ahead of us, there's an empty lot with a large sign advertising acreage and a phone number. Dad says this is the place and pulls off to the street's shoulder. Mom leans forward and squints. Blades of renegade grass sway with the breeze.

"I see what you mean," she says.

"I hear there's gonna be a lot of development out this way," Dad says.

Karson, who is five years old, and I, soon to turn eight, have told our parents we want to be veterinarians when we grow up, and they have started dreaming up a clinic where all three of us— Mom, Karson, and myself—will practice. Our partnership gets off to a rough start when Karson and I, unbuckling our seat belts and squeezing between the front seats for a view, knock heads. Mom says to cut it out. We sit back rubbing our noggins and glaring. Our two-year-old sister Kendra sleeps in her car seat.

It's hard for me to imagine Mom any place but High Plains Pet Clinic; she has a staunch loyalty to habit. But she says she can envision a small brick building with an open kennel behind it where dogs will run, their gray silhouettes bounding after one another. Beyond the vision, patches of land stretch west, ready to be tilled again and paved over. Still farther, beyond this vision, lie cotton fields, their dark rows barreling on forever, neat white blossoms tucked into sheens of green. In his 2014 book *Empire of Cotton*, Sven Beckert writes that the early stages of capitalism often took root from the "unrestrained actions of private individuals—the domination of masters over slaves and of frontier capitalists over indigenous inhabitants." Texas plains Indians were violently displaced to Oklahoma reservations so as to empty the land for the growing of cotton.

But the consequences of empire mislead the eye: cotton fields seem to have always been there. In the distance, long snakes of irrigation hoses sway as they roll forward on fantastic wheels over ground where ancient Gomphotheres once waved their trunks. But no one in my family believes in an old earth. I do not yet know that temperature and wind transformed the Llano Estacado into prairie. Streambeds disintegrated into countless molecules, each containing a single cell from freshwater plants. In its afterlife, bright green algae transmuted into white powder. These fossils, like pale ash, stratified into bands of sediment that collected on top of one another in a layered archive. The alabaster ribbons of this diatomaceous powder are streaked with veins of mud like the staff in sheet music. But there are remarkable places where the dark lines of this earth are not straight: they bend and swerve, pounded into mosaics by now-extinct bison running over the plains. The remains of their vertebra and charred bone were buried in layers of sediment for discovery by those who came later and would marvel that such species of mammals had existed in their New World.

But to my family, the toiled ground is fresh, and there is no past, only future. A long time will pass before I learn to look back.

"There's money in owning land," Dad says. "Especially if there's oil on it."

"How would you know it was there?" I ask.

"You'd get lucky," he says.

"Is this the country?"

"We're not even outside the city limits."

"There any snakes?"

"Probably."

The shadow of a cloud crosses the open land, but light shades of blue fall from the sky toward the western rim of the field where someday a clinic shingle will say "Dr. Blackburn & Dr. Blackburn & Dr. Blackburn."

CHAPTER 3

MY SISTER KARSON AND I are roller-skating on the blue floor at Skate Ranch #1, where, every Friday, homeschoolers get a discount between 1:00 and 3:00. This is another brief window outside our house, an egress I count on every week. Kendra stomps along the perimeter clinging to the rink's carpeted walls. It is not yet summer in 1992, and Mom has recently told us she's pregnant. She presses her baby bump—a boy this time—to the rink's security bars and tells me and Karson to help our younger sister Kendra skate and then returns to her table in the cafeteria and sips ice water. Two women chat behind her. One is saying she wished she'd done home birth, but her kids are all grown now. The other says this will be her fifth. Mom glances back at them.

"Is it safe?" she asks. The woman with the blossoming belly answers.

"Safer."

Mom brings her water over to their table.

Meanwhile, Kendra runs between Karson and me, squeezing our hands and giggling. I tell her to let her skates roll. Karson squints at the cafeteria.

"Who are Mom's new friends?" she says.

"I don't know. But one of them's got all the twins." I point at two pairs of girls, one set with red hair, the other with blond.

Quarter of three, Mom waves us over, and we unlace our skates, slide into our shoes, return our rentals, and emerge blind into the bright afternoon before the public school kids arrive.

A few days pass, and Mom retrieves the phone number she wrote down at Skate Ranch #1 and dials Carol, the midwife. Mom explains that this is her fourth pregnancy, but it would be her first home birth. She waits for Carol to ask pertinent questions. Then she hears the sound of a long falsetto wobble in Carol's throat. The yawn is one of those big yawns that has Mom wondering when it's going to end. Well. It did eventually, but not before Mom makes up her mind. She thanks Carol for her time and hangs up. Was the midwife bored? Lackadaisical? Mom didn't stick around to find out.

Months pass, and I find myself sitting in the waiting room of Mom's obstetrician watching a woman watch a special on sharks. It's nearly September, and my baby brother has made no indication he'd like to join us. It's been two weeks since his due date, and when Mom left me in the waiting room for her appointment, she looked stiff, fully pregnant but also fully apprehensive. "You just wait out here," she'd said, her voice tight. The doctor isn't pleased with her, that much I know. The woman across from me says she saw this episode on sharks before, says it scared her so bad she dropped her coffee. Not this time, though. She's got a good grip on her cup.

When Mom returns from her exam, the tears racing down her face have a life of their own. A knot tightens in my stomach.

"The baby?" I ask. Mom sputters that we need to go home. The silence of our drive is hindered only by a sporadic heave and then Mom's insistence that she's fine.

In our driveway, words reintroduce themselves to her. The baby she carries is absolutely fine; it's the doctor who's got a problem. He wants to induce labor.

"I used to think doctors were so smart," she says and sniffs. She's been reading. Oxytocin can cause a drop in fetal heart rate and strain an already burdened uterus. "But then Dr. Roland says to me that going past due is the thing that endangers a baby."

By the time Mom is held firmly in Dad's embrace, she's angry. "He yelled at me. Yelled and yelled, saying I was willing to put my baby's life at risk. He said, 'You're not the doctor.' Well, I am a doctor. Besides, I have the right to do what I think is best for me and my family."

"You do," Dad says. He rubs Mom's back. I huddle with Karson and Kendra and our parents turn to us, saying that everything is fine.

Perhaps if nothing that came later—my father's diagnosis and its fallout—had ever occurred, this memory of my mother's fourth pregnancy would not have seared itself into my mind with strange foreboding. She believed in the superiority of her own mind to almost everyone else's, but she was also responding to the historic and ongoing insidious ways in which women's autonomy concerning their own health is routinely dismissed or denied. The affront she was responding to was real. But her response also chills me now as I look back. When I try to make sense of my childhood, I see this breach between my mother and her physician as a turning point, marking a clear moment in which whatever trust she had in medical institutions dissolved. With one hand, I wish to reach back into the past and comfort her, and with another to take hold of her shoulder tightly—angrily—and say, *You need to listen to someone besides yourself.* I want to turn to my father and say, *Don't let her do this.*

I remember Dad caressing my mother's back. His expression is calm, sympathetic. He is the only person who can calm her, but he does not refute her suspicions. Rather, he nods in agreement as she says that Dr. Roland has ulterior motives.

"He probably just has a vacation coming up," Mom says.

A few nights later, Mom wakes with contractions. She stands up from the bed, walks past my sleeping father, clicks on the bathroom light, and closes the door. Later, Dad finds her squatting over a makeshift pad of soiled bathroom towels.

"Let's get you to the hospital."

Mom groans. He recognizes the sound. She is pushing.

"Don't," he says.

A few hours later, my father places a hand on my shoulder and gently shakes me awake. I believe, at first, that he has come to fetch me for a morning run. His face is radiant. "Come meet your brother."

The air smells of blood and fresh infant and cleaner mix. My sisters hide their mouths behind their small hands. My eyes cast around the room for the punch line: it's there, sitting in the middle of the bed, cradling a swaddled baby.

Dad prods me, and I climb onto the bed with my sisters like young animals prowling. Mom turns my brother's red, folded, drowsy face toward us.

In the morning, Dad drinks a pot of coffee, then another. My brother sleeps heavily in my arms. I fight my sisters off with my elbows, saying that if they touch his face he'll wake. Mom sighs and picks up the phone and dials Dr. Roland's office. Her voice starts and falters.

"There was no time to get to the hospital."

"Does he have any openings?"

Us kids are sent to the neighbor, and Dad takes my mother and brother to Dr. Roland's. The neighbor retrieves white bowls from a heavy china cabinet and sets a breakfast of Cheerios. Her two boys sit across from us with hair freshly combed and their backpacks at their feet. They chew carefully and their mother addresses no one in particular, saying, "I can't believe your mom just had that baby in her bathroom."

"She said it was easy," Karson says.

When my parents return from the doctor, the red in Mom's eyes makes my own water. My sisters and I gather around her like worried and ill-equipped nurses. Dad holds my baby brother while the girls and I lead Mom to the bedroom. She unburdens herself, sharing details of her ferocious blowout with Dr. Roland. We listen in horror and in turns take her hand and squeeze it.

"He storms into the room and barks at the nurse. He examines your brother—a little roughly, I might add. Then he looks up and says, 'Well?' And I tell him that we didn't have time to get to the hospital.

He goes, 'I don't believe you. Not for one second.'" Dr. Roland all but kicked my parents out of his office, saying he would never see them again, and the receptionist wrote it all down.

I glance at Dad. His glow has given way to ashen fatigue. His eyelids fall and open heavily. He looks like he might drift to sleep holding the baby.

"What did Dad say?" I ask. My father has not heard me. Mom draws back to remember and says, "Huh," as though she'd forgotten Dad was there at all.

"He probably said something like, 'You don't need to talk to us like that.' But we're both very tired." She reaches for the baby, and Dad starts. He passes the baby to Mom and shuffles into the kitchen. I hear the coffee machine grumble.

News of James's arrival rattles the phone. Mom says her thank-yous.

"We actually didn't go to the hospital," she says.

"No. We didn't go to the clinic either."

At his turn with the phone, Dad says, "Beverly did most of the work." He laughs.

Mom's associate, Dr. Bieri, calls. Mom's lips pinch at the corner as she listens.

"He had no right to do that," she says quietly. A warm, stable air rises from her voice, and I post myself in the silence. She squeezes the phone between shoulder and chin, passes the baby to me, walks out of the living room, and says, "I'll tell you what."

The air is drenched with Mom's sobs. She says, "I will not. And you can't make me." Then she is quiet again. The phone clicks in its receiver. She recites: Dr. Bieri was contacted by Dr. Roland, who had been a longtime client at High Plains Pet Clinic. Dr. Roland said Dr. Bieri ought to fire my mother. She is not fit, he told Dr. Bieri, to practice medicine. To my mother, the way Dr. Bieri recounted the conversation felt like he'd chosen a side. She said she would refuse to see Dr. Roland's animals, and Dr. Bieri said he didn't imagine that would be an issue.

"Then I told him I wouldn't see them even if it's an emergency and I'm on call." She pauses to dab her eyes. Dad passes her a handkerchief postscriptum. "And he said, 'Oh yes you will, or I'll fire you.'"

Mom cries that she feels betrayed and says that no one has to agree with her, but they can at least be supportive. She crosses the room and sits beside me on the couch, slings an arm around my neck, and rests her head on my shoulder. I hold her, I hold my brother. He is not two days old. She brushes James's forehead with her finger.

"You know why this has happened, don't you, Kate?"

I search the eyes of the Australian shepherd. He sits at my feet and regards the baby suspiciously. He doesn't know the answer either.

"Because I didn't obey God. He told me to get a midwife, and I just didn't. And why? Because she yawned."

"I see."

Mom lifts the baby from my lap.

"Okay, God," she says. "I've learned my lesson."

Mom sits at the head of our kitchen table–turned–school desk and demands anatomical precision. Open before us are illustrations of male and female anatomy. Today she teaches us about God-planning.

We are not permitted to use any euphemisms for genitals—a lexicon in which she is well versed thanks to the many embarrassed clients whose pets have all manner of injuries near theirs.

"It is not a veevee," she says. "It is not a hoohah or a jay-jay, or a hmm-hmm, a pee-pee, or any kind of food. And it is not a belly button. It is a vagina. And that is what you will call it." Her seriousness and rebuke so curl around her pronunciation of each syllable of "vagina" that I almost apologize for having one. Karson runs from the room with her hands over her ears.

My sister and I know about sex. Karson learned the facts from a neighbor boy and conveyed them to me, to which I said the boy was full of crap. But I fact-checked with my mother, who told me the neighbor boy was correct and then called his mother. Afterward, I moped on the swing set out back for hours.

In this morning's installment of our sex education, Mom opens a book called *A Child Is Born* and points to the wet black translucence of a fetus eye. I study the images of the embryo's amphibious world of liquid and splitting cells. We are to braid the strange science photographed in *A Child Is Born* to the existence of a person. Three years have passed since the birth of my brother and Mom is pregnant again. Mom says she has obeyed God and hired the midwife this time to deliver her fifth child. Turns out the midwife is just laid-back.

Mom explains that God is in control of the womb. Birth control is a sin akin to abortion. I am eleven years old and feel I can safely promise never to have sex in my life. But Mom continues. She and my father have opened their hearts to God's will. His plan eschews human planning and birth control.

"So God decides how many babies you're going to have?" I ask.

"That's right. It's called God-planning."

"If he decides, then why does it matter if you take birth control or not?" Karson says.

"God lets us choose whether to obey him or not."

I am stumped by this revelation: How is it God is more lenient than my own mother? But I am also a pacifist. I let the issue lie.

All life was created by God absolute, all matter by his will. In keeping with her teaching on procreation, Mom's lessons on earth studies usually begin with an illustration of the globe and her finger circling its surface as she explains that the earth came into being in six days and only now exists because of God's continued concern with it.

"Days were longer in the beginning," Mom says. "But not millions of years long. More like thousands."

The creation of life began as a miracle and was complete, for both humankind and the planet, at its beginning. But post-Eden, all are now fallen.

When I was five, my mother described what it was like to be pregnant with me, her firstborn. "I pictured a parasite growing inside me," she said. "Like the ones I used to study under microscopes at vet school." This was around the time she observed me eating a cheese sandwich with my mouth open and declared I was a barbarian—though she would later insist she had said, "You were *like* a barbarian."

Parasites, barbarians. My parents say us kids are blessings from the Lord. But that doesn't mean we are holy. We were born bent to be unbent. Now I am eleven, Karson nine, Kendra five, and James three. Mom presses my hand to a violent punch on the other side of her abdomen. I figure, as Mom's belly expands with her fifth child, this baby will come into the world just as corrupted.

Raise up a parasite in the way she should go. Spare the rod, spoil the barbarian.

Cotton fields spread behind the midwife's house in Shallowater. Trees line a crevasse west of the plot. A garden and trampoline and small barn constitute a yard. The flatness surrounding us is complete, the Llano being the most homogenous region in North America. As the plains climb north, they dip and rise through Colorado, Kansas, Nebraska, and into the southern region of South Dakota, where, at the turn of the twentieth century, hearsay of wells springing up across the Midwest reached Washington. Three geologists were dispatched to confirm what peoples knew twelve thousand years ago: a great source of water lay beneath the center of the continent.

But signs of the Ogallala were sporadic and inconsistent, like the rumors it spawned. Nelson Horatio Darton set out to divine land across Nebraska, where the aquifer flowed beneath counties with Anglo-Saxon names and supplied water for small farms. In his drillings, Darton encountered signs of a seismic history: calcareous grit and soft limestone formed over sixty million years. He created maps of wells, his reliefs of Nebraska rendered like great cardiovascular systems. Rivers and draws flowed through the clay and sandstone and alluvium and sandhills of millennia, and streams, like arteries, pulsed water through every riverbed. Writing of the aquifer in 1898, Darton said, "I wish to apply the distinctive name *Ogallala Formation.*"

Maps of the Ogallala aquifer might have you believe that a vast lake lies beneath the high plains. But aquifers are saturated bodies of rock. They fill like a sponge. Some six million years ago, silt and sediment covered the aquifer and the wind pared shallow slopes into the landscape. When it rained, the pits filled with water, transforming the dry prairie into a wetland of gleaming playa lakes, the wells for the Ogallala. In the wet season, the playas drained slowly through layers of clay to quench the aquifer. In the dry season, the savanna hardened into a prairie with no trees. Short blades of grama and buffalo grass covered the almost featureless plains in what colonizers called an ocean of prairie grass.

To the outsider's eye, water in the southern high plains was always invisible. Playa lakes are small and shallow. Their waters do not roll out to meet the horizon but reflect light in the glades, their shimmering surfaces appearing ghostly. Beholding the land spread boundlessly before him, the conquistador Francisco Vásquez de Coronado couldn't see the shimmering wet surfaces of over twenty thousand playas. When the settlers happened upon one, it took them by surprise. *Lagunas redondas!* Pores for the largest aquifer in the world. But the landscape revealed only a semi-arid savanna, a fleeting place. When, in 1541, Coronado found no gold, he forced his Apache captives to take them east along a path of playas that began in what is now Lubbock.

The midwife's husband built their home, and it calls to mind *Little House on the Prairie.* The air in it tastes like loam and coffee. Carol beckons Mom to the backroom, and they pass a cove with a loft where, at night, four girls sleep. Carol's daughters sit around a kitchen table and consider me and my sisters. The eldest, Eden, older than me by a year, gives me the up-down. I am wearing a sleeveless denim button-down that ties at the waist and white jeans. She cocks her head.

"Want to see our goats?" she says.

Eden leads our entourage of girldom to a modest shed where a considerable nanny nurses her young. Eden lifts a kid and wraps him around her shoulders as though she's just seen the star of Bethlehem. She bends and takes up another and says to me, "Here." The baby goat's bleat could make one cry. Her hooves scuffle against my thighs. Eden stands back and studies my muddied white pants. A smirk spreads across her face.

Carol makes regular house calls and brings her daughters. My sisters and I look forward to their visits. Eden told me that when we met she thought I was some kind of city slicker, but now she thinks more of me. She follows me to my bedroom and sucks in one cheek as she observes my floral comforter. She walks up to the cross-stitches of angels Mom has framed and hung on the wall.

"These are nice," she says. She plops down on the bottom bunk and looks at the ceiling. "Those stickers up there?"

I tell her Mom has mapped the ceiling with constellations and close the blinds and turn the light off. The stickers hint at glow. I point to the long neck of Ursa Major and then the North Star at the tail end of the small bear. There's Orion's belt. There's Gemini—siblings, one mortal and the other a god who begged that the two would never be separated, so they were joined together in immortality in the heavens.

"It's easier to see them at night," I say.

Eden gets up and walks to the light switch and flips it.

"You want to see stars?" she says.

We find Carol closing up her medical satchel, and Eden tugs at her mother's sleeve and whispers in her ear. Carol nods and turns to Mom.

"Can your girls come spend the night?"

By nightfall, we are preparing to camp on the midwife's trampoline. The sleeping bags are rough with use and the smell of leaves and campfire.

"Let me guess," Eden says. "Y'all ain't never been camping before."

Karson, Eden, Eden's sister Ruth, and I climb onto the trampoline outside and spread the sleeping bags across it. The wall of trees is backlit by eventide. Dusk lights up the secrets between the branches. Revelations shift in the leaves. The sun sets and light from stars begins its reveal. I survey the pallets on the trampoline where we sit with our legs crossed.

"You ever worried you'll roll off?"

"Geez," Eden says. She flops back and folds her arms behind her head and says, "First one to see a star wins."

"Wins what?" Karson says.

"Wins," Eden says.

A satellite treks a path above us, and I hear Eden's eyes roll as she explains that it is not a meteorite. Still, celestial bodies turn on the sky's wheel and their millions fall toward us. City light brims to the south. Bands of clustered stars scatter north across the sky's cavern. A dog hulks up the dirt road, her eyes like levitating light. She curls at the foot of the trampoline and sleeps.

Remembering this night, years later, I will also remember a story told to me by my father's mother of a time she lifted her face to the night sky. She had just given birth to my father, her third child, in a military hospital in Colorado Springs. It was 1959, and my grandparents brought their youngest home to a simple yellow house snugged back into a small grove of pines. A cross-section of the bedrock below would have shown every landscape Colorado had been through the epochs—sand dunes, swamp, ocean.

My father's older sister was five years old when she saw in my father's eyes the fathoms of blue that would follow him into adulthood. As he grew and his vision developed, he looked at her with recognition, and Lori came to believe that her brother had not entered her life but returned to it.

Since 1956, the Blackburns had lived only a few miles from Ent Air Force Base in Colorado Springs, the site of the North American Air Defense Command, where my grandfather directed maritime warning drills set amid Soviet invasion scenarios. At home,

Grandma cared for her three children and descended into a psychological fog. Her days were muted, as though she was on the other side of glass. The officers' wives didn't talk about postpartum depression. Night was worse than day, the silence dark and clear-cut. One night she stepped softly around the crib where her growing baby slept. Outside, the mountain air was sharp. She had a clean view of the stars and the Rockies' jagged line. She prayed to Mary, saying, *You have to help me.*

I wake with cold dew in my hair. The sky is gray. I brush the wet top of my sleeping bag. Us girls sit up and sway and stumble on the trampoline mat and climb down. The mutt from the night before laps water from a bowl by the front door. Eden asks if we've ever tasted goat's milk. Inside, she pulls a glass jar from the refrigerator and drinks from it directly, then takes down three cups and fills them and passes them around. Karson remarks that the milk tastes like the goats smell.

"It's good for you," Ruth says and smiles.

The midwife walks into the kitchen, fills a mug with coffee, leans against the counter, and drinks.

"Dog got into the garden last night," she says. Eden and Ruth exchange looks. Carol sets down her mug and from a kitchen drawer retrieves a wooden paddle.

"I am called to beat," she says.

The first sound astonishes me. It comes from the direction of the trampoline. Wood smacking bone. The dog yelps. Another blow lands. The midwife's daughters and my sister and I hold glasses of goat milk in silence under the sound of a wailing dog who knows neither her crime nor the possibility of mercy.

CHAPTER 4

THE DUE DATE FOR MY baby sister is March 12, 1996. Dad plans to run the New York marathon eight months later, in November. On our morning runs, he pants and describes the vision, saying that New York is one of the world's greatest cities. "It's no Lubbock, Texas, mind you. But there's Times Square, tall buildings. Bridges over the Hudson. A big Christmas tree, all decorated." One of the perks of homeschooling, he says, is that I can go with him. "Just flying in, seeing the skyline. There's nothing like it."

It's a testament to how deeply major icons of our culture seep through the seams of the tightest cloisters that I can envision the glow of yellow taxis as Dad speaks. Together, our black boots scuff the wide sidewalks of Madison Avenue. In Central Park, our breath forms a thick mist. A baby sister; a trip to New York; my twelfth birthday—1996 promises to be a grand year.

The notion that God ordained my mother's fifth pregnancy fills me with certainty about the ease with which this hallowed one will enter the world. So it is with shock that I once more wake to Dad's voice in the middle of the night. This time he is saying Mom's water has broken. She is not late, but early. It's a month too soon.

"Come," he says.

Mom trembles on the toilet. Blood, dark and viscous, covers her fingertips. Later she will tell me she had reached inside herself to check for the baby's head, which she could not feel. In the instant of seeing the blood, a surge of panic bolts through me. I believe the baby, which seemed no more alive than fantasy, is dead.

"What happened?"

"Not now, Kate," Dad says. He wraps Mom in a jacket. Carol

has told them to meet her at the hospital. Mom's pain is acute. She doesn't resist.

"I need to go with you."

"You are going to call the neighbors." He takes me by the shoulders. "Breathe."

Karson, Kendra, and James gather in the bathroom doorway, asking what is wrong.

Dad calls from the hospital, saying *abruptio placentae*, the Latin term a clear indication that the voice behind his is Mom's. His attempts to explain are mighty. I hang up and tell my siblings the tubes that fed the baby pulled away. The neighbor grimaces, and my siblings blink like fawns.

"When is Mom coming home?" Kendra says. I shrug.

When she returns from the hospital, Mom is wan, pale, and without her baby. My youngest sister will need support from the natal intensive care unit until she reaches five pounds. She is less than four.

Mom says the medical staff had already started grumbling when they saw her coming. "They don't like me because I'm smart." She leans over a half-eaten sandwich, says most of the staff have been brainwashed by pharmaceutical companies. She doesn't have much nice to say about medical schools either. She intends to care for her infant by returning to the hospital each day to breastfeed her, to hold her skin to skin, and to mount a resistance against the doctors and nurses that will no doubt send each of them in search of dark liquor. She says she needs my father at her side. I turn to Dad. His eyes are soft. Pleading. I pull a strand of hair into my mouth and chew.

"You can do it," he says.

And this is how, at the age of eleven, I become the full-time babysitter for my three younger siblings.

The following morning, us kids gather in the living room and my parents instruct us to follow the house rules, which are modeled after the Ten Commandments. A typed-up list of the instructions is posted to the refrigerator door, though the display is unnecessary: my siblings and I recite the house rules at the start of each school day right before we chorus the Pledge of Allegiance, each of us holding a small American flag. The house rules begin with the first commandment, to have no other gods. But the second commandment—you shall not make idols—has been replaced by the fifth: honor your father and your mother.

"We have put Kate in charge," Dad says. Karson seethes. There are no house rules about obeying your sister. Kendra wraps her body around Mom's leg, and Mom peels her off. She stands back and cries.

"Don't answer the door while we're gone," Mom says, kissing each one of us goodbye. "Call if you need anything," she adds over her shoulder as she walks out.

"Y'all go easy on each other," Dad says. For a brief and final moment of quiet, us kids stare at the closed door. I lock the deadbolt.

This will all be worth it, I think, *when I get to go to New York*. I face the towheads of my bloodline. They scatter.

"No running," I call after them and close my eyes.

In the coming days, the phrase I hear more than any other is, "You can't tell me what to do." Each one of my siblings says it, right down to four-year-old James. But Karson, whose resting temperature is simmer, champions the phrase. On principle, she refuses to do anything that carries a whiff of taking orders. As an adult, she will rest a handgun on a small pillow sitting on her nightstand. As a kid, her sense of independence manifests when I ask her to come set the table. She sits on the floor in the living room, stacking one Lego on top of another in a growing tower. Without breaking concentration, she presses a red Lego to the summit of her empire state, then fishes for another one.

"I'm not gonna," she says. "Because, and only because, you told me to."

When my parents come home in the evenings, I am worn down

to rage, a saucepan of burnt macaroni sitting in the sink, my siblings running around half-naked. I've lost track of who's taken a bath and who hasn't.

I snitch. "They haven't done one thing I've asked them to do."

"She thinks she's the boss," Karson screams.

"That's enough," Dad says. Every single one of us kids bursts into tears. We want to know if our baby sister is better. We want to know when she is coming home. Dad takes an armful of children and sets them on the couch.

"You come sit too," he tells me. He walks over to the television and VCR and hooks up a camcorder. "You'll like this," he says.

The clear walls of a baby incubator appear. Within, a sprawl of skinny orange limbs. A tube taped to the belly. A white diaper so large it can't close around the baby's waist. The view zooms in. An arm appears, Dad's. It reaches through an opening in the incubator. His palm settles on the baby. Nape to hind, she is no larger than the length of my father's hand.

"Is she going to be okay?" I say.

"Oh yeah," Dad says. His quick and easy response reassures me. If something were wrong, he'd know.

As Mary's hospital stay wears on, I get to know the NICU nurses pretty well myself. I call the hospital unit at least three times a day, ratting out one or another of my siblings. A semi-awake part of me wants my parents to understand that, despite whatever medical dictator they are facing down, it's three against one back at the fort. Kendra won't stop touching James. James pulls Kendra's hair. Karson won't lift a finger except to hold it in the air to make her point. One afternoon I call in tears.

"Put your sister on the phone," Dad says. "Wait, hold up, Kate. I gotta go, doctor's coming."

"What'd he say?" Karson says, crossing her arms as I hang up the phone.

"He said to drop the snot."

"Yeah right." Karson turns to Kendra and asks if she wants to play orphanage.

"Only if I get to be a mommy," Kendra says. She's aware of Karson's habit of leaving the orphans in the orphanage and starting a whole other game. The two toddle off to our bedroom.

"At least adopt her," I say. James watches them. A loose muscle in his right eye causes his pupil to drift. It orbits toward his tear duct as he watches my sisters leave. The wandering world of that pupil might as well reflect our whole family. Kendra thinks Karson won't trick her again. Mom is certain her faith gives her sovereign knowledge of the bodies in our family. Dad has a sense of abiding optimism. Because my father thinks all will be well, so do I.

The image of my brother's drifting eye will later come to haunt me, as though it portended the early loosening of our world from the path my family imagined we were so secured to, just as the placenta separated from my mother's uterus even as my parents claimed a holy promise of prosperity. James came to hate his amblyopia. He had corrective surgery a few years after our father died, when he was still young. Following the surgery, he regretted that there existed any photographs from his younger years that showed his eye turning inward. I have sometimes wondered if part of his pain was because of what his eye had seen and couldn't look away from.

One afternoon Dad stays home with us while Mom goes to the hospital. The man wearies at his task. Charged with restoring order to the house, he lasts about an hour. He sits in the green recliner in the living room, kicks up the leg rest, and tells us to go play. Play we do, circled around the kitchen table to compete in a board game called Trouble. The problem with Trouble is Karson won't stop cheating, popping the dice within a plastic dome then moving her blue pegs one too many. She particularly likes jumping my pieces to close in on the win. Since the baby's birth, Karson and I have been entangled in the kind of fights dogs have: we're as docile as daisies until we see one another. Kendra is asking if we can please just play the game, James says he's done playing, and Karson bilks the roll. I lunge and hit her hand as hard as I can. The sound is loud and high-pitched. Everything from the last ten days is in that smack: Mom's thick angry blood, the baby's ventilating tube, Dad's neglect, Karson's hostility, every outburst from Kendra, every glance from James, and the abject, self-loathing sense of failure I've come to feel for my inability to care for my siblings in our parents' absence. I'd done little more than keep them alive—which, as Karson keeps reminding me, they don't need me for.

Kendra rears back in shock. Karson holds her injured hand. It reddens, and so does her face. She gasps as though I've punched her in the gut. My own hand aches from crushing hers. We are both stunned. She grimaces with pain and looks at me. Her sorrow is unbearable. Words of apology jump up my throat, but I stop them. Karson and I, in the same second, remember that we hate each other. She smirks. Her eyes light up. I rush to hit her again, but she jumps up and runs through the kitchen. She's wailing by the time she gets to Dad.

The footrest slams shut. The recliner springs as Dad storms from it. I leap from my chair when I see him. His expression is terrifying—his sleep-deprived eyes wild, his jaw hardened. He jolts me at the shoulders, asks which hand I used, bites the collar of his shirt, constricts my forearm, and strikes the offending hand. Fracture for fracture, commands God. An eye for an eye. My wrist snaps with each crack. Karson blanches. Kendra melts into tears. When Dad finishes, I hold my wrist and stumble blubbering to my room.

Alone on the bottom bunk, I twist my hand. I'd told Dad the wrong one, pointing to my left hand instead of my right. I had done so without thinking. Maybe a part of me wanted to preserve the hand that writes almost daily in a diary, filling pages with updates on the weather and my scrapes with Karson. Maybe I wanted to zap the power of tidy retribution from my father. My wrist gripes when I bend it. I try to roll it and can't. The joints swell.

Shame radiates through my body, and the pain releases a torrent of relief. For every way I've faltered this week, I want atonement: each shout, each narc, each burnt dinner deserves punishment, and though I'm pitiful at caretaking, I can at least be good at suffering consequences. But I also can't shake a feeling of destitution. The memory of Dad's spittle-soaked collar makes my chest ache. My parents have said punishment is a form of love, and no fundamentalist evangelical would disagree. There are plenty of scriptures that support it. But nagging at me is the feeling that Dad broke some kind of promise—a feeling of betrayal that will shadow me into adulthood, when I will wonder at the ways my father suppressed his better instincts in the name of obeying God.

Like my mother, my father believed in corporal punishment, and I was familiar with the strike of his hand across my backside. He didn't discipline me and my sisters often, though he was more likely than my mother to lose his temper and punish us when he did. But the afternoon he clobbered my wrist felt different. He smacked a different part of my body. He acted out of a blind rage, driven not by parental authority but by sleep deprivation and stress over having a baby in the NICU. Looking back, I view the incident not as an anomaly but as an escalation in a pattern of abusive behavior sanctioned by evangelical doctrine. But my father, who was gentle by nature, felt he'd made a mistake. I credit him for being able to elevate his personal code over dogma—most people in the faith would call doing so weakness and unmanly. That was the last time he ever physically punished me.

I remember pressing my left wrist to my sternum and falling asleep.

Dad wakes me and sits on the side of the bed and holds his face. Neither of us speaks or looks at the other. I shudder.

"Let me see your wrist," he says without turning to me. He bends my wrist and I gasp. At the sound, he faces me, his expression soft. Mournful. With the back of his fingers, he brushes my cheek.

"I'm sorry," he says.

My parents name the baby Mary Katherine. When she is a week old, Dad brings my siblings and me up to the NICU floor. I meet the nurse whose voice I've heard so many times on the phone.

"Oh, I remember you," she says.

We arrive at a long wall of hospital glass. Mary materializes in Mom's arms, and I am not prepared for how small she is. A birthmark curves above her left eyebrow in a question mark. She is monarch orange, dark in the creases of her eyelids. As my reflection falls across her, I recall the idea that Mary is a rivet in God's design.

"Why were you crying?" Mom asks me later.

"I don't know," I say, though some part of me does know that, though I have joined my family on Sunday mornings for hundreds of cumulative hours of prayer and worship, I have not recognized the sacred until now. Not in the form of Christ, but as an infant nonetheless, my youngest sister, appearing like a dream on the other side of a wall of glass.

It is late February, cold and dreary on the high plains, the sky a steel brace to the wind, when Mary Katherine is brought home. She enters the house with hints of the fermented aroma of baby, the strong smell of soap, and traces of bitter antiseptic. "Hospital smell," Mom says.

Mary is two weeks old, but time maps strangely onto her, moving forward with chronology and folding back. At two weeks old, she is still two weeks early, and her development is a month behind. I sit in the green recliner in the living room and hold her for the first time. Behind us rears a bookcase Dad built: eight feet tall, crafted of oak, replete with thirty shelves. Its presence assures me of gravity's hold, though my sister feels like she could drift away like vapor. Mom stands nearby.

"You're my second in command," she says. "We couldn't have done this without you." She squeezes my shoulder and then tells my siblings to come to the kitchen for lunch, leaving me alone with my baby sister.

Mary Katherine at last weighs five pounds. I remember the rejoicing when she gained an ounce, the despair when she lost one. Her life had come down to something so empirical—ounces on a scale. Five pounds meant Mary could come home; five pounds meant she would be fine, and our lives would return to normal.

But in my arms, five pounds feels only slightly heavier than air.

I tense with fear as the rest of my family walks out of the living room. Holding Mary feels like trying to cradle a tiny playa. I adjust my arm under her back and she twists away from me. She slides headfirst toward the ground. I seize her swaddled feet and catch her shoulder, my pulse a trapped bird. Mary's head swings above my knees. Her eyes open in shock at the sight of the ceiling.

I tug her back even as I still envision her head breaking on the floor. "I'm sorry," I say between rapid breaths. "I'm so sorry."

She drifts back to sleep, and I fill with fear of my loose grasp, fear of how quickly her body slid from mine.

Over the coming weeks amnesia sweeps over the family, and I beam as Dad talks on the phone with his mother, describing how many meals I can cook on my own.

"We're talking full-blown dinners with salad and everything." He pauses. When Mary Katherine was born, my grandparents offered to drive up from Universal City, a suburb of San Antonio, to help. My parents declined, going into bunker mode. Many years later, I learned my grandparents were hurt by that refusal of their help, and confused. Even now, I see Dad nod as he listens to his mother. "Nope," he says. "Didn't need to hire a babysitter. Got the best in the world right here." He claps me on the back.

Throughout the two February weeks Mary was in the hospital, I held close the promise that I'd go to New York with Dad come November. Each morning now, he runs into the clear dawn. Sometimes I join him on my bike, and he brings Mary Katherine in a jogging stroller and Andy alternates between a trot and balancing his front paws on the crossbar of the stroller to help push it. Mary seems to love the jostle and jerk of the buggy, the bluing of sky overhead.

One October morning I watch Mom put on her face. Of concealing blemish and darkening her brows she's made an art. Her poreless skin is veiled in translucent powder. Her lashes lengthen long and dark brown with each stroke of mascara. She says that she has been meaning to tell me something. I wait. She gets on with it: I am too young to go to the marathon with my father.

I remind her that Dad will be running with two of his close friends, Carlos and Joe, and Joe's wife Anita has a ticket to New York already. We will be together on the sidelines.

"I like Anita just fine," Mom says. "But that doesn't mean I trust her with my child."

My eyes sting. "Can you at least trust me?"

She scoffs. "You're eleven."

In my gut, I feel a pooling, hot and liquid. My beautiful mother is full of grass-fed cow manure. Though Mom found me old enough to leave my younger siblings with me as their babysitter for almost two weeks, she is saying I am too young to travel with Dad. Although so many of my feelings about this time in my life will change in the coming decades, my resentment over this hypocrisy will remain consistent over twenty-five years, a hard stone I carry with me. Whether she lies to me or to herself, I cannot tell. I am young, she's right, but I can see how she rewrites her code to suit her convenience. I cry. Mom shrugs.

"You'll go when you're older."

That night Dad takes a stab at comforting me. Tucking me into bed, he tells me I am the greatest help to him and Mom. I roll away, convinced that my ability to cook and monitor playtime has worked against me. I have to stay in Lubbock because I am too young, but also, paradoxically, because I am so reliable. It's a betrayal that sits as well with me as pineapple, a food that comes charging right back up my throat when I eat it. Dad rubs my shoulder. I plot to skimp on the vacuuming, to wash dishes slowly, with plenty of clanging.

"It's going to be cold in New York, you know," he says. "And you would have had to get up very early, way before daylight." I snap around to face him.

"I get up early to run with you."

"Come on, Kate." He sighs, folds his hands, presses them to his forehead, and drops them to his lap. He seeks my hand and holds it. The side of his face glows in the lamplight. He tells me that there will be many more marathons. He describes how hundreds of runners will gather at the Verrazzano-Narrows Bridge. He's heard some will be wearing expensive coats, and at the signal to start, they'll just drop them onto the street. He's run many marathons, including the White Rock in Dallas and the San Antonio, but this will be the first time he's participated in the New York City Marathon. He will join over twenty-eight thousand runners. I imagine the thunderous sound of everyone's feet. "It's crazy," he says.

On marathon day, he will finish in three hours, forty-six minutes, with an average pace of an eight-minute mile. Some people will be cheering from the sidelines. That's where I would have been.

"Next time," Dad says, "I'll take you."

CHAPTER 5

DESPITE THEIR BRAVADO, MY PARENTS were shaken by Mary's early arrival. While they refused the help offered by my grandparents, they also talked about lacking a strong Christian community. We'd been church hunting for most of my life, jumping from one congregation to another, my parents seeking what they called true Bible-based teaching and coming up disappointed each time. There was the small congregation, filled exclusively with other home-school families, where women weren't allowed to speak. Mom said she didn't feel at home there. There was a church that met in a bank; one that met in an old basketball gym; one that met in the home of a skinny man with an animated Adam's apple in his throat. I watched the knot bob up and down as the guy claimed he needed no other job than to lead a small flock. Then he glanced at a nearby sleeping dog and said that were it not for the call to do God's work, he'd love to have the life of a dog that slept all day. Afterward, I overheard Dad say it was hard to respect a man like that.

These were fledgling churches claiming to have broken the yoke of doctrines that strayed too far from the teachings of the Bible. My parents, raised Catholic, converted to evangelicalism in the Year of Our Lord Ronald Reagan. No more intermediary between God and man. But my parents never fully embraced the evangelicals' saved-by-grace-alone theology, which was sluggish by comparison with Lent. Grace alone was for the lazy. Religion was regiment. They brought the discipline from Catholicism to their evangelical rebirths. It was like throwing gasoline on the Holy Spirit.

With each failed church hunt, my mother became increasingly convinced that she and my father were solely responsible for their children's spiritual education—as they had concluded with every other aspect of our upbringing. One evening my parents call us into the living room and tell my sisters and me that we will not be going to Sunday school at any future churches. Mom says she has read the scriptures closely.

"We are supposed to worship together, and that means literally. That doesn't mean babies going off to nurseries, kids going off to Sunday school, teens sneaking off to youth group, all while parents stay in the sanctuary. Church shouldn't divide up the family."

She says that sending us to Sunday school would be an abdication of her parental role. I find myself wishing I had a less responsible mother. As a homeschooled child, I'd found Sunday school to be one of the few places where I might meet other kids.

"You'll meet other children when they get out of Sunday school," Mom says.

We walk into the small, dank sanctuary of Grace Church for the first time in 1996, when Mary Katherine is not yet one year old. The building was once a funeral home—a *ha-ha* held dear by the congregation. A woodcut of the continents hangs on the east wall of the sanctuary like a military map, a reminder that God makes disciples of all nations. Of those nations, about seventy white people and one family of color are represented, mingling near their seats. I fidget with my dress when I see how small the sanctuary is. There will be no way to even bow my head without everyone noticing. We walk to the front of the church where the only empty row of seats remains. Although my trip to New York has been canceled, my twelfth birthday still hovers on the horizon. My braces have recently been removed, and I run my tongue over my smooth teeth.

A keyboardist and two guitarists take the stage at Grace Church and worship begins. There's a drummer too, and though his kit is behind a noise barrier wall, the beats drown us in white noise. Above the stage, a cross is lit from behind. Then a projector screen drops over it, and the song lyrics for "This Is the Day" appear.

Mom leans over and glances down our row to make sure my

sisters and I are singing. Kendra is busy wide-eying the congregation, her gander rolling over each adult, pausing to take in a shiny bald head, a gaudy watch. Mom reaches past me to rattle Kendra's shoulder. I wince with a flicker of rage. There are many reasons why, as adults, neither I nor my siblings will attend church, and they could all be distilled down to Mom mouthing the words, "You need to sing."

A woman crosses the aisle with her eyes on my mother. I resist the impulse to wave her off. *You're wasting your time*, I want to tell her. Instead, I fold my arms. The woman taps Mom on the shoulder. Her name is Jo Marshall.

"You can take your little baby to the nursery." She smiles down at Mary Katherine.

"No, thank you," Mom says. Jo looks at my brother. He is sitting on the floor taking dollar bills out of Mom's purse and counting them.

"What about him? He might enjoy playing with the other children."

"He's fine with us."

Jo smiles again and says, "We're glad you're here."

Mom smiles brightly at Jo, and I see the chance to meet new friends disintegrate into ash. Mom turns to me, eyes gleaming. She preens whenever she gets the chance to buck expectation. Am I not proud? Awkwardness passes through me like a sour taste. I swallow and look away.

Worship ends, and a stampede of children pass us. Jo turns in her seat and nods in the direction in which all of them are skipping. I look at the red carpet, my black buckle dress shoes, my ankle turning as the two women continue to exchange smiles like flying daggers.

Kids between the ages of five and thirteen clamor toward two doors at the back of the stage. Some of them eye me and my siblings curiously as they pass. My brother stops playing with Mom's wallet to watch them bounce by. One girl pauses at the stage and bids me join her. A nervous smile spreads across my face, like a dog baring her teeth. The girl flinches and vanishes into the back of the church. The doors close.

A middle-aged man, Pastor Shawn, steps up to the stage and grips the podium with bent fingers. He begins with a few announcements: The Culvers are hosting a Bible study on the Book of Revelation. There's going to be a potluck next week. The sign-up sheet is by the water fountain. Pastor Shawn pats the wisps of his comb-over and smiles.

"It's time for share-time." He steps down from the stage and slowly ambles around in the front of the church. "Are there any other announcements? Any needs for prayer?"

The congregation is silent. I scan the group, unsure of what's happening. A man stands. He's dressed in worn Levi's and a plaid collared shirt. Kelly speaks straight through his nose, says he hasn't been around much, we might have noticed. The congregation chuckles.

"It's planting season, and me and Jesse been going sunup to past supper." He points his thumb at a skinny boy of about fifteen who's sitting in a row of boys at the very back of the church. He's leaning over his knees with his hands clasped and head bowed. He looks up with the ice-blue eyes of a Husky.

"Forecast is what it is. But we know who's in control." The cotton farmer nods at the ceiling.

"Amen," Pastor Shawn says.

Kelly sits. Someone in the crowd says, "Oh, all right." The keyboardist, a short, corpulent man named Jerry, scuffles up and adjusts his glasses. "Brenda put me up to this. We've got a praise. I passed my qualifying exams last week, and I want to thank God, by his blessings and grace. I'm also grateful to my wife." Jerry turns and places a hand on Brenda's back. "And thanks to my kids too. They're somewhere around here." The congregation claps. Jerry waves us down and sits.

"Anybody else?" Shawn raises his eyebrows and surveys the room. "Okay," he says. "God is good."

The embarrassment and disappointment I initially felt at being barred from Sunday school gives way to a tingle of sport. Each Sunday there will be the boy with blue eyes. Each Sunday will involve share-time when, in the name of the sacred, church members will air their requests and gloats.

We've been attending Grace Church a few months when one of the pastors announces that he's stepping down from preaching. Back in 1982, Randy Ward had been the one who led a small caravan from Houston to Lubbock to found a church. Randy looked made for televangelism—he had a paunch, a thick mustache, a fiery gaze that twitched with thought, and the charm of a car salesman who strikes you as out of place in the dealer's lot. He was the kind of straight-talking guy you could trust. As he sped over the blacktop to Lubbock, he dreamed of a megachurch, his message broadcast on radio, his willowy wife draped in glossy new outfits each Sunday.

But Grace wasn't destined to be a megachurch. Pastor Shawn wraps an arm around Randy as he explains he needs some personal time. "I need to find myself again," Randy says. He has a Winnebago. He's going to drive up to Canada. Members of the congregation gather around him and place hands on him and pray. Mom's eyes squint a little and move across the prayer group, her eyebrows two flat lines.

On the way home she shares her opinion. "I guess Randy's wife is just supposed to take care of their children until he 'finds himself.'" She makes quotes with her fingers. Dad nods. I watch Thirty-Fourth Street go by. We pass a bookstore called Adult Books and the teahouse where Jo works and Sunset Church of Christ. I think of Randy, the way he stood at the front of the stage, puddling in midlife crisis. When I look up, I catch my mom's eye watching me in the rearview mirror. I see the reflection of my face beside hers. I am calm and smiling and playing dumb. She smiles and glances away.

My ability to conceal my reactions has the benefit of rendering my eleven-year-old self almost invisible during share-time. The adults around me seem to assume I'm not listening, or can't comprehend what they're talking about, or won't remember. In this way, I learn the art of the humble brag, boasts posed as "praise reports." The person who dominates in this category is a thin-framed woman named Cherry Stewart. She is the wife of a state representative who won on his credentials as a certified accountant promising to lower tax rates. Together, Cherry and her husband have four, by their account, highly accomplished children.

"Our oldest, Jane, won at regional gymnastics last week." Cherry's praise report is followed by perfunctory clapping. Mom holds Mary Katherine and doesn't applaud.

"We're grateful to God," Cherry continues, "for protecting her and giving her favor. She placed first on uneven bars, and her team won floor." The farmer's son Jesse locks focus with me and smirks. It makes me feel incredibly mature to share an inside joke with a boy who's three years older than me. I roll my eyes.

Another week, Cherry asks for help defrosting her freezer while her husband is down at the capitol protecting families and small businesses. It was commonly known that her husband was up in a deer stand when Cherry gave birth to their fourth kid, but a few people offer to assist with the freezer anyway. Mom will remember Cherry's defrost ask for years. As we walk out into the church parking lot, she shakes her head. "Like no one else has anything to do," she mutters. "I have an idea. Why doesn't Blake come home and defrost his own freezer."

Before climbing into the van, I turn to see Jesse. He stands in a group of church boys with skateboards. His hands are in his pockets. He nods my way and then looks at the ground.

Jesse's father speaks at the next share-time. He stands and starts crying. I can barely make out his words. Jesse's head is bowed.

"We need to pray for Randy," Kelly says. Randy Ward. Last I knew, he was still in Manitoba, camping in his recreational vehicle. But no one asks why we need to pray for him, everyone closes their eyes, and Pastor Shawn requests that the Lord be with Randy.

Before we leave the building, Mom stands in a huddle with

some churchwomen and rubs the space between her eyes. Then she gestures to us kids and says it's time to go home. In the van, she tells Dad that Randy met a woman online.

"And guess where she lived? That's what all this soul-searching was about. Yeah. I thought it was weird when he said he needed to find himself. I'm going, why does a man need to drive all the way up to Canada to do that? Well. And poor Jeanie. She's had to get a job driving a school bus."

That evening I stand in the doorway of Mom's bathroom. She's washing her face.

"What do you think will happen with Jeanie and Randy?" I ask.

"I don't know," Mom says. Her eyes sweep the doorway and she mouths the words, *Are your sisters around?* I shake my head. She waves me over and whispers.

"The women at church were saying Randy demanded blow jobs from Jeanie. Yeah. Every night for months before he left her. You know what those are, right?" I lie. My ears burn as she tells me anyway. Mom went to great lengths to prevent my exposure to expletives, bikinis, and sex only to turn around and explain fellatio. I am to be shielded from the vague morality of prime-time TV, but not one iota of what drifts across her brain. I want to beg her to stop. As she says the word *suck*, I back away in horror, a response that seems to satisfy her.

That night I lie in bed crying at the very idea of a blow job.

It will take me years to understand that my mother looked forward to share-time the way I did. It was salacious. And for her, something more. She could flatter herself that she didn't have such problems, couldn't conceive of them really. Showboating one's woes wasn't for her. She could safely promise herself to never speak at share-time.

CHAPTER 6

A PAIN BELOW DAD'S WAISTLINE caves him at the commode. It burns to urinate. His bowels urge. He sits. The smell of blood and shit. He tells himself it's runner's hemorrhoids. Back in January he passed his annual pilot's health exam. His doctor agreed, *runner's hemorrhoids*. At thirty-eight years old, Dad can run a six-minute mile, a personal record. But the ache is new. It's May 1997, six months since the New York marathon, four months since his last physical. He flushes.

It's embarrassing to toilet like this at his parents' home on Sherri Avenue in Universal City where he grew up. The blue tile porcelain bathroom; the towel cart set with the warm glow of a lamp: his mother's pristine housekeeping the same as it always was. After drying his hands, he takes a moment to straighten and smooth the towel. Glancing at his reflection, he pauses. At five-foot-seven, he is not a tall man. Born of sturdy, dense stock. A fast running back on the high school football team. Thick calves and thighs. Bulky if he doesn't watch it, but he does. But now, at thirty-eight, he is, for the first time in his life, slim.

Out back, Grandpa sweeps the pool with a long pole net, and Grandma takes her coffee at the patio table, her mug hovering over the paper. Dad walks into the kitchen and fills his own mug. He notices one of his parents' Medicare pamphlets lying on the counter. The front flap reads: "When to Call the Doctor." He lifts the tract and reads on. It's an efficient text. He recognizes his symptoms. When the screen door hinges gripe, Dad replaces the booklet and Grandma appears with a small yellow mug.

"Refill?" Dad says and lifts the coffee pot.

My grandparents' kitchen opens to a lounge with a large window overlooking the pool. The bar is crafted of large mason stone. Behind it, crystal glasses sit on glass shelves. Light from the pool flutters across the walls and ceiling. Above the long end of the bar hangs a framed photograph from the day Dad joined the Air Force. My grandfather swore him in. Along with their DNA, Blackburn men pass down a military lineage. My grandfather's father also had a career in the Air Force. In the photograph, Dad and Grandpa are dressed in uniform and face each other. Dad holds his right hand aloft as he takes the oath his father took, just as his father's father had done before him, just as James, my brother, will do many years later, after both men from the photo are gone.

Coffee in hand now, Dad follows his mother out back past the photograph. Its glass pane reflects the pool and the glare of the gray figures that gather at its edge.

Following his visit to his parents, he asks Mom if he should see a doctor, and the woman who could find almost any reason not to, says yes.

But all I know at the time is my parents have departed for an appointment saying Dad's stomach is bothering him, and now my sisters are refusing to do math. I'm loading them down with just-wait-till-Mom-and-Dad-get-home threats. Karson colors her nails green with a marker. James retreats to his room. Kendra has an announcement: she has finished her math lesson. She slaps her notebook closed and dashes off. Mary walks into the dining room having eaten half a black crayon.

"That's it." I hoist Mary to my hip. "*I* have an announcement. All y'all can stare at your math books for the rest of your lives. See if I care."

"Fine." Karson shoves off from the table and stomps away.

I turn to my baby sister. "Now, about you."

I have a right mind to flood my parents with the morning's report when they walk in, but the expression on Mom's face knocks me dumb. She is pensive, her mouth drawn. I've seen this same countenance after she's read a grim lab report or asked a client to leave her dog for a series of X-rays—times when a litany of medical jargon does little to stop the client's eyes from clouding over.

Mom grins at me with the world's most half-assed bluff, and I file the morning's offenses in my cranium's backlog.

Searching Dad's face, I look for a sign of worry. Instead, I find an expression I've never seen before. I catch my breath. He is blanched.

"Your dad's going to be fine," Mom says. Dad nods numbly as she uses the word *polyp* and takes great pains to explain the human large intestine. Every nerve asks that I cover my ears.

He's going to get a scan next week.

"It's pretty routine," Mom says. Her voice cracks. My tears detonate.

Dad grabs me and presses his face to my head.

We eat dinner, bathe, dress for bed, and pray. My sisters' sleeping breaths count the seconds. A murmur surfaces through the calm. It trails from the kitchen; I am certain of it. I slip from the bed. At the corner of the hallway, I hear Dad's voice. He's on the phone. I wait for the sound of reassurance in his voice but instead he pauses, speaks again.

"Maybe bad," he says.

The lawn is freshly mowed. Inside the house, the wafting aroma of Mom's spaghetti sauce graces the air with oregano and garlic. In the guest room, the bedsheets have been turned back.

A blade of light glances off my grandparents' white Lincoln. They park at the curb.

A torque of despair turns in my stomach at the way Dad draws his mother into his arms. There's a tumor in Dad's colon. That's all anyone knows. Mom has continued to say they've caught it early, and Dad has agreed and recovered his nonchalance. But my grandmother's hands pass over his back and pause.

Mom buzzes with questions about my grandparents' drive, with particular interest in the conditions of the road.

"How long did it take you?"

"About seven hours," my grandfather says.

"What can I get you all, something to drink?"

I pray against her water monologue. Mom likes to say we have good water; she means our privately filtered system. Our water, she claims, is so pure you can taste what isn't there. No microbes, no industry pollutants, nor, good Lord, any arsenic or fertilizer runoff. She says city water gives a tell in the skin and teeth, like cigarettes. In time I will understand she is more right than she knows. In the present, I wish that we had something more than water to offer my grandparents. Back in Universal City, they might have sipped sherry from crystal glasses. But now, they follow Dad to the guest room, each with a glass of water. It's five o'clock somewhere. Not here.

Looking back now from the distance of twenty-five years, I imagine that once inside the guest room, Grandma downed her glass of water and said something like, "That ought to take the edge off." Humor, rhetorical shrugs, that was the Blackburn way. She would have then set to work placing her folded slacks in the empty dresser. Perhaps her mind darted as it did when she later talked to me about the last year of her son's life: he'd looked robust as he strode across the yard to greet her. When she took him into her arms, she thought, *This has got to be some sick joke.* His firm young body, a promise. The dying don't feel like that. She knew.

In 1963, while my grandfather was stationed in Baumholder, Germany, my grandmother discovered she was pregnant with her fifth baby. She found it remarkable to be bearing a child at the age of forty-four. A surprise, a welcome one, and she offered her belly to her four children when the baby kicked. But as her due date neared, a doctor said there was no longer a heartbeat. He told her to go home and wait. She had to carry the baby to term.

Back at the base, she lay in bed and listened to the baby-boy chatter of Johnny and Bobby as eleven-year-old Lori cared for them. Their voices reverberated down the hallway. Grandpa had left with their eldest, Tommy, to drive out to the station's bunkers, where he routinely checked on the well-being of the troops and thanked them.

Perhaps as she waited, Grandma thought of the night sky in Colorado Springs. By comparison with waiting for a stillborn, her postpartum in the foothills of the Rockies was a penumbra, a dull scrape. I imagine she knew her body would never be empty of remembering. Not when she birthed a child who had died inside her. Not when she stopped bleeding. She was a lifelong Catholic, Order of the Sacred Heart, and she was a woman of faith, but what words came to her then? When a pain bloomed in her abdomen, it must have felt like the kind of beginning, bleak and unknowable, that separates epochs. She named the stillborn Paul. My grandfather accompanied their son aboard a plane across the Atlantic to Arlington's National Cemetery, where a soldier can bury his children among the fallen. My grandmother was not there for her son's burial.

I'm not aware that she used words to describe her feelings about being expected to stay behind, but in her remaining life she never visited Paul's grave. Some members of the family think she felt unacknowledged in Paul's death—perhaps by the military, who treated the baby as Tom Blackburn's son. Perhaps, even, by my grandfather, who soon returned to Baumholder and focused on his rise to colonel. There were also practical considerations—she had four children already to care for. And once the Blackburns returned to the states for good, Virginia was a long way from Texas. Perhaps my grandmother felt no marker could match the scale and brutality of the loss she had endured, especially after feeling she hadn't been acknowledged but cut off.

She refused to bury another child. As she grappled with the looming details around my father's health, she clung to a memory of him as boy, a promise that he would outlive her.

In 1971, when Dad was twelve, Bobby ten, my grandparents took the boys on a cross-country road trip from San Antonio to the Grand Canyon. The colonel stopped somewhere in the Southwest to fill the family's big brown Lincoln. Always a Lincoln. Always an American-made car. Grandma fanned herself with a map in the backseat, while Bobby flipped through the pages of a comic book he'd memorized. Next to the colonel, my father sat up brightly, eyes cobalt and bright as quartz. He pointed to a diner across the highway and asked for money to buy ice cream. Those blue eyes. My grandmother's were cut of the same crystal. Her mother's too. Whenever people remarked on the Irish origin of Kennedy, my grandmother's maiden name, she was quick to mention that her eyes were her mother's. "From the Danish," she'd say. But she didn't tell anyone she was afraid of going blind. Her mother was losing her vision. Worn vessels had opened in her retinas and were leaking blood. Macular degeneration. The condition was hereditary.

Dusk ignited the horizon, a resin line above blacktop. A lighter snapped. Ash whisked through the open window as Grandma watched her son run across the highway to the diner. He held his elbows akimbo, but his gait was smooth, as though he were much older.

My grandmother liked to think she'd also inherited her mother's resilience. Dorothy Kennedy was born in Racine in 1920. The oldest of five children and the only girl. *Little old me*, she used to say. Daughter of a salesman, an Irish immigrant, a drunk. Whenever Dorothy heard of people saying they had depression, she scoffed. Depression was using your four-foot-eleven frame to shelter your mother from your father's vitriol after he'd spent his earnings on whiskey down at a bar called Nick's. It was lying awake at night in a house in Mansfield, Ohio, just praying you wouldn't hear his feet stumble up the steps. Drinking wasn't an addiction. It was a personality, and AA couldn't cure that. Her father was what they call *recovered* by the time she brought my grandfather home in 1946 to meet him, but she knew he was still the same man. You don't recover from who you are. When her father died in 1956, she didn't attend his funeral.

My grandmother thought of herself as the kind of woman who knew enough to know when you had it good. When, in 1966, Grandpa got stationed at Randolph Air Force Base and they found a place in a suburb outside of San Antonio called Universal City, it sounded right—*universal* signifying to her not the cosmos but a modern system of highways and underground pipes. Places like Universal City were under development everywhere, their green lawns, strip malls, and good schools manifesting the standardized

American dream come true—for a white man with a salary and a family. Twenty miles from downtown San Antonio, Universal City was only 2.7 miles from Randolph Air Force Base, my grandfather's last station before retirement in 1969. But Universal City could have been anywhere in the United States.

Not everything came up rosy. The war in Vietnam threw its shadow over those early years in Texas. In 1967, a year after they moved to Universal City, a fire consumed the USS *Forrestal*. The aircraft carrier was stalking Vietnam's north shore, preparing to attack. Aboard the vessel, young Navy ensign John McCain readied for combat in an A-4 Skyhawk fighter jet. Then a parked F-4 Phantom launched an errant Zuni rocket that struck the Skyhawk's 400-gallon fuel tank. Petroleum slapped the deck a few feet away from where the future US senator stood. The leaked fuel lit up a path of fire that, in ninety seconds, reached parked jets with pilots strapped inside. Officers on foot scrambled for hand-held extinguishers. The CO_2 did little more to stop the fire than their own breath would have done. Inferno trapped the pilots inside their planes. Then the flames detonated at least one 1,000-pound bomb, killing the men who were chasing them. The explosion set off a chain of combustions that blew through the length of the 1,091-foot flight deck and sent half the supercarrier to hell. The conflagration burned for at least seventeen hours, killing 134 sailors and injuring hundreds more.

Never again. The Navy joined forces with the company 3M to develop a new aqueous film-forming foam (AFFF) that could stop petroleum fires.

The magic ingredients for the foam were a group of chemicals that had a carbon-fluorine bond—the strongest bond in organic chemistry. Perfluoroalkyl and polyfluoroalkyl substances (PFAS) had high electronegativity, low polarizability, and long carbon backbones. These properties made PFAS ideal ingredients for non-stick products. My grandmother didn't know about PFAS, but she did own Teflon pans and Scotchgard, some of the more famous household items in which PFAS were present.

Though other formulations of AFFF existed, the foam that 3M

exclusively developed and sold between the 1960s and 2002 dominated the market. It was created using an electrochemical fluorination process to produce a long carbon chain that reinforced the strong carbon-fluorine bond. Among PFAS, this group, called perfluoroalkyl acids (PFAAs), were a powerhouse substance. They were *highly* chemically and thermally stable. They would become some of the most environmentally persistent, bioaccumulative, and toxic PFAS on the planet.

Over fifty years later, certain PFAAs, including perfluorooctane sulfonate (PFOS), perfluorooctanoate (PFOA), and perfluorohexane sulfonate (PFHxS), would constitute three of the six forever chemicals targeted for regulation in drinking water by the Environmental Protection Agency (EPA) in 2023 because of their hazardous health impacts. But in the 1960s, 3M branded its foam "Light Water," as though its presence on the planet would be just as ephemeral and life-giving as those elements.

Petroleum fire had no effect on light water. It was the other way around. Light water spread through fire without disintegrating. The foam resisted heat and every other type of chemical bond. It spread through petroleum fire like a blanket. In some drills, the foam could snuff out flames in less than thirty seconds.

The response to the *Forrestal* disaster was distilled to acronyms: the DOD contracted with the manufacturer 3M to produce AFFF. Light water was distributed across the nation's military sites, and PFAS entered the environment on a global scale.

With a good feeling sometimes came a foreboding. Back on the interstate in the Southwest somewhere, Grandma looked across the highway.

My father was holding an ice cream cone and waving from the other side of the interstate. He looked far away. Something inside her reached for him. The asphalt between them stretched too wide. The highway swayed, distant and thin, like a telephone wire, and her son perched on it no larger than a bird. His waving hand was a flame flickering on the time line of his life. Sometimes a woman is given God's view but no power to do anything about it. A blood vessel ruptured in Grandma's periphery. A cloud of crimson. A red car careened toward her son with the silence and intent of a meteorite. How long had that rock flown through space before gravity turned it into a four-cylinder bullet? Red is the last color you see before you lose all sight. She leapt from the car and ran toward the highway. She shrieked. To look? To back away? A horn. Her son turned to face it, and she couldn't help herself: she closed her eyes. There are some things you see but can't watch. Don't look at the sun or the dying.

When my grandmother's eyelids lifted, my father's hair was dancing in the car's red wake.

CHAPTER 7

THE DINING TABLE IS TRANSFORMED from its homeschool function to a long banquet set with nine drinking glasses. Mom sits as stiff as a latched spring—a posture that for her and my grandmother must stir memories of the first time the two women met.

In 1979, when Dad brought his fiancé home to meet his parents, she sat on Grandma's couch starched as cotton duck canvas. Grandma observed that Mom was as beautiful as her son had said. Rightly so. She was also shy. Or rude? It was hard to tell. Had John really met her while out two-stepping? Grandma's questions bounced off Mom's one-word answers like a tennis ball off a wall. The most Grandma got out of her was a startle when she asked if Mom would like a cocktail.

"I'll have a water, please," Mom said.

Dad attributed Mom's social conduct to her intelligence and held her in awe. No room existed where Beverly Jacobs was not the smartest and most handsome, and his parents' wet bar was no exception. To heck if she was shy. He'd heard a fair amount of too much talk from people with less than nothing to say—and he ought to know, he joked. His own talents included gab. Sitting next to Mom that afternoon in Universal City, he rested a reassuring hand on her knee and served conversation into the air.

About meeting my grandparents for the first time, Mom said they were kind. With shame she admitted to sleeping with Dad before they were married. Upon arrival in Universal City, she feigned virginity at first, insisting that she and Dad take separate bedrooms. But Dad simply joined her after everyone had gone to bed. My grandmother's knock on the bedroom door came midmorning. "She just asked if we'd like some breakfast and treated me with the same generosity as she had the day before." Though Dad said his parents really didn't care—remember, he told her, they're laid-back Catholics—Mom always held that after finding my parents in sin, Grandma had a right to shun her but didn't.

My grandmother takes the chair next to mine. I inhale mint, something floral, and the whisper of booze. We bow our heads, and she folds her hand over mine, a civil gesture, as she doesn't care much for the impromptu prayer of the nondenominational. Dad thanks God for bringing his parents here safely and for the delicious food.

"And thanks for the good news we'll be getting tomorrow," he says. Grandma's hand tightens.

The prayer ends and my grandparents cross themselves. Kendra scowls at the gesture.

"Kendra," Mom says. "Take a roll and pass it." This gets the assembly line going: pass the rolls, pass the salad, pass the noodles. Praise abounds for the sauce. With only a tilt of the head, Mom and Grandma could lock eyes, but neither one of them do. I find myself between them in the role of buffer, though against what I can't rightly say. I smile too hard, laugh too loudly. When all else fails, I abide in the study of condensation dripping down my glass.

In years prior, whenever we drove down to Universal City, Mom hauled along a case of bottled water. Plumes of bacteria and toxins, she'd say, contaminated Universal City's municipal water—"but don't tell your grandparents I said that," she'd add, as though that was not exactly what the cartloads of Ozarka communicated. I wonder now if Grandma observes the glasses filled with reverse osmosis water and notes her daughter-in-law's ability to take something as easy as water and make it hard.

My plate is almost clear. I sop up the remaining sauce with bread.

"I think I'll come with you tomorrow," Grandpa says.

"Thanks, Dad."

"I can help with the kids," Grandma says.

I wait for Mom to say us kids are pretty used to watching ourselves. Instead, her tension gives way to frenetic cleaning up. Mom can bounce a dinner gathering faster than songbirds flit rainwater, setting plates to table, food to plates, plates to sink. Some might call it anxiety. Mom? She calls it being polite. Tonight her manners are torpedo-grade. Someone makes a joke about stepping away before they end up in the dishwasher too.

My grandparents vanish to the front of the house, my parents to the back, the hallway stretching between them like a chronology of family history. Some points on the time line are known. From my perspective as an adult now, my parents' biography joins like a stream with other time lines that course together in a floodway.

In 1973, six years after the *Forrestal* fire, Air Force workers across the globe doused enflamed model planes in white foam that, from a distance, looked like sea-foam covering the ground as if a tide had just pulled away. A gray and quiet calm settled over fields where only seconds earlier flames had licked the air. After each drill, the fields were washed down as though with soap. What became of that pristine landscape? Light water seemed to vanish for good into the ground. There was little concern about the safety of releasing chemistry's strongest bond into land and water; Air Force environmental scientists suggested that powdered charcoal could weaken the PFA molecules in the foams. Then water could finish the job by diluting them.

That summer of 1973, Dad strolled hand in hand with his neighbor, Robin. She was tall, slender, brunette; Dad balanced on the street curb, as though walking a beam, so as to appear closer to Robin's height. In the evenings, the neighborhood kids caught now-rare fireflies and sealed them in canning jars, releasing the insects on their last gasp. At night, Dad tapped on Robin's bedroom window after everyone was supposed to be home and asleep. She'd sneak him in, and the two would huddle over her record player and listen to the soundtrack to *Grease*. But Robin knew he didn't love her. He always talked about her older sister Christy, sighing over how beautiful she was. It tore Robin's heart out. When they began high school that fall, the two joined different circles of friends— Dad went with the jocks, and Robin gravitated toward the local kids whose families weren't military.

In Houston, Mom started high school in a freshman class of over eight hundred. Devoting herself like an underdog boxer to the study of math and chemistry, she became the highest-scoring student in both and broke the class curve, provoking the eye rolls of her classmates. She sat at her desk as straight-backed as she did at the piano bench back home, every groan of a nearby peer music to her ears.

In 1974, studies conducted at the environmental health lab at the Air Force base in Kelly, Texas, found that increased exposure to AFFF advanced death among fish; the implications for human health were present and concerning. Researchers suggested that an oil separator could help decompose and oxidize the foam before it was released into oceans and freshwater.

Dad started dating a cheerleader, and Robin took up with a boy who studied with her after school. One afternoon her beau looked up from an agonizing English assignment and saw Robin gazing out the front window. He turned to look. Across the street, Dad was waxing his 1970 silver-and-green Ford truck. Robin's boyfriend waved his hand in front of her face, said, *Hey, over here.*

Mom got a job cleaning cages at Beechnut Animal Hospital in south Houston. The owner of the practice, Alan, took notice of her acumen and her soothing way with animals. She told him she intended to go to veterinarian school, and he taught her how to draw blood and translate a profile. He showed her how to see inside a small animal with your hands. Under the head of a surgery lamp, Alan talked Mom through the steps of removing gallstones from a dog who was sedated and prone and not much like a dog so much as a skeletal heap breathing under blue surgery cloth. As he used his hands like eyes in the cavity of the dog's abdomen, Alan narrated a journey from bladder to intestine. Mom nodded. The clinic was the only place where she felt like she belonged. She murmured to us once that her dad never really liked Dr. Thomas because he knew Mom had come to think of the veterinarian as her father.

In 1976, a Navy report gestured toward desires for "improvements in environmental areas" where AFFFs were discarded after use. No regulation governed their disposal. Later, this approach would be called "uncontrolled."

Meanwhile, Dad made captain on the Judson High School varsity football team. He was small but quick, and he could take a hit. His teammates described him as a tough little running back. He liked to holler like wild from the sidelines. He got into Texas A&M, and Robin went off to the University of Alabama. No one remembered who said goodbye to whom.

In Houston, a student from the yearbook committee stopped by the lab, and as he set up a photo of the science club, Mom drifted to the side, like she didn't know where to stand. The photographer tried waving her in, then gave up. She wore a long-sleeved coat that day, one with wide faux-fur lapels. It made her feel stylish, though she sweltered in it. A part of her was hiding inside that wool shell—and doing a terrible job of it. But another part of her had something to say. Beverly Jacobs didn't swear, but she was one hell of a cuss. She wore the coat to say she didn't give a fuck. She was so out of there.

In 1978, the Navy completed a study on the environmental repercussions of firefighting foams, stating that it was difficult to determine the biodegradability of the carbon chains because 3M refused to disclose relevant data on AFFF concentrates, stating, "The constituents of the AFFF formulas are trade secrets." The report concluded that the foams were likely toxic, but only at volumes much higher than the military deployed.

Dad finished his first year at Texas A&M as an ROTC cadet.

Mom entered Texas A&M University with enough dual academic credits to skip freshman and sophomore years; she then fast-tracked by completing two years of prerequisites followed by automatic admission to veterinarian school and an honorary bachelor's of science. "Two-year wonders, they called us," she'd go on to say.

There were only two such wonders in 1979: Mom and some guy whose name she would never be able to remember. While in vet school, she started attending a few evangelical services with her college roommates. Though she didn't join any church officially, the political voice of the rising Christian right was saying things that sounded right to Mom. Morality was as absolute as the absolutes of organic chemistry and mathematics. Mom began to pore over her Bible just as she did textbooks on canine and feline infectious diseases. For her, there was no distinction between the study of endocrinology and the study of God, not because they were both complex, but because both were subjects she could rigorously rationalize.

When she went to college, Mom didn't want to get married, didn't want a family. She planned to graduate and move back to Houston to join the veterinary practice where she'd worked as a technician in high school.

"But God had plans of his own," she said later. "I met your dad." The two encountered each other at a honky-tonk two-stepping. They were dancing with other people, and then the caller called to change partners. They were engaged three weeks later.

In 1981, Dad graduated with a degree in civil engineering and a C+ average. He swore devotion to the Air Force and joined the flight training program at Reese Air Force Base in Lubbock. Mom drank Pepsi as she drove the 428 miles from College Station to Lubbock, her eyes lit up by her scandalous behavior. Whether her transgression was premarital sex or drinking Pepsi—and which she considered more illicit—would remain an enigma.

Dad's first posting was with the Forty-First Rescue and Weather Reconnaissance Wing as a hurricane hunter—or "typhoon chaser," as he was called on Guam.

It is a testimony of Mom's infatuation with my father that she was willing to follow him to Guam. I was born in the island's naval hospital in 1984, with perfect timing: Reagan would withdraw the government's invasion of families just as Mom was beginning one.

Meanwhile, she arrived at her nondenominational faith through osmosis, claimed the Moral Majority as her political party, read the Bible, and sought out others doing the same, from College Station to Guam and back to Lubbock.

In 1985, a Navy study reported that at least two hundred million gallons of AFFF wastewater were generated annually by the Navy and Air Force. The waters were not so much disposed of as left behind to let nature clean up.

I was a year old when my father was dispatched once more to Reese Air Force Base. Mom fell in love with a house on a cul-de-sac just a mile south of a white church that stood alone in a field of cotton.

In 1989, the Air Force circulated an internal report stating that ponds in Colorado Springs were contaminated heavily with run-off from fire-training areas at Peterson Air Force Base. Commercial and personal uses were prohibited at one of the ponds. The report recommended that the DOD address the disposal of firefighting foams.

My parents feared that politicians, not generals, would control future international conflicts, just as they had the war in Vietnam. Only fools would trust the federal government after that, they said.

Dad gave seven years to the military, then joined the ranks of the commercial air carrier American Airlines, trading his green jumpsuit for the company's winged insignia and epaulettes. When friends said, "Wow, congratulations," Dad said that he was a glorified taxi driver.

Mom joined the practice at High Plains Pet Clinic as Dr. Bieri's associate. She began working Thursdays and every other Saturday.

There are also chapters in my parents' biography we don't know—mystery in some secret and colorless spaces between points on the family time line.

Mom has said that some details from her past are locked away in a box, and she fears that, if she opens it, she won't be able to close the box again. Her childhood remains mostly a mystery, though there are clues—in how she clings to my father, in how she encircles herself with her children like a ring of lights—suggesting that she's never stopped protecting the girl who grew up in Houston. What is she shielding herself from?

My father's adolescence is a glissando of golden boy, covered with thick swaths of nostalgia. But what from his youth doesn't fit this picture?

Around the time when Dad took the job at American, 3M filled two undisclosed industrial containers with so many variants of carbon chains that future toxicologists would suspect over two hundred formulations existed but knew how to test for only sixteen of them. The Department of Defense and 3M claimed there was no way to tie exposure to PFAS to disease, and the EPA would not take steps to set maximum contaminant levels for "forever chemicals" in drinking water sources until 2023. What actually endangered lives? Fuel-fed fire. Now that was an obvious cause and effect, at least to the DOD and industries like 3M. Internal reports on PFAS were locked away in a box.

But the PFAS released into the environment couldn't be sealed up. They became euphemized as "forever chemicals," a term one can at least pronounce if not comprehend. The ability of PFAS to repel oil and fire is also what endows them with their durability. The chemicals are described as "forever" because they do not break down but rather persist indefinitely, accumulating in water, sand, soil, and blood.

Lights out. My body twitches. Who can bear the wait till morning? I lie in bed and try to quell my fears, thinking, *By this time tomorrow, everything will be back to normal.*

Something hangs in the air, traces of a lit match, a feeling. My thoughts return to my father's prayer and the flinch of my grandmother's hand. What was she afraid of? I consider my mother, moving relentlessly through the motions of the evening, the wooden spoon bobbing in her back pocket. Her moods make me sensitive as long-wave radio, but tonight I couldn't quite read her. My grandmother watched her too. The Blackburn family refrain on Mom is that she's smart, if unconventional. Years of phone calls to Lubbock, I imagine, have been followed by my grandparents making martinis and saying, "Beverly's smart and John adores her. Now pour another."

The next morning Dad and I stand under the basketball hoop on our driveway. He gestures to his ribs, saying if the cancer hasn't spread, he'll seek medical treatment. It's likely his colon will have to come out, and chemotherapy will wipe out any renegade cells. "They'll pump me full of chemicals, Kate. Give me a permanent bag."

"I just know it hasn't spread," I say. I tell him I know he is going to be okay. Hugging the barrel of his chest, I believe he will be.

The van pulls away with my parents and grandfather. My grandmother watches them from the front porch swing and doesn't set the swing to lilting. I pass her and walk inside to make breakfast.

I mix the sugar and flour. There are no eggs in the refrigerator. Everyone groans for pancakes. "Oh, you big babies," I say.

We watch a movie and finish it. The phone rings. Dark lipstick smacks on the other end. The woman's name is Annie Buckley. "Yeah, I remember you," I say. She's an old neighbor who once intervened when an umbrella drug me down the sidewalk during a dust storm when my scheme to take flight went awry. She's calling from the edges of our social circle, proving Dad's bad news has tumbled out, as though blown around by wind. But Annie and I chat about her freckled son instead. She is saying Nick-something when my parents pull up to the house.

At first, Dad looks like he might return even more confident than when he left. In the story about the diner on the highway, my grandmother always describes Dad laughing as he crosses back over the tarmac with ice cream melting on his chin. But two decades later, he pauses under the basketball hoop. The moment hinges between two possibilities. I will nothing to move. Annie will not say one more word. My siblings will stay seated on the living room floor. In this instant of light, it seems so simple an act of willpower, to keep living the life we know. But something swings open in my chest and heat rises.

I hold my breath. My eyes sting as I push back. My childhood will end when I exhale.

CHAPTER 8

A BREEZE WICKS THE BASKETBALL net. Dad folds. Grandma catches his head to her chest. My mother's hands cover her face and she shakes. Annie's voice is cut off half-sentence when I punch the Talk button.

My parents enter the house. Dad's weeping frightens us. He sits at the desk chair in the schoolroom. My siblings tug at him, their cries terrible. Dad reaches for me, and sobs catch in his throat. I jerk back. Two dark creases fold in his forehead. He steadies my face in his hands. "You are so beautiful," he says. Someone wretches. Vomit splatters the floor.

Mom disappears and returns holding her Nikon. She shuts one eye, aims the lens, says the light will be better outside, and directs us to the front yard. I hug my knees at the porch step, my siblings huddle next to me, and Dad settles his arms across us. Mom documents. The shutter clicks. At the sound, I know these pictures will be unbearable. Between shots, my sisters and I sniffle and rub our eyes, and then we smile something wretched.

Mom passes me the camera and says that she hasn't made it a point to get enough pictures of everyone. She says that she just needs to do a better job. She wraps her arms around Dad's neck and pulls his cheek to hers. The faces of my parents are luminescent. In the future, theirs will be the only photo from this afternoon I can bear seeing. Their expressions could be collapsed into a potboiler: raw and stricken and in love.

The day has given way to its hours, and I am learning time's disregard for shock. My sisters and brother each wear the same bewildered expression. They look abandoned. James picks up a toy cowboy and looks at it. The pupil of his right eye turns toward his tear duct. Kendra clings to Mom's leg. My grandparents have closed themselves inside the guest room.

I wind the kitchen window's turn handle to open it as Dad walks into the backyard cradling the phone. The pitch of each number bleeps as he dials his sister, a long-distance call to Murfreesboro. He crosses and uncrosses his legs with, I imagine, the swing of her big voice. Even if she were here, I would strain to make out the words in Dad's throat he has to pause to release.

"It's not his best book," he says. "Jack Ryan is president, and the villain is basically Saddam." He pauses. Nods.

"Well. I'm dying."

"There isn't much else to say."

He mumbles.

"I said I don't want to spend the rest of my life with my head in a toilet."

Behind my father, a ponderosa spires into the sky in flagrant disregard of Lubbock's decree of flatness. A white crane sometimes weighs down its tallest bough, but today the tree's empty branches bristle in the hot stillness. In coming years, I will wait at the kitchen window for the crane. I do not know at the time that the water bird is one of the sandhill cranes that migrate by the thousands to the lunettes of West Texas and find refuge on the banks of the shallow lakes seventy miles northwest of Lubbock. In coming winters, when one appears, I will think of my father.

Dad hangs up, reaches for the tennis ball at his feet, and throws it for Andy. He turns and sees me at the window and waves.

The facts of Dad's cancer are rather clear. Metastases from a primary tumor in his colon have spread to fifteen lesions on his liver. The masses are too large to cut away—they would take the whole of his liver with them. A colectomy could become an option if, with treatment, the principal growth shrinks. It expands rapidly now:

the bleeding in Dad's stool is caused by the tumor breaking through the colorectal wall. Chemotherapy might at least put a pause to the multiplications. Radiation could delay what everyone agrees would be a too-early death.

In fragments I learn that at the internist's office Dad studied the images from the computed tomography scan. "Are you sure you have the right guy?" he asked.

My grandfather murmurs to my grandmother that the internist told Dad to go home and pack his bags for the hospital. If a combination of chemotherapy and radiation works, the doctors can operate and remove the masses and Dad will still have some liver left. Intensive treatments would follow, making Dad sick enough to need hospital care. But the process might give him more time. There was a chance of living another year or two. Decent enough to take the bet.

"It's not up to us," Grandpa says.

"Yeah, well."

For me, the diagnosis creates a murk I stumble through, as though walking down our long hallway in the dark. I keep saying "legion" instead of "lesion," a slip that brings to mind the biblical story of possession. In the New Testament, Jesus performs an exorcism on a man whose body has become dominion to fallen angels. Christ asks the demon its name, and the suffering man speaks on behalf of his tenants, saying, "I am Legion, for we are many."

"I understand your mistake," Mom says. I've found her refreshing her makeup in her bathroom. Powder keeps turning to clay with each attempt to erase her tears. "The cancer is legion in your dad's body," she explains. To seek a cure, we must change the diagnosis.

Dread swells in the house like a chronic, dull ache. I hug my arms to stave off a cool slant of shade everywhere. I find Grandma sitting on the front porch swing again. She places a manicured hand on my leg. Her blood pulses like a stream of butane, her touch a lighter. "Your mom and dad are very religious. Very religious." Her mouth twitches. "They will do what they think is best."

Before bed, Dad asks his parents if they'd like to join us for bedroom prayer. They would. From a seat on the ledge of my parents' bed, they reach for Mom's hand and for Dad's and for the children's, and in this way we form a ring of trembling arms that spills from the bed to the floor. Mom's Bible is open to the Book of Job. She reads that Satan roamed the earth and God asked if he'd noticed Job, the most upright of men. Indeed, the ruler of the world had. He noted that Job had everything a person could desire, making his righteousness easy. Mom reads on, "Satan answered the Lord, 'Put forth your hand now and touch all that he has; he will surely curse you to your face.' Then the Lord said to Satan, 'Behold all that he has is in your power.'" Mom pauses and looks up from the text. "You kind of think, it'd be nice if God didn't point out Job like that." She reads on. When Job entreats God to relieve his suffering, God asks, "Where were you when I laid the foundation of the earth?"

"It's important," Dad says, "that no matter what, we all keep believing in God. His goodness and his plan."

We walk down the hallway, Grandma between Kendra and me, Grandpa shepherding Karson. At the door to our bedroom, my grandparents kiss each of us on the forehead and urge sleep.

In bed, my sisters and I are quiet. The solar system glows overhead.

"Are you scared?" Kendra asks.

"No." I tug her to me and wait for her to fall asleep.

Thirsty, I am quiet as I leave the bed. The air in the hallway is cool. A line of light shines under the guest room door. In the other direction, my parents' voices purr. What if I were to find my way quietly to their bedroom? Surely, I would hear my father comforting my mother even as she assures him that death is not part of God's plan.

And if I were to press my ear to the door of the guest room? Perhaps I would hear questions that have followed me into adulthood: How was it that two grown, college-educated adults of good intention and sufficient means came to plead holy in the face of facts? By what logic does one arrive at a healing mysterious and corporeal?

In these questions I hear the note of contempt I sometimes picked up in my grandmother's voice, a scorn masked politely as confusion. Only now, I recognize the disdain as my own. *Literally?* my millennial brain squawks at me. *We thought God would literally heal Dad?* The question is the stuff of my sleeplessness.

And yet, living apace with the what and how of my childhood in hopes of unearthing the why, I arrive instead at a glass of water.

I see my younger self in the kitchen. She flips the light on and fills a drinking glass. In the window above the kitchen sink, her reflection lifts the glass and drinks.

The buzz-click and ring of dial-up connects Mom to the World Wide Web, and the same tenacious mind that gained her early admission into veterinarian school now works in the predawn hours like a sieve, filtering through testimonies of raw-juice and sodium-free recovery, bone marrow and omega-3 wonders. Supplements, she reads, often diminish tumors. Book titles leap at her: *How I Beat Colon Cancer* and *Alternative Cancer Treatments*. There might be a way around chemotherapy. Thank God for the internet. She reads claim after claim about supporting a cancer patient's immune system as God works a miracle. The rapid click of the keyboard drifts through the schoolroom, past the kitchen table, and into the kitchen, where Grandma fills a coffee filter and sets the maker to brew. The smell of the grounds mixes strangely with the patter of Mom's typing.

Mom sits back in her chair, and the printer spits forth paper. She takes it from the tray and gets right back to work. The thrumming of her keyboard lets loose a drumline as persistent as her will through the house, pausing only so Mom can say, "It's time for school." No news on earth will keep us from homeschool.

My siblings and I say the Pledge. I get to work diagramming

sentences—subject, verb, present perfect, direct object. My grandparents' shoes click in the entryway. The front door whines open,
ticks shut. The phone is the chattiest creature in the house. I answer.
"Blackburn residence."

"K.D.? Karson?"

"K.D."

"I can't tell any of you kids apart. Is your dad home?"

Dad takes the phone. Crosses and uncrosses his legs. "It won't,"
he says.

"We're figuring that out."

"I know."

Friends who call keep saying Dad's diagnosis makes no sense.
Men like John don't get cancer.

For the span of Dad's life, more than thirty years, 3M made
statements like that refrain—*Men like John don't get cancer*—but
company representatives put it this way: *The weight of scientific evidence does not show that PFAS cause harm to the environment or people at current or historical levels.*

The words *perfluoroalkyl* and *polyfluoroalkyl* sit strangely on the
tongue; hostile to pronunciation, they mute the speaker, ward off
the listener. No one in my family would have known how to say
them.

An internal manual at 3M claimed that PFAS were toxic as
early as 1950; as 3M secured patents for its formulations, company researchers found acute oral toxicity among exposed rats. As
the DOD distributed the foams to military bases across the world,
scientists informed 3M that the substance builds up in blood. It
rewrites DNA, and the new codes produce cancer. But 3M suppressed studies that demonstrated the carcinogenic toxicity of perfluoroalkyl and polyfluoroalkyl chemicals.

Dad's diagnosis feels like it occurred years ago, but it's been two
days. My sisters and I cry in fits. Kendra follows my parents into
every room, afraid to be away from them. My five-year-old brother

talks less and less, as though the mounting pressure has crowded out whatever he might have said. I think back to the girl who couldn't make pancakes because there were no eggs. I want to warn her, but what would I say?

My grandfather approaches my father and asks if they can talk. The two stand at the front window and fold their arms and take in a view of the lawn. The mailman passes down the other side of the street. I pin myself to the doorway of the kitchen and listen. Grandpa says doctors make mistakes. The one at American Airlines should have caught this. The local internist seems competent enough. But.

"We should get you a second opinion."

"They're just going to tell me the same thing."

Grandpa waits. He speaks again. The severity of Dad's diagnosis seems unlikely. There's no family history of cancer. Dad doesn't smoke, or drink, or eat poorly. He's so young, so healthy. The company doctor missed it. But that doesn't mean the whole medical establishment should be abandoned. My grandfather hasn't lost hope. Medical treatment could add time. Who knows? Maybe years. Sure, the road ahead would be less than ideal. But wouldn't that be worth it?

"That's not good enough," Dad says. He envisions training for marathons, playing with us kids, continuing to fly. Faith is not only an alternative treatment plan; it's the promise of prosperity. A life full of bounty and boundlessness, an extension of the kind of existence he had already been imagining he could have. He doesn't want a life's remainder of chemotherapy treatments, brittle bones, skin like paper. Time served wearing gloves to open the refrigerator. His immune system weakened, making him vulnerable to other illnesses, cancer itself an ambiguous disease made up of a twisted knot of maladies. Flailing through treatment only to die anyway? That's no cure. "Chemo would kill me before the cancer does."

"You don't know that." My grandfather goes on. He and my grandmother feel they have been supportive of my parents' unusual choices—theirs to make, obviously. My parents call them, saying they want a midwife, want a compost tumbler, want to homeschool. Okay. My mother is smart, anyone can see it. She could teach the children geometry and English. If she insists, she could teach them Latin too. The children have no idea who the Beatles are, but college will teach them. My grandparents are pleased and even a little surprised with how well everything has been turning out. But when Dad calls saying *cancer*, my grandparents load up the Lincoln and bootleg a bottle of red wine to Lubbock. This isn't about lifestyle. It's about life.

"You can't just do nothing."

"Faith is not nothing."

Before dusk, my parents walk down the length of our block and stop in front of a yard full of cacti. Mom drops her gaze and shakes her head as though she's been struck again by the news. She reaches for Dad. I've never seen them like that.

"What are they doing?" Kendra says.

"Come here," I say. She twists out of my grasp, tears plowing down her cheeks. Grandma stands next to me and watches Kendra's body grow smaller as she runs to my parents.

"She's scared," Grandma says.

Later, when James is a teenager and Kendra is sneaking painkillers and slipping out of the bathroom window at night, James will come sit next to me on my bed.

"Strategy," he'll say. "Kendra has no strategy."

Even as children, it's true. And true for everyone in my family. Though cancer binds us to the experiences of hundreds of thousands of others, watching Mom and Dad at the narrowed end of the sidewalk, I feel they might as well be standing at the edge of a plank, about to drop into no-man's-land. Strategy. None of us have one. We've given up any strategy of our own for God's plan.

My parents walk back holding Kendra's hands. She skips between them and rubs her nose on her shoulder as if nothing is wrong after all. Then Mom yanks Kendra up by the arm and thrusts her toward me. Her teeth clench. "Your dad and I are trying to talk." Kendra bellows. She grasps Mom's thigh, and Mom peels her off.

"She's all right," Dad says. He stoops and gathers Kendra. Karson and James crowd him. I swing Mary to my hip and press into the fold. I feel what I've come to fear most: Dad's chest heaving.

"Let's just everyone go inside," Mom says. Her head shakes in infinitesimal vibrations that are terrifying to behold. Kendra prods her.

"I'm not angry," she says. Kendra grabs her by the hand and pulls her to the house. I don't understand why she isn't more afraid of our mother. The woman seems to be hardening into an implacable version of herself. I look at Karson. She brings up the rear. Her chin quivers.

Inside, the plans my parents discussed at the end of the block become clear. Mom opens her address book. She calls Pastor Shawn. "Eight o'clock's not too late," she says. She calls Kelly the cotton farmer. She passes the phone to me. "Call Brad and Susan."

Susan answers. "I just put the boys down, but Brad will be there. Tell your mom I'll be praying from home."

Brad's patrol car pulls up first, right behind my grandparents' Lincoln. "Am I in trouble?" Grandpa says.

"These are just some people from our church," I say. He grunts.

Kelly and Jesse show up and step out of their pickup and cross the lawn in their boots and work denim.

"Sally come running out, saying you called. We come straight from the field," Kelly says.

Jesse eyes me quietly.

Pastor Shawn parks his Astro van and walks inside and extends his hand. "You must be John's dad." Next, he reaches toward Grandma. She takes his hand between both of hers and thanks him for coming. I sweep the room for my parents. Nothing. The kitchen too is empty. Talk in the living room forces itself until Mom's appearance at the entrance to the hallway snuffs the chatter. Her eyes are wide and tired, but she looks ready to bark a command. She seems thinner, and something else about her is altered. I don't recognize the change, but my body does. My muscles still. A message rises from my gut. *Look calm*, it tells me. *Watch. Don't move.*

"John's in the back." She turns with a rigid face to my grandparents. "This will only take a minute."

Static electricity would feel calmer. Grandpa slides his hands into his pockets. Grandma pats the pastor's hand and lets it go. She watches the men from church tuck their heads and follow Mom. My siblings and I trail after them.

No one speaks as we walk down the disturbing length of the hallway. The men's shadows glance off the portraits of my family hanging on the walls.

Dad is sitting on the edge of my parents' bed.

"Hey, John," the pastor says. "Heard you got some news." Each guy takes a turn clapping Dad on the back. They crowd the privacy of my parents' bedroom, the deepest part of the house. Jesse positions himself next to Mary Katherine's changing table. The men nod as Dad talks and moves his hands, saying God has other plans.

"Beverly and I been talking. What if faith isn't our only option? What if it's our best option?"

Someone chips in a hallelujah. Something inside me calcifies to rock, but when Jesse glances at me, I smile. Dad smiles too, and rolls his lips together. Gravitas settles over us. The charge is great. Face death and defeat it. Pastor Shawn spreads his long, crooked fingers in the air. My sisters and brother and I bow our heads. I close my eyes and see my grandparents in the front of the house, standing quietly by the fireplace. Perhaps Grandma imagines a blaze inside it, sputtering sparks, cobalt blue at the heart of each flame. How many places around the world had the military moved the Blackburns to, then stationed them elsewhere and moved them again? *Active duty* is being acted upon. During the Korean War, my grandmother's first role as an officer's wife was to accompany the base chaplain bringing the news of a man's death to his wife. To her, my grandmother, fell the task of helping the bereaved pack and depart within two days. A particular fear grew in her with each visitation: she dreamed of a cold fog spreading from the homes of each widow till it covered every military base and claimed her, the messenger. What exactly does her daughter-in-law think she cannot understand? She too has prayed for the life of her husband. She too has prayed for the life of a child. Maybe my grandmother thinks of the night in Colorado when her sorrow was so profound that she felt nothing but the bleakness of it. And then perhaps she thinks of Paul. Her son.

She reaches for the phone, dials my aunt Lori, says, "We've been cut out."

At the back of the house, Pastor Shawn prays. "We ask you to cure John."

Mom's and Dad's voices rise above the rest. Amen.

CHAPTER 9

MY GRANDFATHER LOADS THE TRUNK of the Lincoln. Five days
have passed since Dad's diagnosis, three since the prayer circle. It's
Saturday, a good day for driving across the state. My grandmother
takes her coffee and sits once more on the swing. She looks ahead;
her expression reminds me of Dad's stare, of how he looks when
his thoughts carry him elsewhere and he inhabits two places at
once—memory and the present, the unseen and the seen. I wonder
if Grandma is praying. Perhaps she is making a wager.

If her son lives, she will forgive his wife.

We take one another's hands. There has been no discussion of
what happened the night of the prayer circle. Conversations about
my father have ended. Grandpa no longer asks to speak with Dad.
In silence, my grandmother and I sit together. I want to tell her that
Mom lives in only one world, her own. But we both already know
that. I want to say something, but when I open my mouth to speak
a sob escapes.

Mom is baking chocolate chip cookies for her in-laws' trip. "It
will be good to get the flour and sugar out of the house anyway,"
she says. She spoons dough onto a baking sheet. My sisters and I
crowd her, each with a spoon in hand. Mom steps to the oven, and
my siblings and I pounce on what's left in the bowl.

"I need to get through," she says bumping past us kids. She runs
the sink and juggles words into the air, about the oven temperature,
the cooking time, the plant watering, the vacuuming. With morti-
fication, I watch her strip the guest room bed. Grandma walks back
inside with her empty mug and observes the bare mattress with a
blank expression. What could offend her now?

In farewell, Dad holds my grandmother in a tight grip. His father wraps his arms around both of them. Once, Dad flew a route to Chicago on the same day that his parents had a layover in O'Hare. He gave his parents a gate number and time. They stood at the terminal window and watched their son land the aircraft. He taxied close enough for them to see him wave from the cockpit.

My siblings and I hang back. Dad opens the car door for Grandma and says something. The door clips shut. My grandparents' hands flicker as they pull away. Dad wipes his face. He watches the spot on the street where a second ago his parents turned.

The next morning, when we enter Grace Church, I feel the congregation's massive gaze. The row we usually sit in—stage left, three back—has been left empty for us. The length of worship feels both interminable and too short. With each song, Dad uses his collar to pat his eyes. Mom's mouth twists in the corner. She pushes her hair back and rubs a place behind her ear. My face is dry. I haven't cried since my grandparents left, and watching Mom and Dad, I realize that I can't anymore. I consider Dad's diagnosis again, I remember the way his forehead balled like a fist, I picture my siblings' blanched faces and heavy quiet. The recent memories exhaust me, but my eyes are drained. I press my temples and wish I were anywhere else. I feel the presence of the men from the prayer group, and my headache worsens. They have been to the most private part of our house. I don't now know how to meet their eyes. I feel Jesse's gaze and avoid it.

Worship ends and the children flee the sanctuary. Pastor Shawn makes announcements. There's going to be a church yard sale to support missionaries. The men's breakfast will meet as usual on Tuesday at 6:00 a.m. at the Lubbock Breakfast House—be sure to get one of their Texas-shaped waffles. Thin laughter responds. Shawn pauses and steps down from the stage to stand level with the front row. He presses a finger to his lips and lowers it.

"Prayer requests?"

Someone releases a choked sob. Then there's another. Then the pattering of someone who, now that he's started crying, can't stop. The sound of dread breaching everyone's throats pulls the starter to my panic. Some hidden part of me has believed that nothing from the last five days has sunk its teeth into reality, but the tears of the congregation convince me: my father is sick, and he may die. Glances flash our way. Dad clasps his hands and leans over his knees. He lowers his head. No one stands. Shawn looks at the floor.

My pulse gives chase. From the corner of my eye, I see my father rise to stand. His voice shakes. "Some of you already know. . . ." He grips the seats in front of him, the couple sitting there already leaning away. He summarizes the last week. "There aren't a lot of medical options. We are still figuring out what to do. But we believe that, you know, I've got a lot of years left. A lot of years."

"Okay, John," Pastor Shawn says. He gestures to the congregation. Everywhere I look, people cry. There are no tense backs, no chins aloft, nor any faces beaming forth faith. No one says to praise God for his promises. A cloak of grief falls over the congregation. Chairs creak as men and women stand and stumble over. Here come Kelly and Jesse. Here come Sharon and Blake. Jo and her husband, Brad and Susan. Jeanie Ward. Shawn drapes his arms over Dad's neck. Hands press to my shoulders. Fingers spread on the back of my head. My sisters and brother and mother disappear under spread palms. My body softens and folds away from the ceiling lights. I kneel and dig my nails into the rough fibers of the church floor. Under all those arms, I lean into a cool dark and the soft bubbling of my father's emotion. I hope this is the space of miracles. I am certain it is one of tenderness.

Now that my father's body has opened to disease, it has also opened to the touch of so many hands. "And your hand, God," he says. "Reach down and touch me."

Shawn's voice rises like smoke, no more than a whisper. He weeps. "Father, please," he says. "We do not know your ways. But we ask you to be with John and Beverly and all the kids. Work in him, whether through medicine or your divine intervention."

The awning of arms thins. Seats refill. Mom's back is stiff as timber, as though her posture alone could deflect any condolence. She wants no pity. The grace she is interested in is God's. His the only mercy. In prayer she cried, but she did not tremble.

In my seat, I hug my limbs. While Dad is trapped in his body, I feel loosened from mine. The diagnosis hardens into fact, and a key in my gut turns, locking me away from the taste and smell of my instincts, the sound and burn of my father's predicament. I recall my anatomy lesson years ago when an artery emptied into the cat's chest. "A bleeder," Mom had said. Something in me has bled out. In the hollow of my chest, a wild shriek insists that Dad will be healed. I think it is the voice of God.

CHAPTER 10

I TWIST THE AMERICAN AIRLINES insignia between my fingers. The feathered wingspan with the "AA" logo at its heart looks more than vaguely military; most of the pilots who don it are ex-Air Force. Dad's uniform is freshly dry-cleaned and sheathed in plastic. He is dressed in belted black slacks with a precise crease down each pant leg. His formal button-down has three silver stripes on the epaulettes, marking his rank as first officer, a captain's copilot, second in command. He drops a worn copy of his flight handbook into the suitcase, covers it with crisp white dress shirts, and secures the garment straps. He will depart in the afternoon. After this flight, the company will change his status to disability and suspend his commercial pilot's license.

He buffs his polished Oxfords with a brown horsehair shoe brush and presses his feet inside them, then slides a wood-handled lint remover into an interior pocket. Without thinking, I put the metallic tip of the pilot regalia to my lips.

"Here," he says. "You can chew that up when I get back." He pins the badge above his left breast pocket. Holding his pilot's cap by the round top brim, he lifts the curtain of plastic protecting his coat and folds it over his arm. I ask to pull his suitcase down the hall.

Up till this final trip in May of 1997, my father's salary approached a commercial pilot's average annual salary of $120,000. Then he called his supervisor to update his health status.

But my parents don't talk money with me. What I know is what I overhear. In the days leading up to his last flight, they murmur: disability pay will cut Dad's income in half. Mom will have to take on relief work at clinics citywide. What will become of homeschooling? Mom openly doubts that my father can handle it. Based on the mayhem transpiring Thursdays and every other Saturday, he's inclined to believe her. Even with Dad's newfound calling to discipline, he tends to punish when he's lost patience; given he's a pilot accustomed to choppy weather, it's simple to avoid angering him. It's also easy to push boundaries—hopping up regularly for bathroom breaks, wandering off to the backyard for a personal recess. Offering to "help" by whisking Mary Katherine to the playroom. But Mom? She remarks on the unique quality of days when no one needs a beating.

Dad calls his supervisor. Says he's still running in the mornings and feels no different than he has for the last two years—the length of time, his doctor guesses, there's been a tumor growing in his colon. One of the more devastating facts of my father's diagnosis is that colon cancer tends to be treatable if caught early. Dad had misidentified the symptoms of the disease, thinking they were signs of his ability to run.

"But still," Dad says. He argues that the effects of medical treatments are moot: he is not going to do chemo. Why not let him fly until he becomes ill from the disease? *If*, he adds, that happens.

The hub supervisor for Dallas–Fort Worth regrets to say that it is a matter of liability. If something happened on the flight, God forbid, and word got out that the copilot had cancer, American Airlines would forfeit revenue in litigation. The supervisor, for one, would lose his job faster than the aircraft's legal fire could be put out.

Dad's mental health, the supervisor continues, is also a consideration. Suicide rates among cancer patients are double the national average. The side of the Rockies can beckon a pilot who's dying slowly.

The phone comes down, hard.

My siblings and I sit at the front window and watch for Dad. Summer heat warms the glass. I squint into the glare. I'm not frightened that my father won't return; I'm scared that he will. I want the person from a week ago to reappear. The man I hope will come home isn't diagnosed with a degenerative disease. He hasn't been identified for Satan's attack. Over him no prayers are offered. His tears mean devastation, and so he doesn't cry.

He once took the family to New Mexico, where we drove to a lookout point in the Sierra Blanca Mountains. A valley of treetops opened beneath us as a shadow climbed across the foothills. The mountainsides blushed in the sunset. The white peaks rose holy above the sun. Dad walked ahead of us to the railing while holding Mary Katherine. He whispered something to her. In that moment, I caught a glimpse of the man who flew aircraft into the skies, a private part of him. He faced the mountains as my father, but he was somewhere else too, in the sky as a pilot, the skies his refuge, where even lightning is not a threat. "Lightning is only a problem if you're grounded," he once said.

One of my sisters gasps. His blue truck appears on the road. We run over each other at the door, and Mom says, "One at a time." He is still in uniform, his cap on, his coat draped over his arm. He lifts his suitcase from the truck bed. For a moment I think I have my wish and I reach for the pilot. But the man I touch is trembling. My father is home. This isn't how I wanted him to return, but I cling to him anyway. He splinters with grief. He turns his face to the deep blue vault of sky and weeps.

I have begun to imagine what it might be like to attend school. I would be in the eighth grade. In cultural currency, I am bankrupt. But I can also picture a room with desks, my peers seated, my place in the back row. I can imagine what it would feel like to be away from the house: like cool air on the back of my neck.

Mom cries that forcing her children into public schools is part of the devil's plan; it's one of the reasons Dad's got cancer. Upending our home education is an evil scheme to destroy our household. "Satan hates families," she says, a phrase she could have put in the memo line of every check she's made out to the lobbying group

Homeschool Legal Defense Association. To give up homeschooling would be to accede to Lucifer's whims. To move into a house with a shorter hallway would feel like a big old step in the wrong direction. What about the additional children God was planning to give her? She condemns the brainwashing of the liberal curriculum as though it's already taking place.

I have no plans to burn a bra—I just got one. But I am smart enough to keep quiet about my fantasies of escaping the house and listening to boy bands and using the vocabulary of friendship.

Dad cleans the surface of the kitchen counters. He worries the corners. He stresses over the peeling caulk. I ask if he is glad to be home more. "Well, sure," he says. "I just wish it was for a different reason." He assures me that it will only be for a few months. Until then, I imagine, our house will be spotless.

Before long, he calls his daughters to our bedroom, positions himself on all fours, and peers underneath our bunkbed.

"How hard is it," he begins, "to look under here every once in a while?" He reaches into the dark and constructs a word problem of days divided by number of items flung into squalor. "If you clean this out more than, I don't know, once a month, you might get back to having a full closet of shoes. Has anyone been missing this doll?" He jiggles a rubber Water Baby with peeled paint where an eye should be. Us girls snicker behind our hands. Dad will have the space under the bed immaculate by the end of his lecture. If he's feeling long-winded, he'll vacuum it too. We are plenty brat enough to wait him out.

He lifts an empty single-pack carton of Gatorade grape powder concentrate. Lord knows how long it's been under there. Whoever mainlined it didn't share.

"What's this lemonade doing under here?"

"That's a Gatorade," Karson says.

"You know what I mean." Dad turns to Kendra, who, at the sight of the carton, springs to point like an English setter. "Do you have something to say?" Kendra wags her head, her bowl cut a pinwheel.

"Maybe this is why you've been bouncing off the walls," Dad says. He chucks the carton at the trash can and misses. All three of us point to the spot where it lands.

The company supervisor calls and asks if the problem is money. He's done a little digging. It's possible to set up a pay pool and offer instructions to pilots on how to donate vacation days, if they're so moved.

A week later, the supervisor calls again, saying his faith has been restored, not in God but in pilots: over a year's worth of days have been donated.

Dad leaves and returns with a FedEx box of note cards he made on Printshop software on the home computer and sent off for printing. A Texan, a copilot, he will send a thank-you to each pilot whose name appears on a list he requested. There are over a hundred.

I watch Dad's pen move and visions of carrying a backpack and eating lunch with friends evaporate. In exchange, I hope, some semblance of normalcy will return. Maybe Mom was right anyway—maybe public school would have rent our family apart. Dad's neat, angled print fills each card. He designed them personally so as to add to the inner flap a scripture from Romans: *In all these things, we know that we are more than conquerors through him who loved us.*

I offer to help write addresses. My cursive loops stammer. Lord, I dread each lowercase *b*. No one looking at Dad's uniform print would doubt his precision with a line, but each name I write strays down the envelope. I miss the ruled paper of my diary and composition notebooks, lines that might help to stabilize my hand. My mind too. My body is at war with itself. I'm torn between wanting to be home and wanting to leave it: part of me wishes to be near Dad, and another part is clawing to get away. *What about him?* I wonder. Does he long to be sent away with each sealed envelope? I pity him. Does he have any idea what it's like to live in this house full-time? At this point, do I?

CHAPTER 11

DAD FILLS A PAGE WITH math proofs, his pencil gliding along. I utter complaint. He tells me to think more spatially.

"Well, I'm not a spatial thinker."

"It's not your forte because you don't do it."

"My point exactly."

"The point, I believe, is mine."

I roll my eyes.

"See there? That was a slope with coordinates."

He brushes the page with x and y equations in a hand downright graceful. Each letter and number follow a consistent slant as his left fist moves across the graph paper. He mumbles. "Slope is equal to change in y over attitude. Delta Kate is three over delta y. And there you have it." He slaps down the pencil and holds up his scheme. "The slope of a smart aleck."

"At least one of us finds geometry useful."

"And just how do you plan to get into Texas A&M? Great looks and a good personality won't do it like they did in my day. May I suggest you apply yourself to scholastics." He stands. "Holler at me when you're finished."

"Wait. I'm ready to work."

"Now we're talking."

Grounded full-time, Dad has become my official math teacher—a post he is frankly more suited to than Mom, who, despite her insistence on homeschooling, has no patience for teaching. Flexible, multi-modal pedagogy strikes her as full of loopholes for lazy students. She plans meticulous lessons with the aim that over twelve years I will learn to write and divide decently enough to enter a public university. She holds that intelligence is inherent, and genius a genetic rarity. I inspire in her no aspirations of sending me to Harvard. Not even Rice. Vanderbilt, she once told me, is a very impressive school. The conversation ended there.

While Dad maintains that his children ought to honor our heritage as proper Aggies and pursue our education at Texas A&M, Mom murmurs that Texas Tech, with its generous admissions policy and proximity to our house on Eighteenth Street, will suit just fine. My siblings and I are lucky, I will understand later, that our parents have college degrees. They are both first-generation college students. And unlike the parents of most of the homeschooled children who pass by on their roller skates at Skate Ranch #1 on Friday afternoons, university has been normalized for my parents. They believe they are preparing us for academic success, not trying to avoid it altogether. They just also want their daughters to attend university as godly, virginal creationists who keep curfew, wear bras, become veterinarians, and move back home to live near their mothers.

Despite these goals and Mom's background in the sciences, she holds forth best in the humanities. My Latin lessons revolve around translated and abridged versions of Pliny. Because Mom believes that literature ended when women started wearing pants, I read across the Victorian canon. Mom teaches that Thomas Hardy is dark; Emily Brontë is better than Charlotte, but both are depressing; and Dumas and Dickens are loquacious (from the Latin word *loquor*, meaning "to speak"; now conjugate that in the pluperfect).

Mom says Latin will give me a jump-start in following in her footsteps to become a veterinarian, which I quite want to do until I meet my lessons on the formation of proteins with consternation. Mom balks. To her, my inability to remember the difference between meiosis and mitosis comes down to one thing: a poor attitude. "There are only a few people on this earth who can read something once and understand it. You need to study," she says. "Diligently."

But no matter how many times I pore over splitting cells, I don't comprehend them very well until I read a description of cancer. I come to understand the proliferous life span of mutant cells that change fundamentally and outpace healthy ones. Cancerous cells reproduce with a desirable if not miraculous perfection. In time, I will read Siddhartha Mukherjee's nuanced point that cancer has mastered what modern human beings strive for: proficiency, boundlessness, immortality. But before I intellectualize the concept, I experience it as Dad begins to rock in his seat whenever he helps me with math.

A pressure is growing in his abdomen. He forgets I'm listening and describes the pain to Mom as a dull and constant ache. They circle back to the gastroenterologist, who palpates Dad's colon and says that the mass is expanding. It will soon block him. The doctor recommends an out-patient procedure that involves a laser cutting away parts of the growing tumor and cauterizing the laceration.

Mom continues her search for answers online and prints a claim that prayer and healthy food can put cancer into remission. But the process can take months. My parents agree that it could still be an act of faith to carve away some of the tumor. It will give God time to work. Meanwhile, I understand mitosis not only as biological process but as mathematical calculation. I translate Pliny: *We have divided God.* I think of *cellula*, meaning a "cell" or "monastery." In the nucleolus of my family, I recognize the same contest between biology and sanctification.

Dad comes back from the procedure walking stiffly. His inhales are clipped. He holds an orange vial filled with white pills prescribed by the doctor. For pain, he explains. He places the bottle in the cabinet holding vitamins. He collapses in the green recliner and waits for the codeine to kick in. It does and his body softens. Dad suggests that we go for a run in the morning.

The next day he meets me in the schoolroom wearing khaki shorts and a baggy T-shirt and apologizes. "Maybe another morning," he says. He asks if I need help with math. He opens the cabinet above the toaster, pops the orange vial, shakes its contents into his palm, and lifts them to his mouth. He swallows.

Within two days, he feels the relief of the diminished tumor and, accompanying the reprieve, a desire to travel. His sister is due in Universal City to see their mother. Dad calls my grandmother, says, "Tell Lori I'll be there tomorrow."

The visit comes as a surprise. Dad had told Lori his pain had become too acute to travel. But with the latest laser surgery, the pressure has receded.

My grandparents and Aunt Lori sit by the pool. Lori's three kids water-fight; she ignores them. The family's ability to not talk about what is right in front of them is remarkable. Dad eases himself into one of the patio chairs and hesitates before sitting down completely and finally unflexing his arms. *Has anyone in the family finally watched* Braveheart? Lori says it's too violent for her. *What's wrong with* When Harry Met Sally? Dad rocks forward, presses his palms to the top of the table, and lifts himself slightly. Someone tells him to go ahead and take his pain meds. But he hasn't brought them.

"And let y'all tell all the jokes? I don't think so."

"We would have gone easy on you," Grandpa says.

"I wouldn't have felt like I was here." Dad glances at the pool. "Kids say I get codeine eyes," he says. He exaggerates a dazed look. His family chuckles. Grandma lifts her martini, takes a sip, drinks it down, lifts the skewer from the glass, and eats the olive. Bobby is driving over from his house a few blocks away. Dad's oldest brother, Tommy, is in St. Louis; there hadn't been enough warning time for him to get to Universal City to see Dad. Perhaps neither of the brothers minded too much. They weren't close.

One of my cousins climbs out of the pool and foot-slaps up to the table. Dad holds thumb and finger to his eyelids, says, "If you press your fingers like this, your eyes will pop out." He makes codeine eyes again.

In the morning, Lori thanks him for coming. She knows it wasn't easy. He says that she would have missed him too much. She says he couldn't bear letting her have all the fun. Quiet settles between them. Their parents will appear soon to say goodbye. Lori asks Dad if he's heard the one about the man in the flood. Not Noah—another man, another flood. The man was drowning, and he begged God to save him. A tree appeared, and the man ignored it. He asked God to save him. Then a boat appeared, and the man dismissed it, saying God would save him. When he drowned and got to heaven, the man asked God, "Why didn't you save me?" God said that he had sent a tree and a boat.

"My point is," Lori says, "God made medicine." She takes Dad by the shoulders. "You still have options, John."

Dad kisses her forehead.

Dad scores my math lesson with an A and writes *Good job* across the top of the page. He believes in positive reinforcement, having been something of a mediocre student himself. He calls his sister, and she asks for a cancer update. He finds me and holds out the phone.

"Tell your aunt how many times you've read *Pride and Prejudice.*"

I progress to pre-trigonometry as the burden in Dad's bowels returns; the pain sets him like a metronome wand rocking back and forth. My eyelids flutter at the clicks of his chair. I want to take hold of him and say, *Stop.* With a rigid faith as my guide, I am left with little else to say. But I do not say it.

One morning I focus on the textbook open in front of me and tune out the clicking of Dad's chair. His touch startles me.

"What?" My voice cuts the air.

"I've said your name twice. This is how you show your work."

He slides his scratch sheet to me and studies me with a softness that threatens to topple my resolve. I wish he would slap me instead, but the man who chastens me has departed into the past as well. I push the explanation back.

"I think I get it."

He nods. He checks the numbers once more, hesitates when he comes to the bottom of the page, and runs his pencil through his hair and across his lips. For a thin moment, I hope we can forget what I've just said and he'll mark the page once again. But then the chair clicks, clicks, clicks.

"You know," he says, setting his pencil aside, "I think I need to go and sit in the living room." He rises to leave. "You sure you got this?"

"Dad, I'm fine."

CHAPTER 12

MOM MAKES BREAD TO SAVE Dad's life.

It doesn't sound as extreme at the time. Dad's cancer is so aggressive that we blame the devil; our desperation has done things to our perspective. Mom calls it faith.

"God is healing your dad," she says. "And we can show our faithfulness with some healthy eating."

In healing's delay, my parents research ways to purge Dad's body of anything that might hinder God's work, embarking on a diet revolution that makes paleo-heads look indulgent. The fruits of Mom's research come to bear: we are called to abandon red meat, white rice, white sugar, white flour, corn syrup, corn-anything. Mom romanticizes the change as though we are harnessing some unadulterated time when people lived off the land and never cussed.

One afternoon she returns from Well Body, Lubbock's de facto health food store, with paper bags full of lentils and carrots, basmati rice and beans. The world's evils came through additives. Preservatives are cancer feeders. Raw vegetables can wage war on tumors.

Boxes arrive, filled with mineral supplements. Mom replaces Tylenol with ground algae, and the vitamins shaped like Flintstone characters with bottles of echinacea. Kendra frets her fingernails down to their beds watching Mom throw out the last of the cereal and flatten each box.

"Stop chewing your nails," Mom says.

"What are we going to eat?" Kendra says. I lightly pinch her earlobes.

"We're going to starve, silly."

The kitchen is transformed. The montage of porcelain canisters are emptied of their powdered sugar and flour, and shelves of tomato sauce and pasta are replaced with white gallon buckets of organic honey. The refrigerator brims with greens. Mom reads literature suggesting that salt is fodder for malignancy. Our diet flattens to bland.

A box of a loose-leaf red tea arrives. "Itzhak tea," Mom says, boiling water. After the tea steeps for twenty minutes, she pours herself a cup and takes a sip. Her mouth presses into a grimace.

"All righty," she says. "That's going to take some getting used to." I ask if she intends to drink the tea too. She says that she does. "He shouldn't have to do this by himself."

Pastor Shawn drops by for a visit and surveys our pantry. He scratches his bulb of a forehead.

"How you going to get your kids to eat like this?"

"Hunger," Dad says, as much to himself as anybody, "is a powerful motivation."

I view the contents of our pantry like a to-do list I can manage. Under different circumstances, lentils three nights a week might test a palate raised on Betty Crocker. But should food be a form of prayer, I hold legumes holy. Asked to eat them, I'll lift each spoonful and say, "For Dad." Like my parents, I take solace in an actionable faith, in having something to do. You couldn't pay me to eat an Oreo.

The changes in the kitchen spread into the living room, where the bookshelf Dad built stands, a reflection of his love of carpentry and obsession with thrillers. He used to spin yarns from their plots in G-rated versions that left me, at twelve years old, breathless. I often tried returning the favor, offering up synopses of *Rebecca of Sunnybrook Farm* that could test the patience of a guardian angel. When I committed to reading *The Count of Monte Cristo*, Dad preempted my spiel by offering to read it too.

Dad now occupies himself mostly with reading the Bible. Meanwhile, I count down the years till I can sink into Robert Ludlum's novels. The brazen titles of Dad's books line the top shelves like the liquor cabinet of literature. Dean Koontz is Jim Beam, and Clancy could be Beefeater's—not that I know to think of them this way. If asked, I would say they were simply the best books of all time. On one of the top shelves is a worn and rippled copy of *Lonesome Dove*, Dad's favorite novel. The lower shelves boast Mom's medical textbooks from her years in veterinarian school. Heavy yearbooks from 1979, '80, '81, and '82, my parents' time at Texas A&M, line the lowest shelf of the bookcase.

Space along the bookshelves is cleared—why not say it in the passive voice? A force moves in our house beyond human agency, though surely the hands of my father move the books, just as the hands of my mother clear the pantry for sacks of wheat berries. Evangelical texts about supernatural healing appear along with books on the merits of raw juice and bone broth. Next to Benny Hinn's *Miracle of Healing* is Susan Baxter's *Immune Power*. A.B. Simpson's *The Gospel of Healing* sits beside a book whose title will haunt me—*Sharks Don't Get Cancer*, a text that has led Dad to drink ground shark cartilage diluted in water.

Anyone surveying the bookshelf could see that our family's arc begins when my parents meet in college, rises through the making of a family, and falls with Dad getting cancer.

Kendra lies next to me and sighs. "I miss sour cream chicken."

From the top bunk, Karson mutters, "I miss macaroni and cheese."

"You miss burning it to the bottom of the pan?" I say. "Because I don't miss cleaning up after you."

"Hey." Karson's face appears upside down in the space between the bunks, her hair a long red curtain.

"You're scaring me," Kendra says.

"You want to know what I really miss?" Karson says. "Cookie dough. I want a big, big bowl." She springs her arms wide. Kendra squeals.

"I used to dream," I say, "of the biggest bowl of cookie dough. Like big enough to swim in." We laugh, and then I press my lips together. Worry tugs at a spot inside me that's been worn raw. I picture Mom walking down the hall, her tiny frame all filled with rebuke, God having woken her because of course He hears everything.

"Y'all are going to wake up Mom."

"Oh no." Karson flips and planks on her back. The ceiling fan hums. The constellation stickers dim.

"She sleeps like a feather," Karson whispers.

"Lighter than," I say.

"Whatever."

In the morning, the din of Mom's computer keyboard is replaced with the blare of the industrial-grade juicer that excretes pulp through something similar to an industrial-grade anus, an observation I keep to myself. Dad drinks down the liquid and says it's the kind of taste you get used to, praise God.

At the end of each day, I weary in the final minutes between waking and sleep when gales send shudders down the length of the house. I believe I can hear wind cross the broken plains, roaring through Oklahoma and New Mexico—the same gusts that whipped the panhandle into the sky in one day: April 14, 1935. On Black Sunday, dust filled the lungs of livestock and people, igniting a pandemic called dust pneumonia. "The simplest thing in life, taking a breath," writes journalist Timothy Egan, "was a threat."

Breathes there a person of rough country anywhere whose soul is not shaped by wind? Gales lifted dirt loosened by the plow, and federal funds came rushing in to drill over two hundred new wells that bored into the Ogallala across the southern high plains to find water that might settle the dust. Though, in 1997, dust pneumonia is a thing of the past, my breath tightens in my chest. In the still darkness, the quiet between squalls—a silence more terrifying than ruined dirt—holds my greatest secret: my fear for Dad's life. At dawn, dread winks in the swirls of dust on the windowsills.

Karson climbs down the bunk ladder and slips into bed next to me and Kendra. We have only minutes before Mom will walk the hallway, rap on the open door, and tell us to get ready for school. Before we dress, comb our hair, and appear at the kitchen table ready to recite the house rules, Karson speaks.

"I saw something last night," she says. She describes a woman, with the tail of a snake, wrapped around her feet. She tried to shake the woman loose, but she laughed.

"Then I said, 'in the name of Jesus,' and the woman vanished."

"It was a demon?" Kendra says.

"I'm going to go tell Mom," Karson says.

That afternoon, Mom takes the olive oil she bought at Well Body and pours a little over her fingers and makes crosses with it above the doorways to the bedrooms and bathrooms, praying softly in words I can't make out.

The doorways blessed, the library altered, the kitchen readied: the next step is bread. Mom determines to grind the wheat herself. She chooses, without hesitation, an electric wheat grinder over a hand-mill.

"Let's not get carried away," she says.

The WonderMill Electric Grain Grinder, a bona fide staple for bread makers, looks like it was designed by NASA. Mom stuffs bright orange earplugs into the sides of her head and flips the switch. At first, my siblings and I stand back in awe as Mom scoops a cup from a five-gallon bucket of wheat berries and pours them into the grinder. But the machine is as loud as a broken fan belt, and we go flying from the noise. Wheat berries swivel down a vortex in the grinder's open dome, disappearing in a steady scream, where they pop and powder against the blade. Then there is the sound of a chain choke and the grinder stutters to a halt.

"Doggone it," Mom says. She unplugs the machine and digs the snagged berries out with a butter knife. "This is supposed to be the best," she mutters. I assume she is talking about the mill's brand, not the process of grinding flour to make bread. She still has the earplugs in. I wouldn't have asked anyway.

Baking bread is an act of faith. The important parts are the unprocessed ingredients, authentic in their heartiness and nutritional value. But there is an inherent flaw in the grinder's design. The funnel for the wheat berries swallows more berries than the grinder can grind. The blade jams. Even when Mom manages the wheat berries' flow rate, the ground flour builds up unevenly in a short white bucket. Without finding a way to level out the flour as the grinder runs, the pulverized grain spews all over the counter— a massive fresh-ground-flour explosion in our own personal dust bowl.

It happens all the time.

Mom's solution is to post Karson or me next to the grinder. The key is to shake the bucket enough to level the incoming wheat flour, but not so much as to detach the container from the hose, causing the same carnage we are trying to prevent. Once, I swivel the bucket too far to the right, disconnecting hose and bucket. I am sprayed with flour before I can flip the switch. Mom hides a laugh behind her hand as I blink through the dust. Another time I miscalculate how long the mill has been running, and the bucket's lid pops off. A film of white powder covers the counter and floor. This time Mom is not amused.

"What were you thinking?" My broom tracks lines across the tile, and Mom lists off what I already know: She is going to have to start all over. Now she will have to rush. Don't I understand how important the bread is?

No amount of apologizing seems to convince her that I comprehend her grievance and grasp the larger purpose of the bread—how it is central to Dad's recovery. How preparing it is the act of obedience God requires to intervene. Each time I screw up the wheat berry–to–grind ratio, it is a personal affront, a spiritual failure, as though I'm not committed fully to making Dad well. I need to do more.

I collapse in my room. Afternoon light cuts through the blinds. I am chilled as though by fever. Contemplation of the daylight smears with images of Dad in the green recliner bent over a tray of homemade bread and home-juiced carrots. *Home home home*

home—the prefix to everything in our lives. Scripture reels in my head like an earworm.

Karson finds me.

"You hyperventilating?"

"I don't know."

She sinks into the bed. "If it's your stomach, I can bring you a trash can."

"I don't know."

She exhales loudly and settles on her back. I roll over and work to slow my breathing. Above us, a series of blue bars bolster the top bunk.

"Sometimes 7Up can help."

"I doubt that we are going to be drinking 7Up for a very long time."

Though Mom is from Houston, she might as well have descended from the German-blood settlers who, in the 1930s Dust Bowl, refused to evacuate West Texas, despite surveyors' observations that the high plains were unfit for cultivation and uninhabitable by anyone whose survival relied upon agriculture. The Comanche followed their hunt across the plains to live. But when the land didn't shine green, settlers dug houses deep into the sod, and the infantry trapped the Comanche in Palo Duro Canyon and captured their horses. Drought had always been a season in the high plains, but settlers named it plague. When rain didn't fall, there was water underground to make sand out of grass, wheat out of sand, miracle out of curse. Call that which is not as though it were. What choice did they have, the settlers asked themselves. Money in the bank stretched no further than the three hundred acres they'd bought for next to nothing, their life's savings. Besides, the land was theirs. Also the well underneath it. Made available for sale by a canyon turned into an indigenous people's graveyard.

White settlers landmarked their acres with stakes, lest they lose their way in the ocean of grass that brushed their knees; otherwise, they might wander in oblivion across the Texas panhandle. *Llano Estacado*, the staked plains. Everything they owned staked to dreams of prosperity in a desert of the country's making. Nothing to do about the cloudless sky except fill it with belief.

But belief takes a sign. Mom teaches me that.

Over time she perfects the bread. It becomes the stuff of legend. Neighbors request it. Church members hold her a little tighter when she appears with a loaf in her hands. The bread becomes a regular birthday gift to friends who respond with thank-you notes, writing, "There is nothing like your bread, Beverly." It is a fitting signature for Mom. Ten cups of fresh-ground wheat berries sweeten the air as she pours six cups of lukewarm water into two tablespoons of yeast and sets the mixture to ferment. Then comes three-quarters of a cup of honey, two teaspoons of salt. The bread hook's two steel arms whip the dough to belly soft, inhaling for a double rise. She divides the dough into five steel bread pans. The loaves, once baked, have a shelf life of less than a week.

To say the fresh-ground wheat bread my mother makes is best on the first day would be an understatement. To begin, this is true of all bread. But Mom's bread is unlike any other. It rises to a stiff dome, filled with the sweetest air. I burn the pads of my fingers turning the not-yet-cooled pan with one hand and, with the other, sliding the loaf out. The bread tears like fine cloth, but more porous, more alive. A serrated knife causes the loaf to fold on itself before the bread cools. My three younger sisters and little brother press behind me as I prepare a slice for each of them. Even Mary Katherine smacks her lips. One loaf disappears before the other four cool, dissolving into honey in our mouths, exhaling yeast when we swallow.

But what makes Mom's bread distinct is our longing, which rises in steel pans. This is the bread that God will use to rescue Dad. His lungs draw in the bread's aroma deeply before each daily bite.

There was a time when the air holding up the sky was so pure it healed people. Sanatoriums blossomed throughout Texas, Oklahoma, and Colorado, beckoning to men and women of means whose lungs had blackened in the industrial air of urban Britain. *Breathe in the clean air*, pamphlets advertised—the dry heat in the shade a balm, cool as a hand. But clear skies didn't dump rain, didn't turn over wheat bushels. The windmill was a fine invention when the wind cooperated, but the gusts were fickle.

In drought, our white ancestors made their own thunder. We shot dynamite into the sky, believing that the explosions would draw rain. Faith took the shape of cannon flame splintering into sparks of fire. Smoke held promise of apocryphal clouds that thinned into lines at the horizon—the high-pitched ringing in everyone's ears a prophecy.

The Llano Estacado plateau rises from the Gulf of Mexico at a slope so subtle that only water knows it. The sediment crests at just over three thousand feet, far enough away from the sea to have forgotten it. Mom doesn't like the ocean, not since she was a kid and got caught in an undertow at Galveston that threatened to fill her lungs with saltwater and sand. Didn't have to tell her twice. She comes to know how Lubbock's altitude determines the length of time bread dough takes to double. Our house fills with the earthy smell of wheat, the fragrance of Mom's resolve, a force well suited to the 100th meridian west, the line where desperation and backbone meet. When I think of bursts in the sky above West Texas, I think of my mother. A strong will recast as willingness. A demand for blessing. See? Here I am. Making bread. Lighting the sky on fire.

CHAPTER 13

MOM WEAVES BETWEEN THE KITCHEN and the computer desk, between bread and verse. At her keyboard, she types up scriptures in Times New Roman fourteen-point font and prints them on blue index cards. She is boycotting metaphor. Where the Old Testament prophets wrote *heal*, they meant it literally.

Looking back across the space of over two decades, I want to slow down here and try to get a clearer picture of my younger self. Where is my own movement amid the bustle of my mother's? I can picture myself leaning against the doorway to the schoolroom, watching her type. I feel the air part as she brushes past me to check on the bread. But memory offers glimpses of little more than a statue of a twelve-year-old.

The details around my mother sitting at the computer desk crystalize. They reveal the intensity of the time, my awareness, and my ability to deeply observe, but the spotlight on my mother also keeps my dismissal of myself in shadow. I was not, at the time, paying close attention to what I thought or the physical sensations passing through my body.

Though I had inherited my father's love for story, I often didn't consider myself a prominent actor in the narrative of my life. Like my mother, I would become obsessed with words, but I did not at the time try to find the meaning for what I was experiencing. I am grateful for what I remember. But memory is itself a storyteller, and my memory did not, in moments like these, consider me one of the main characters. I am keenly aware, in retrospect, that my recollections are often shorn of the one remembering.

A part of me was coping with trauma by going numb. It's also true that, while my parents loved their children, they did not often think of us as persons with reflections of our own. My mother in particular rarely asked me what I was thinking, feeling, or needing. I was even less attuned than usual to my inner feelings in the early days of my father's diagnosis because that's where doubt might reside. I could will myself to believe in a miracle if I ignored my senses and instincts, which perceived the changes in my father's body.

But what's not there in my recollections tells a story too, and I can feel in the absence of a fuller portrait of my younger self a painful irony: the presence of a young girl's attempt to survive.

The graveled post-smoker, post-sinner voice of evangelical Joyce Meyer rattles from Mom's portable stereo. Meyer teaches that a good attitude is the prerequisite for material blessing and physical wellness. The Bible is no mere book of stories. If you want heaven's favor, you've got to believe God's word is alive and well and sharper than any two-edged sword. *Hallelujahs* and *glories* gush from the speakers. Mom pauses and turns the dial for the volume clockwise. Her typing resumes in a flitter, and Meyer swoons, saying, "Now that's good preaching. God's speaking through me tonight." A shower of applause responds.

For an example of blessing, one need look no further than Meyer herself: her net worth will eventually approach $8 million. She travels from megachurch to megachurch in a private plane. In response to criticisms of her wealth, built on donations, Meyer says there is no need to apologize for receiving God's benevolence. I'm bent over *The Return of the Native* at the kitchen table, pondering the number of times I've heard my mother apologize for anything.

The typing ceases again as Mom turns the pages of two enormous texts lying open before her. One is a faux-leather-bound biblical concordance; the other is the good book itself. Mom scans the concordance and holds her finger to a reference and then flips through the Bible, searching out every instance of the term "healing" and its Hebraic synonyms.

The walls surrounding the computer desk are lined with bookshelves filled with curricula on math, grammar and spelling, history. Next to her, the printer whirs with promises of God's power to cure.

The scriptures are familiar. Few are the preachers who have missed a chance to belabor this one: "Jesus was bruised for our iniquities, cast down for our transgressions. By his wounds we are healed." The verse sits at the top of Mom's blue index cards. She claims that, despite its ubiquity, the verse is misunderstood by most people. "They think it's just talking about the healing of the soul. But the definitive original Hebrew includes physical healing. And it's present tense. We *are* healed."

Move over, Joyce Meyer.

Mom asks me to hold the deck of scriptures as she tapes each blue card to her bathroom doorway. "Place my words like a seal over your heart," she says, channeling the Old Testament. "Write them on your doorways. Meditate on them in your coming and going." The doorframe fills with blue cards and the words blur into one another until the sentences form a floating ribbon above the doorway my parents will walk under each day. Whenever I seek out my mother in the morning, knowing well her routine of facewash, toner, moisturizer, curlers, foundation, eyebrows, lipstick, I will stand under this banner of belief.

West Texas is the land of the literal; Lubbock is surrounded by flat towns with names like Plainview, Levelland, and Brownfield. But my family is kicking language into high gear. Words of healing are our vernacular.

I turn one of the cards in my hand. "Is anyone among you sick?" it reads. "Let them call the elders of the church to pray over them and anoint them with oil in the name of the Lord. And the prayer offered in faith will make the sick person well; the Lord will raise them up." The speaker is James, a disciple who is thought to have been the first martyr for Jesus. Well. There have been many since.

I pass the card to Mom, and she tapes it to the left corner of the doorframe. I stand back to see if I can make out the words from James from all the rest. I can.

Pantry revamped. Bread baked. Doorways adorned. Our house is primed for miracles. Then a bulge appears under Dad's right rib.

It emerges under his shirt as he reaches into the cabinet, pushes aside vitamins, retrieves the codeine, and quaffs two pills. The lump looks like a pocket of air. When Dad relaxes, it disappears. *There was nothing*, I tell myself.

Then I see it again. Dad is shirtless and sitting on his bed, studying its shape. This time the bulge does not vanish. There is a strange malformity to it, as though a fist wants to punch through his skin. Dad looks up and our eyes meet. His lips part in a grimace. The blue cards twist above me.

I believe Dad's illness is a test of our faith, a suffering with purpose. My immaterial conviction will manifest in the material wonder of Dad's restored health. When God heals him, we will give up the spare diet and throw a pizza party.

But a different materiality crops up, filling me physically with dread. In trying to deny the sign of trouble in my father's body, I dismiss the warnings in my own. My body tightens like I've been caught off guard, and the spook won't slacken. I can't relax. My muscles, bones, flesh, and nerves feel bound not to belief but to a truth before my eyes: Dad's liver is swollen with cancer.

I feel words cast about in my chest. I try to catch them and speak. *The prayer offered in faith will make the sick person well.* But the language wafts away. In my hand warms the memory of the cat's liver. I shift my gaze elsewhere and Dad pulls a shirt on and Mom says it's time for prayer.

Her glass of water glows under a table lamp. The yellow lampshade casts the filtered liquid in a sickly hue, an image I will recall twenty-two years later, in 2019, when I see a picture of the old hangar at Reese Air Force Base next to a headline in the *Texas*

Observer that reads: "Nearly 500,000 Texans Live in Communities with Contaminated Groundwater. Lawmakers Aren't Doing Much about It." Journalist Christopher Collins makes clear that in 2019 Texans were only recently becoming aware of forever chemicals contaminating their public waters.

The article broke less than a year after a report from the Centers for Disease Control and Prevention (CDC) recommended a safety threshold for PFAS that was ten times lower than the current standard set by the Environmental Protection Agency (EPA). The recommendation was significant because it suggested that many more people were at risk than previously thought from overexposure to PFAS. Internal emails from unidentified White House aides revealed that the Trump administration and Scott Pruitt's EPA suppressed the CDC report for over three months, attempting to prevent a "public relations nightmare" for the EPA and Department of Defense.

Collins writes that Lubbock was a prime example of the kind of place where people who had lived on or near military sites were exposed unknowingly to the by-products of firefighting foams through water that they showered in, cooked with, and drank. Those most at risk resided within an area three miles east and northeast of the base site, because PFAS migrate in the direction of groundwater. My family lived beyond that radius by a few more miles, so when the CDC selected Lubbock as one of eight Texas sites for a two-year study on the health impact of PFAS, my family was not considered for a number of reasons: our residence fell outside the geographical location; we drank filtered water at home; and my father was diagnosed after he retired from military service.

In 2021, I contacted the Air Force officer who worked on the PFAS study and requested an interview, specifically asking if we could talk about pollution in the Lubbock region and the communities participating in the study. I was hoping to hear about the exposure of military personnel who had worked on the base while serving on active duty. In an email, he told me that he was the right person to talk to, but that all interviews had to be organized through Air Force Public Affairs. He forwarded my request to the said public relations office, which told me that they could not discuss any history of chemical use. "We are conducting investigations into the presence of PFOS/PFOA in the environment, its impact on drinking water, and identifying/implementing strategies to manage PFOS/PFOA in drinking water," Air Force spokesperson Mark Kinkade wrote in an email. He explained that the officer in charge of the investigation in Lubbock had "limited knowledge of historical use of foam at the installation, and it is based on whatever records may still exist."

He told me to direct questions regarding public health effects of PFAS to the CDC's Agency for Toxic Substances and Disease Registry (ATSDR) team, whose study on Lubbock concluded in 2022. That study found that two types of PFAS associated with firefighting foams were detected in participants' blood at rates higher than national averages. The higher levels in older participants indicated a longer duration of exposure, though the report makes clear that it cannot account for exposure *preceding* 2017.

When I read that, I contacted the CDC manager for the Lubbock study to ask if he could confirm that military personnel who were on active duty at Reese Air Force Base during the 1980s were likely to have been exposed to contaminated drinking water. He forwarded me to the same officer who was blocked from speaking to me back in 2021, the one whom the public relations director said had limited knowledge of the historical use of the foam. The CDC manager wrote that the Air Force officer ought to have "excellent knowledge of the historical sampling activities." I was frustrated, but I tried emailing the program manager again. When my email to him was ignored, I returned to Christopher Collins's description of forever chemicals: "Even if they don't kill you, they'll definitely outlast you." And I recalled the image of Mom's glass of water on her nightstand.

I remember her climbing into bed and pulling the comforter up to her waist. We read again from the Book of Job. I know better than to ask about the engorgement below Dad's rib. I know I will be reminded that my doubt—not cancer—is the problem. The arch of a tumor, the increasingly acrid smell of Dad's body, my constant, anxious sweating: these details are the stuff of theater, shades of evil taking on forms of the world. The reality is God's word. Qualms, not growths, are the true danger. A part of me finds comfort in this admonition, but my mouth runs dry.

Tonight Mom reads a passage from Job that begins, "Since his days are determined, the number of his months is with You; and You have set his limits so that he cannot pass." We pray. I bend to kiss Mom good night.

"I know you probably want to sleep in your room," Mom says, "but it would mean a lot if you kids would camp out in here."

I look to Dad. He picks at a place on his thumb. Anger tears through me before I can swat it away.

"Why?"

I expect Mom's strike, but her voice continues in a soft tap. Her eyes brim. She pleads. I tilt my head. Her intent is as clear as the page of a book. She wants to tell herself I will sleep in her room because I have chosen to support her. She prefers this to what we both know: if I say no, she'll make me do it.

"I need you. It helps when you're nearby."

A current twitches down my back. After a day's long work of belief, holding the lid to the grinder, reciting verses, ignoring my father's groans as he rocks a chair that doesn't rock, I fall into bed. The work of school, of tending my siblings, and most of all, the task of prayer, the labor of showing no lapse in faith—all this presses my body into the mattress. Looking into Mom's troubled face, my eyes sting—with pity or resentment or both. With the clarity of lightning, I understand that I need those few minutes in my own room before nightmares claim me; in this same instant, I know those minutes have been taken from me. My palms sweat. I shudder and look away so Mom can't see my rage and grab my chin and pull it into her breath.

"I'll need to get my own water."

"You can just have another sip of mine."

She searches my face as I drink. Her expression shifts. Now that I've given her the story she wants, she's ready to bite to protect it. I lower the glass.

"Did you get enough?"

"Yes."

"How about a 'Yes, Mom'?"

"Yes, Mom."

I open the cabinet at the end of the hall and pull down a pile of quilts. Karson is dutiful. She takes one of the blankets and shrugs as if to say, *What did you expect?* Kendra squirms in her blue nighty, caught between excitement and anxiety. Was this a slumber party or the apocalypse? Both seem likely. On the floor, she curls at my hip, warm as a puppy. James and Karson flop down on the other side of us. Mary Katherine sleeps in the bed between Mom and Dad. The rest of the house fades.

Mom clicks her table light off. A nightlight blinks on. Next to Mom's drinking glass, a digital clock radio gleams with red numbers. In the morning it will sound at 6:00 a.m., tuned to Positive Encouraging KLOVE, Christian radio. Illumined only by the nightlight, the water in Mom's glass glows yellow. Years later, my memory will settle on this image as a harbinger—not of things to come, but of what had already seeped into our lives. Faith, it's said, can move mountains. What can cleanse porous rock?

The chests of my siblings rise and fall in quick, soft movements. I hear the deep breaths of my father, though whether he sleeps, I cannot tell.

CHAPTER 14

A GASH, RIMMED BY CHALKY powder, yawns in the wall of the homeschool room. Did I hear the blow? Flakes of sheetrock have settled across a tray of math manipulatives. I peer into the opening.

"It's time for school," Mom says, marching by. The spoon in her back pocket looks especially eager. She says we'll talk about the split in the wall later.

A frying pan clamors on the burner. Mom turns the control knob and asks who wants eggs. Karson volunteers to make them and steps around Mom and opens her palm for the whisk. She is ten years old, but cooks with the confidence of a matron. The eggs burn to the bottom of the pan.

"Let the pan soak," Mom says.

Kendra walks into the schoolroom and pauses under the puncture in the wall, as though it has something to tell her. Whatever it says sparks a fire. She storms into the dining room and pulls back her chair with a scrape and pouts. Mom's response is instantaneous. She tells Kendra to get up and lie over the chair.

"May I ask why?"

"No, you may not."

Mom presses the flat of her hand between Kendra's shoulder blades and sweeps the spoon up. It lands with a soft thud. Karson and I eye one another. It's then that I notice the strange lumps in Kendra's underpants, like little mushrooms.

"What on earth is in your pants?" Mom says.

"Nothing."

"Stand up." Mom tugs my sister's elastic waistline back. "You take those rags out right now." Kendra whimpers and pulls one soft diaper rag after another from her underwear. Mom turns to me and cups a smile behind her hand. "She thought I wouldn't notice," she says.

Kendra is slow and reluctant to remove the rags. For this reticence, Mom says her beatings will double. Kendra howls. Mom says that if she keeps hyperventilating, the number of hits will triple. Kendra screams. I grip the table's edge. A smirk spreads across Mom's face as the rags pile onto the floor. I want to smack it off her face. I thrust my chair back.

"Spank me instead."

Mom cocks her head, amused. "I'll get to you next."

She takes her time with me, landing the spoon and pausing to bring the swing through before lifting again. I wince and rock forward with each strike, but this whipping is nothing—I can see Dad's swollen liver and I don't cry. I turn about to face her and press my lips between my teeth.

"I can tell you're upset," she says. She mimics rolling her lips together.

Mom told me once that her own mother beat her with a two-by-four spiked with nails. She laughed when she described it, how she jumped in the air with each puncture to her legs. She insists that spanking is different and speaks in cliché, saying it hurts her more. She does it because she loves me.

I bite down harder to fight the tremor. Mom wants me to cry. A book in my parents' bookshelf entitled *To Train Up a Child* says that a child's tears are manipulative, proof of noncompliance. If my eyes leak, she'll hit me again. I am grateful for my power to stop feeling the fresh soreness spreading across my body.

"Come, give me a hug," she says, her voice mellow. She pulls me to her and though she holds me with gentleness, I stop feeling that too.

"Now, let's get to work." She sighs. "We're already running behind."

Dad falters past the dining room table carrying a cut of drywall, a utility knife, and a level. I spell words as Mom dictates. Dad saws at the edges of the hole in the wall, wipes the white dust away, and checks his lines with the level. Then he puts down his tools, walks into his bathroom, and closes the door. When he returns, he resumes with the blade and evens the lines of the opening. He fits the square of new sheetrock to the frame. The opening is still craggy, but suitable for spackling. He walks back to the garage and comes back carrying a bucket of DryDex.

"Can I get a hand real quick?"

Mom grumbles. She joins him in the homeschool room and helps to hold the drywall in place while Dad seals the edges. The patch of new wall is gray and will remain unpainted.

Later that afternoon, Mom beckons me to the kitchen. The vitamin cabinet doors are open. Her hand holds the prescription bottle of codeine. Dad rests in the recliner, out of view and asleep. Mom whispers. The other night she found him raking the shelves for his pills. She made a remark, then walked into the schoolroom. He followed her, spun her around, drew his face toward hers, and hissed, "Don't tell me what to do."

Mom told him that he'd been taking too many narcotics. Then he stood back and punched the wall.

Codeine relieved the pressure in his lower back and the urge to strain, the feeling that the tumor could fall from him if he just pushed enough. It aided his sleep, giving him temporary relief from his duty to bear his curse. The night of their brawl, he'd woken up in pain.

"But the pills are demonic," she tells me. Taking them opens Dad's body to possession.

"God's word says the true believer cannot be invaded by an evil spirit, unless that believer be ill." Sickness had made Dad vulnerable to a demon.

I glance at Andy, who's looking at us through the hexagons of a baby-gate that keeps him in the laundry room. His ears lift. He huffs and rolls to his side.

When Mom confronted Dad the day following their spat, he said he didn't remember it. She showed him the hole in the wall, and he said he couldn't recall making it. That was all she needed to hear. Dad's memory lapse, she reasoned, was caused by an evil spirit acting through him; he hadn't been the one acting out at all.

She passes me the orange vial. Alarm sounds through my bones as she opens a stepladder, climbs it, bends at the waist, and cocks her head to make sure Dad is still sleeping. Should he wake, he'll be looking right at Mom's reflection in the microwave door.

"Here." She waves me over, beckoning for the vial. She lifts herself onto the balls of her feet and pushes it to a far back corner. The vial vanishes from view. She closes the cabinet, steps down, and folds the ladder.

"I could see it in his eyes," she says. She describes his appearance as feral, his teeth clamped shut. She grabs me by the shoulders and tightens her jaw to show me. I find it easy to imagine a demonic power with Mom's nose brushing mine, her stare bearing down on me.

"I get it," I say, shaking free of her grasp.

"If the pain gets really bad, we can give it to him. It's not his fault, but he's not himself when he's on them." She says that she will tell Dad where the meds are. A lie, and I know it.

While awaiting sleep on my parents' bedroom floor, I slowly replay the scene of Mom hiding the codeine. Her weighty use of *we* settles on me. I stiffen. We are bound together in a test: we must uphold my father's faith. If I fail, my mother will know.

The dark square of my parents' bathroom doorway opens above me. Beyond it, I know my mother's razor sits on the bathtub ledge. The handle is ribbed, metal and heavy, the blade casing black. Burning within me is the memory of the time I went behind her back to shave my legs. It was almost two years ago, I was eleven. Eden had told me shaving my legs would feel amazing. I remember walking into my mother's bathroom, opening the cabinet beneath the sink, retrieving a sanitary pad, and leaving. I had begun a miserable early puberty, with cramps and a breakout of acne. My shirts stretched taut across my chest. Mom said I had elevated hormone levels because of steroids in dairy products and took me to Walmart to buy a bra. When I shuffled back from the dressing room sobbing because a woman walked in on me, Mom sighed.

"Oh, K.D. It's nothing that woman hasn't seen before."

I curled up on my bed and pressed my knees to my chest and rolled on top of my breasts in agony. Once a month for years to come? I cried. Mom sat next to me.

"This is ultimately a good thing," she said. Still, she forbade me from shaving before I turned thirteen, a deadline she designated for puberty based on absolutely nothing. "Everything changes after you shave," she mourned. "Even the hair doesn't grow back the same." Everything was already changing. I was tired of pants, but wearing shorts embarrassed me. I wanted to impress Jesse, who acted like he couldn't decide whether to tussle my hair or blush.

My sisters found my body curious. At night, the three of us squeezed into the bathtub. I sat closest to the faucet and tried to make a wet washcloth stick to my chest. One evening Kendra peeked around my shoulder.

"You get back there," I said and jerked forward. She giggled. "That's it." I climbed from the tub, wrapped myself in a towel, and splashed my way to Mom's room to announce that I could not take baths with my sisters anymore. Mom did little to fight a grin of amusement from spreading across her face. I seethed.

"You don't need to cry," she said.

The next night I locked myself in the bathroom and showered alone. Thunderous raps sounded through the door. I pictured my two sisters taking turns pounding as the other shook out her wrist. I soaped my hair once, then twice. The strands were heavy as I toweled them. I pulled a comb through my hair and watched myself in the mirror. I noticed that my face, always round during my childhood, was elongating, and my hair was growing darker. I was sure I would not grow up to be beautiful. But it felt good to be alone. Under the bathroom window, I leaned against the wall and rubbed lotion into my legs and then tried out doing nothing. The banging stopped. The room steamed. Above me, outside air sneaking through a crack in the window frame whispered across me. I could have stayed in that bathroom for hours.

Mom's knuckles percussed the door. I opened it, and she stood there, clutching her wooden spoon. Every muscle in my body tightened.

"You know you're not allowed to lock the door," she said, her hand beckoning me to come forward. She told me to drop my towel. I grasped the frame of the bunk bed. The sound of each strike of wood on flesh slapped the air. My sisters watched, deepening my shame and educating theirs. If I cried out, Mom would continue. I crushed my lips with my teeth. The embarrassment was immediate, and worse than the physical pain. When she stopped, I gathered my towel from around my feet and wrapped it above my small hard breasts.

"It's fine if you want to shower by yourself, but if you can't be grown-up enough to follow the rules, you can take a bath like a child." She waited.

"Yes, Mom," I said.

I didn't cry until she left the room. Karson's arm came around my shoulders. Kendra hugged my waist.

The next morning, a green bruise rose from my thigh.

A few weeks later, Eden told me she just ran a shower and snuck in the razor. "Your legs are going to feel so smooth. Call me after you do it." I pressed the Talk button when Mom walked into the kitchen. I smiled at her. I had won the right to take a shower alone, so long as I left the door unlocked.

The problem was the distance between Mom's bathroom and mine. Our house was deceptively large. From outside, the white brick ranch looked humble, with a single carport and basketball hoop. But inside, the foyer opened to a lengthy hallway that connected the bedrooms. When I stepped into the house for the first time, I wondered, *How far does this house go?* The explanation was simple: a previous owner had extended the hallway to add on three more rooms and two bathrooms. But even after living in the house a while, the long hallway still frightened me. I often flaunted one of the house rules—thou shalt not run inside—and sprinted up it in sheer panic. "You always feel," my sisters and I would say to one another, "that someone's following you." Karson often snuck up from behind and whispered, "Run."

My parents' bedroom lay at the end of the hallway and the bedroom I shared with my sisters with the bathroom attached sat up front. The trickiest part of shaving my legs would be carrying the razor back and forth in the hallway undetected.

It was easy enough for me to identify the day for transgression— a Saturday morning when Mom was at the clinic and Dad was away at work. This was, after all, two years earlier, when Dad still left for work and I still planned my little indiscretions—listening to rock 'n' roll, locking the bathroom door, and, my greatest yet, shaving my legs.

But Mom's eyes had a way of watching me even while she was away—through the blue pairs set in Karson's and Kendra's heads. My Judases. I would have only a few opportunities. I thought through the Saturday morning schedule. There would be *Winnie the Pooh* at 8:30, but Mom wouldn't have left yet. There would be snack time at 10:30, which required a referee. I only had till noon. If we started a movie at 11:00 and I got up to leave, someone would surely ask where I was going. Still, the movie window was my best option.

The following Saturday morning, I watched my siblings drink down the milk they'd used to sop up graham crackers. A mess of crumbs lodged in the corners of my brother's mouth. I held up the VHS cases for *The Little Mermaid* and *Rescuers Down Under*. My mistake. Karson and James wanted *Rescuers*. Kendra chose *Little Mermaid*. The three demanded a trial. Chances were slim that Kendra would recover from the rejection of her choice. I quoted a time-honored line from my mother: "Either y'all agree or we aren't watching anything." Karson rolled her eyes.

"You think you're the boss?"

"How about this. What if we watch *Little Mermaid* and everyone gets another graham cracker."

"Chocolate ones?" James's eyes beamed.

"Chocolate ones."

The vote shifted to three-to-one.

Mom's razor was a three-blade Gillette. I found it resting in its usual position: the corner ledge, left of the faucet, handle pointed to the back of the tub. In my hand, the razor was cool, a little heavy. I pressed it carefully to my thigh as I walked—cautious not to run—down the hallway.

The bathroom fan roared. I all but hushed the faucet. My heart raced and a still small voice, my own, told me not to do it. It was in dismissing this voice that I found gratification. In the shower, I worried I'd betray myself by dropping the razor, my clumsiness heard in a stone clang reverberating throughout the house. But I passed the neat blade over my skin without any incident but one: I sensed I was maturing by years within only a few minutes. I felt older instantly. I wondered if maybe my mother was right, a revelation that delighted all the more because my pleasure would have horrified her.

I lathered my legs with shampoo, cut a nearly even path through the suds, and tracked my fingers up the smooth trail. Afterward, I sat naked on the bathroom rug, and ran my hands over my legs. My skin glowed. The bruise on my thigh from when Mom hit me after I locked the bathroom door had healed completely.

I returned the razor to the corner ledge of Mom's bathtub and turned it so the head faced the faucet. I walked into the living room before Ariel had turned into a human.

"You showered?" Karson said.

"Yeah, real quick."

Later that afternoon, Eden's giggle teased the line between us. "Told you," she said.

Glorious was the Sunday that followed. I pulled on stockings and zipped up a floral dress with a skirt that flared at my waist. When I walked into the sanctuary, I preened up to Jesse before service. Never mind that my legs were still hidden; I had the glitz of my secret. I asked about the farm. He gave a confused smile.

"Planting's done. Maybe this year we'll earn more than we spent, 'cause I'm due a raise."

I nodded and shimmied a little. Bewilderment crossed Jesse's face. He arched an eyebrow, scoffed, looked at the ground.

"Anyways," he said.

We both glanced down the row of church skater boys.

"I better go sit down," I said and trounced down the center aisle to my seat in the family row, feeling Jesse's eyes the whole way.

Later that week, Mom's voice bolted down the hallway. I found her perched on her folding stool in front of her vanity mirror, lit by a frame of round lights. Freshly showered, her hair was twisted in a towel. She plucked her eyebrows with a silver pair of tweezers she'd owned for fifteen years. She sometimes said those tweezers were her oldest prized possession and her children would know which of us she most favored by whom she willed the tweezers to. Her razor sat dully on the bath's ledge. I stood in the doorway of her bathroom and waited. Only Mom could turn tweezing into the hands of an interminable clock.

Just once did she loan the tweezers out. One afternoon a woman named Amanda from Bible study, who described everything from the sunset to a baby bib as "awesome," chirped that her baby girl had a splinter festering in her arm, and Mom offered her the tweezers. When Amanda didn't return them for two days, Mom said she should have known. "Amanda has always been a flake," she said. Mom drove the ten minutes across town and knocked on Amanda's front door. Amanda looked confused, but Mom didn't care. "So what if they're a pair of tweezers. They're good ones, and they're mine."

I thought about Amanda nearly every time Mom brought the tweezers out of her makeup basket. Most people underestimated Mom's doggedness. I usually didn't make that mistake. As I watched her, I told myself I had accounted fully for her obstinance when strategizing my first shave. I'd made sure my siblings were glued to the television set, sated with sweets and milk. I wore socks to walk the hallway. I cleaned the blade. But as Mom shaped sleek dark arches above her eyes, I winced as she held me waiting. I could see that an idea had already formed into a boulder in her mind, so steady was her precision as she leaned into the mirror, so complete and unhurried her calm.

She set the tweezers back in her makeup basket. "I know you shaved your legs."

My mind raced. I stood dumb in the doorway, feeling like she'd caught me in the act, a shining razor in my hand.

"Do you want to know how I know?" She turned from the mirror to face me. "God told me."

She pinched her lips to the side as though hearing the words fresh from the Lord again. I felt I heard them too, in a deep voice: "K.D. shaved her legs."

A sobless, steady stream of tears ran down Mom's face. At the time, I believed she cried because I'd deceived her and ruined part of my body, a double offense alarming enough to warrant God's intervention. But after that afternoon, I came to understand that she didn't just call me to the bathroom so that I could be filled with guilt. My mother wanted me to understand that God shared an omnipotent line with her. Nothing escaped his notice, and nothing escaped hers.

My mother and her holy panopticon.

Now, two years later, I lie on my parents' bedroom floor, bound to my mother in a charge to guard my father from the temptation of his own flesh. Can we, my mother and I, trust God enough to keep his promise of healing? Will we falter, delay a miracle, cause my father to open himself once more to the devil's hold? My mother won't. Will I?

How clear the corners of each room appear as I walk through the house in the days that follow; how sharp the angles are. Each doorway, each frame hanging on the wall. Light gleams on glass panes, flat and clipped. I inherited Dad's perfect vision, his blue eyes. Under my feet, the floor feels firm. Beneath me, time reverberates up from the Ogallala through deposits of agate, chert, flint, jasper, opal, and quartzite to support my task. My mouth is dry with responsibility, and my hands seek something to busy themselves with.

The house seems to change in sync with my father's body. The skin on his shoulders and arms loosens from bone like an ill-fitting suit. His chest caves in; by contrast, his legs fill with fluid. From dust to dust we eventually return. But first to water.

Dad calls me to his recliner, passes me a white pair of compression socks, and asks for help pulling them on. I kneel. How utterly devoid of muscle his limbs have become, yet his calves and thighs are thick. His feet feel made of clay. He bends to pull the stockings up his calves, then gestures toward a pair of sneakers.

"Leave the laces untied. Please." With an effort, he lifts his foot. I work free the tongue of his shoe. Does he think of the Saucony trainers he used to slip on each morning, Andy's joyous cries, the click of my helmet buckle? My feet are like his: middle toes webbed and longer than all the others. We are both slender of foot, with slight arches. I push the images aside. An imprint from my fingers remains around his ankle.

He cries softly. I stand and walk out.

Mom and I are in the front yard pulling the weeds that crowd the serrated petals of dianthus.

"Pitting edema," she says.

"What is pending edema?" I say.

"Pitting. *Pit-ting.* Blood isn't flowing like it should through his liver." She explains how the excess fluid gathers and turns skin taut and bright. That's why Dad's legs are swelling. Mom's eyes are red with strain, as though she has looked upon Dad's swollen legs from a distance of years. She isn't like Dad; she can only live in one place. Perhaps she's flown ahead in time and already inhabits a world where Dad's illness is a memory. I have to stop myself from envy, one of the deadly sins.

Even with Mom's explanation, I continue to mispronounce the

term to myself. *Pending*, I think. Waiting. He awaits his healing. We all do.

But the test of my faith also pends. The pills sit in the high cabinet, a presence more than a concrete object. They seem to watch me whenever I walk into the kitchen. If necessary, I will wait out my father's pining for relief, bolstered by righteous understanding and the knowledge of good and evil. If I give him the codeine, I hand him to the devil. The failure won't be his, but mine.

CHAPTER 15

WHEN JAN STRATTON PRESSES HER manicured palm to Dad's forehead, light from her silver bracelet flecks across his face. Jan has the gift: God channels healing through her as if she is a vessel.

Lubbockites come to Thirty-Fourth Street seeking boot repair and kung fu classes, thrift shopping at Goodwill and the Salvation Army. Thai food at the Bangkok Restaurant and barbecue at J&M's. Porn at Adult Books, a gray box of a building across from my family's own Grace Church. For prayer on Thursday nights, some thirty or so worshipers sit in the green pews of the old Baptist church to hear Jan Stratton croon holy in services called "Miracles on Thirty-Fourth Street."

Jan is a dignified healer. Veins rope her hands, and her fingers sparkle with rings. Set off by pearl earrings, her hair is teased to a high silver bob, bringing her even closer to God. She is dressed in a pleated business dress and shod in sturdy leather heels. At the touch of her hand, full-grown men fall to the floor. Slain, as we say, in the Spirit.

I've never been so moved by God to collapse. Just about anything, I believe, would be preferable. Watching Dad at the shallow steps of the altar, I wonder if he will join the fainters near his feet. Two men in suits, the elders, are ready to catch Dad should he be overwhelmed.

Mom says people falling supine is mostly hooey. "It isn't so much a faint as they get pushed over," she once explained, beckoning me over so she could wide-hand dunk my head to the ground. My knees buckled. "See?" she said. "Now just imagine a big old man doing that." I couldn't argue. If a preacher with the body of a former linebacker made the altar call, perhaps the real test of faith would be withstanding the healer's meaty hand. But Jan Stratton is no big old man. Her touch is soft, and when folks pass out in the Spirit, the two elders lower them to snooze on the floor.

Despite my trepidation, a part of me yearns to know what it's like, those minutes of unconsciousness—how like a dream, how changed the dreamer. Should I overcome the inhibition bolting my hind-end to the pew and fall prostrate in the presence of the divine, I think I would be forever altered. But every time they wake, the slain walk back to their seats like it's just another night on Thirty-Fourth Street. Average they are when they approach, and average they remain when they return; though I search for it, I see no hint of disappointment at this outcome. Dad at least will report back from the floor and tell me what I most want to know: that the sacred dream follows you after you wake. That he is healed.

"The Lord is near to the downtrodden and the broken," Jan says. "Rest in his presence." She hums along with the pianist. "Come, Holy Spirit, with the healing power of your word." From the way Dad stands, I know his eyes are closed. From the way he holds his hands open, I know he weeps. He doesn't fall to the ground.

At "Miracles on Thirty-Fourth Street," the jubilation of fellow believers stays quiet. No one spouts visions. Jan doesn't overpower. The volume of her voice doesn't rise. She utters only cadences and song, only prayer. Jan's harmonizing comforts. Would that her voice could follow my family home.

Mom curls into a whimper as Dad stands before Jan and she sings over him. I've seen Mom look afraid, her fear signaled by the ramrod of her spine, her strained neck belying her insistence that all is well. But this evening she looks worn out. Almost helpless. I touch her arm.

"I'm okay," she says. "It's just hard right now."

My family seems to allow ourselves to be vulnerable at Jan's prayer meetings, where an unsteady faith provokes no satanic attacks. There is no judgment for weakness. Mary and James concentrate on their coloring books, Kendra brushes the hair of a baby doll, and Karson and I fold our hands in our laps. Jan calls the sick forward, and her hand brushes their temples and their necks, as though to cool a fever. Men and women mourn gently when she prays. At "Miracles on Thirty-Fourth Street," the pressure to perform radical belief abates, and we briefly become the fullness of what we are—a family of seven hardly apprehending what is happening to us.

Jan comes to know my family. She calls to Dad by name and welcomes him when he approaches in supplication. One evening Dad returns to his seat and keeps on praying, his head bowed. A man behind us settles a hand on Dad's shoulder. Dad turns.

"God's told me to pray for you," the man says. He introduces himself. Roy. Here is his wife, Loretta. Her voice is as soft as Dolly Parton's. She bends to hug me and leaves a swath of foundation on my cheek. In this gathering, Dad hardly stood out as a desperate man, but years later Loretta will say she never forgot the first time she saw us. "Your family took up the whole pew."

Dad and Roy lean toward one another, and Roy rests his hand firmly on Dad's back as Dad explains why we're here. Roy answers, saying he himself suffers from an impaired heart: a heart attack did something to his heart's back chambers, and only the front part is working.

Roy's prognosis is grim. Cardiologists have told him that the risk of future heart attacks is high. Even so, at the age of sixty-two, he has lived much longer than expected. Roy and Loretta have known Jan Stratton for some years and find her calling true. Each Thursday, Roy prays for the miracle of just one more week. And because he keeps on living, he believes his purpose on earth is unfinished. When he saw Dad tonight, God's voice filled, not his ear, but his heart, which, split between this world and the next, punched him in the sternum. He knew he was at the right place at the right time.

"Thank you, Brother," Dad says, though Roy is old enough to be his father. They grasp each other's arms.

"Doctors say I don't have much time," Dad says.

"That's all right, man," Roy says. "I've only got half a heart."

CHAPTER 16

A GLASS JEWELRY CASE HOLDS three sterling silver rings. Warm light shines evenly across them. None cast a shadow. I point to the one with a cross carved clean through the band. The ring looks much smaller on this side of the glass. It doesn't clear my knuckle.

I am here to pick out a present for my thirteenth birthday. The ring should be ready by then, a woman in a black blazer explains as she wraps the fourth finger of my left hand with a thin soft tape measure.

"All James Avery jewelry is customized," the clerk says. "We'll get you measured. Will you be wanting an engraving?"

Mom leans near me and smiles. I am on the precipice of womanhood. I will promise to abstain from sex and get a razor.

"Yes," I say and bring a folded piece of paper from my pocket. The verse inside is written in Mom's delicate cursive: "Let no one look down on your youthfulness, but rather in speech, conduct, love, faith, and purity, show yourself an example of those who believe."

The clerk retrieves an order form and writes my name across the top. *K.D. Blackburn.* "That whole verse won't fit, of course," she says. "What most people do is engrave the reference on the inside of the band. Or sometimes they choose a word." I punt the idea of wearing a ring inscribed with the word *virgin.* Mom nods and points to where she's written the scripture reference. 1 Timothy 4:22. The clerk writes it down and hands Mom a carbon copy of the form.

Promise rings glint from the fourth fingers of the folded hands of most of the young women I know in Grace Church. Many of us remember when we worshiped without the keyboardist Jerry, who sat that solemn morning among the congregation with his family. Side-eyes darted off the musician and his teenage daughter, who hunched next to him. I remember biting a place inside my check, so thick was the tension inside the sanctuary.

After the last kid disappeared to Sunday school, Pastor Shawn raised his hands in invitation to share-time. The silence was not nearly soft enough. I looked to Mom. She appeared to be the only puzzled adult in the room. Her eyebrows were furrowed, while everyone else just glanced down, waiting. Then Jerry stood. He placed a hand on the shoulder of his daughter. She pushed the thick frame of her glasses up and dabbed her eyes with the cuff of her sweater. Brenda, her mother, was crying too. Jerry cleared his throat and said that his daughter was pregnant.

"We know this wasn't God's original plan." His voice wobbled. "There's been a lot of grief, a lot of repentance." I looked away. The gossipy high I usually experienced at share-time gave way to dread. A flush crept up my chest and crawled toward my neck. The lights above me felt too close, too hot. I looked at Mary Katherine. Her eyes pooled with apprehension, perhaps in empathetic response to mine. *She shouldn't be here*, I thought. She was still young enough to escape the heat I felt swallowing me.

"But we know God works all things for good," Jerry said. "A baby is always a blessing. My daughter is here to confess and seek God's grace. And to ask forgiveness of you all." He gestured across the room.

"Amen," Shawn said. I tried to take normal breaths. Jerry's daughter cried harder. She was separated by at least four years from me, and isolated further from every girl in the room by this. Those nearest to her huddled around her to pray, but they couldn't close the distance: she sat alone. The soon-to-be mother pressed her face into her hands and shuddered.

At the end of service, I brushed past Jesse. I didn't have a full grasp of what had just happened in service, but I knew he had no clue.

"Hey," he said. I kept walking.

A few months later, the women at Grace Church announced they were going to throw Jerry's daughter a baby shower. Mom balked when the shower invitation arrived in the mail. "It's one thing to offer prayer and support. It's another to act like nothing wrong happened."

Mom's seemingly endless disappointment in her fellow believers was convenient in this case as there was no social function she detested more than a baby shower.

"All the tedious games, the chitchat with acquaintances," she said, throwing the invitation in the trash. She had never accepted a baby shower for any of her children. Motherhood was a job, not a game of matching adults to their infant photos.

"You just sit there and ooh-and-aah over every gift. You're expected to join in diaper costume contests. I guess some people enjoy it. But I never cared much for a baby shower."

Now, as my birthday approaches, my promise ring takes on more than its traditional implications for sexual purity. Maintaining my virginity feels simple compared with the daily task of mustering enough faith to pray down a physical healing. I begin to associate the promise ring with a purity of faith so crystalline that my father's recovery will be guaranteed. The stakes for me have little to do with losing my virginity. That's not what Eve did. Her sin was to cause a man to fall from God's good graces.

My cake is sweetened with molasses. Dad notes the moisture. Crepe streamers decorate the ceiling. A camera flashes.

"Could you warn me first?" I say.

"Just trying to catch you in the moment," Mom says.

I scowl and stick out my tongue. The shutter clicks. My sisters guffaw and show their tongues. Someone says the molasses has spiked our blood sugars.

"I can't believe there's any sugar left in my blood," Karson says. Mom offers a lesson in glycemia. I receive flannel pajamas, a paperback copy of Catherine Marshall's *Christy*, and a blue pull-over sweater from Mervyn's. I leave to put on the sweater. When I return, Mom lowers the camera, a glint in her eye. Now is the big moment. I've saved the gift from my parents for last.

"Go get K.D.'s gift," Mom says.

"I don't know where it is," Karson says.

"Well, it must be under all this tissue paper." The paper rustles, hits the floor, balls up in my father's fist, drops in the trash can. The table is cleared, and still no ring has appeared. Mom says to hang on and she walks down the hall.

Dad lifts the copy of *Christy* and thumbs to the opening page. His eyes follow the sentences, and he turns the page.

"This is pretty good," he says. He is determined to stay at the table for the duration of my party even if it means waiting through a scavenger hunt. His sacrifice is palpable. He sways forward in his chair. His torso is shaped something like a pear. The skinny frame of his shoulders widens to a round belly, raised on his right side where the liver swells. His thirty-ninth birthday—we were both born on the twenty-seventh—is exactly two months away. A bloodless yellow color shades the palms of his hands and his finger-nails. His inhales are short, as if he is holding himself still; when he moves, his breaths snap.

Mom reappears and says everyone needs to stop what they're doing and help look for my present.

"Karson, you wrapped it," Mom says.

"I left it in your room," Karson says.

I glare at my sister. Her face falls.

Dad grimaces, stands, says he'll look in the living room, and walks to the bathroom.

In this evening's prayer, Mom thanks the Lord that I was born and asks him to show us where the ring is. Then, as we do every night, each one of us reaches a hand toward Dad to petition his healing. I say, "Amen," and open my eyes. My father's face is drawn, his smile feeble. He says that he loves me. "Happy Birthday," he says. My stomach pitches. My hands want to strangle something to death.

Lights out, Karson lies next to me on the pallet. "I didn't lose it, K.D." I roll to my other side.

I dream that I am walking toward our house. A gale catches me up, lifts my body, and thrusts me forward. I eat gravel. I'm no closer to home. I take a few steps, and the wind throws my body again, knocking me out of breath. I drop. I wake up wheezing to catch my breath. Blankets gather at my feet. My pulse races. My forehead glistens with sweat.

In the morning, I unroll a loaf of bread from its plastic wrap and slice a piece. Kendra requests toast. James too. My eyes meet Karson's, and she looks away.

The bread bounces out of the toaster, and I spread honey across it, take a bite, crunch, consider, and say, "I had a weird dream last night."

Mom pokes at her scrambled eggs.

"Well?"

"It felt like there was a wind inside my body. It kept kicking me up high. I felt so angry."

Mom lowers her fork, says, "Huh."

Come afternoon, Mom finds me lying on the bottom bunk with my new novel. She crawls in bed next to me and rubs her hands together. "Cozy under here," she says. She looks up at the crossbars holding the top bunk. "You ever hit your head on those?"

"I've learned not to." I dog-ear the page and close my book and wait.

"Well. I wanted to talk to you about your dream." She asks me to describe it again.

"The thing is," she says, "I woke up in the middle of the night because I heard something. A growling sound. I got out of bed and walked over to where you kids were sleeping. Your head was kind of shaking. Your teeth chattered, and there was like this gargling sound. Do you remember anything like that?" I do not. I can tell from the way she nods that it's the answer she expects. "It didn't sound like you. But then I prayed over you and it stopped."

I picture Mom hovering in her light blue nightgown.

"What do you think it was?" I say.

"I think it's pretty clear. You say you were angry."

"More than I've ever been."

"Anger can open you up to attack. The sound I heard was a demon." I breathe deeply. Something about what she's saying begins to fall into place. The way the wind launched from my rib cage, how it vaulted me into the air like a rag doll. Maybe it was a wicked spirit. A flare of anger returns. I am not pure, but possessed. Or maybe my mother is holding me hostage by a chain and tugging at it. Either way, I feel I am a prisoner, the bars above me not so much a bolster as a gate. A quiver starts in my chin.

"Oh, don't worry," Mom says. "I prayed it out. There's no demon in you now."

I find Karson bent over puzzle pieces spread across the coffee table. The green recliner groans with Dad's movement. He stretches out one leg, then another. He moans. I sit down next to Karson.

"I know it's not your fault."

She folds into my side and rests her head on my shoulder.

Pastor Shawn preaches from the Book of Mark about the healing of a blind man. Jesus led the one without vision away from a town, spit on his eyes, and placed his hands across them. The man looked up and said that he saw men like trees but walking. Jesus put his hands across the man's eyes again, and when the man looked up once more he saw everything clearly. "Now go forth in truth," Pastor Shawn says. After service, Jesse approaches my parents. They look at each other and nod, and Jesse waves me over.

"Can you come with me for a second?"

He's recently turned sixteen, and this is my first intimate glimpse of his blue, rusty Datsun 280Z—the closest look I'm allowed to get. The sound of the church boys' skateboards slurps to a halt.

They kick up their boards and hang back to watch. Jesse opens the metal jaws of the trunk. My stomach is flurried as he retrieves two long paint sticks bolted together with fabric between them. He holds this construction upright, the sticks part, and Jesse vanishes behind an enormous fan fluttering open.

I hide my mouth behind my hands. In the scene on the fan, blithe cranes parade under a pink sky. In the right-hand corner curls a delicate black calligraphy.

"I think it's Chinese," Jesse says. He tells me that he was in Dallas for a kung fu tournament. "They had these on sale. I don't know. This one made me think of you." He folds it back together and passes it to me. "Happy birthday."

I smile, then look down and shake my head and stutter.

"I love it."

One of the skater boys rolls over to us. "Let's have a look at that." I unfold the fan. The boy steps off his skateboard, cocks his head, and gives the fan two thumbs-up. He claps Jesse on the back, then his skateboard slaps the concrete and he skates away.

Jesse says that he better get going.

"Thanks for thinking of me," I say.

"It ain't no thing."

The fan takes up darn near the whole dresser surface. To brace it, I press a small jewelry box against one end and corner an angel figurine at the other. The top of it arches across the bottom of the window. Karson stands next to me. Air conditioning threatens to topple the fan.

"I thought we weren't allowed to have boyfriends."

"He's not my boyfriend."

"He's your crush?"

"Something like that."

"Well. We're not allowed to have those either."

Mom calls for us, her voice excited. We tell each other to *go go go* and hurry down the hallway. Mom stands by the coffee table, which is cleared of everything but a small white gift box with a silver ribbon.

"How did you find it?" I say.

"I didn't. It was just sitting here."

"The whole time?"

"There's no way it was here the whole time. We checked everywhere. No. I walked in, and it was just here."

I stoop at the table and open the box. A silver ring with a beveled cross gleams back at me. I slide it onto my left ring finger and turn my hand in the light.

"God answers prayer," Mom says. "An angel must have put it there. That's the only explanation."

"Told you it wasn't me," Karson says.

Dad asks to see it and takes my hand. "That's nice." I thank him and remove the ring and point to the engraving on the inside: *1 Tim 4:22.*

"That's all there was room for," I say. Dad tilts the ring to read the print. I want him to know the abbreviation is all I require. I hardly need the reminder. I stand proud and bright before him. He will not falter because of me. Inside my bones ring not God's words but Dad's: *Better to be a woman with nothing to recover from.* If turning thirteen means I am becoming a woman, I will become such a woman.

Yesterday's fouls give way to the orderliness of having found the ring and sliding it onto my finger.

"Let's read the whole verse," Mom says and hops up. She is giddy. She thumbs through the pages of her Bible, then stops and runs her finger down a column of text. Her brow furrows.

"Let me see the ring." She reaches for it, and I twist it off and hand it to her. She turns the ring to read the inscription and looks back at her open Bible. She says, "Uh oh." She passes me the ring.

"I gave the lady the wrong reference. It was supposed to be first Timothy four-twelve. Four-twenty-two doesn't exist."

I cough up a laugh.

CHAPTER 17

A GERMAN SHORTHAIRED POINTER DIVES into the clinic's glass wall with a hard clang, and Dierdre laughs. She says she's laughing so hard she's crying Dr Pepper.

Mom hollers from the clinic office.

"The Freidman dog," I say.

"Well, put him back."

I drag the dazed pointer to her cage and double-check the lock. She whines.

"I know you don't want to," I say. She thought she'd escaped into the full tent of sky. I understand. I also leap at the chance to break away from the confines of my life, embracing any mileage between me and my ailing father. For this purpose, the clinic suits. I reach between the cage bars to scratch the captive's nose.

Mom comes in and asks me to bring up a cat that's yowling across from the pointer. Looking at the cat's wolverine claws, I start sweating.

"No way."

"You afraid?"

"Aren't you?"

"She's not a horse, is she?"

Mom's been afraid of horses ever since one bucked her when she was about four years old—one of her earliest memories. In veterinarian school, she almost quit during the large animal rotation, which involved no shortage of poking and agitating beasts of burden. She went to the program supervisor and said she couldn't practice on horses. You will, the presiding doctor told her, or you'll fail out. She often mentioned her large animal rotation, a kind of origin story. Whenever I've asked her how she managed to pass, she says she doesn't know. She just made herself.

Mom now scruffs the cat. The tabby spirals in the air.

Thursdays are school days, but Mom deems my time at the clinic hands-on learning. She's managing to keep up with home-schooling despite Dad's worsening condition. What she judges to be the downside of public school education continues to motivate her. Contrary to the popular belief that homeschooled kids are antisocial, my mother contends that it's public school kids who are socially inept, with their partiality toward interacting only within their age group. At the clinic, Mom finds that I'm good with animals and praises the experience I'm getting at talking to adults.

I discover I have an uncanny ability to remember the stuff said between relevant information. I can recall not only a client's name but also that her brother's deployed and he's crazy if he thinks she's giving the dog back when he returns. I am void of cultural references, but at the clinic my flytrap memory is welcome. I need not know one reference to *The Simpsons*.

Instead, I remember that Bill Spragg's schnauzer is named Molly and that Bill played stand-up bass when he used to could stand up; his favorite bassist is Ray Brown. He brings me a recording of Oscar Peterson. I remember that Eleanor Bradley has had fixed and fed nearly sixty-three cats but has only one dog, a chihuahua named Toto. I remember that Lawrence Harrison stole his Maine coon from a neglectful neighbor and named him Little One. Lynette Boar has three mutts and two biological sons: one is a doctor and the other is, as she puts it, clinically insane. The last of her children is an adopted daughter who accuses Lynette of spending more money on her brother's mental health than on anything for her. Lynette roars, *If that girl wants to go into lockdown, there are any number of hospitals that will take her.*

"You interact with folks here you'd never see anywhere else," Dierdre says. "It's not animals you need to be good with at a vet clinic. It's people, and there're some weird ones."

Who could be weirder than me? I think. I got angels hiding my jewelry.

Another perk of my thorough inquiries: no one asks about my life.

I lean on the treatment counter and visit with the vet tech Sabrina. She's a college student at Texas Tech and aspires to be a veterinarian. She has a soft underbite and laughs at the end of each sentence, joke or no. Mom doubts very much that Sabrina will ever become a vet, once saying, "The girl is too timid."

Sabrina tutors me in the art of scrubbing shit from cages. I follow her to the kennel reserved for large dogs who are convalescing from surgery or who have become dangerously ill with distemper, renal failure, carcinoma, or some flummoxing combination of symptoms. A golden is in with diarrhea. Her tail beats the wall and loose stool corrupts the cage. Sabrina leads the retriever into a fresh run. Together, she and I consider the beige carnage of stomach upset. Mom pokes her head in.

"Is there any plant life in the vomitus?" she asks. The retriever has a record of ingesting foreign bodies like she's got a death wish. Sabrina bends over the bile, says she doesn't think so. Mom walks all the way in, glances at it herself, confirms. I glove up, lift the spoiled towels, hold my breath, drag out the rubber mat, spill blue cleaner, and attack the concrete floor with a scrub brush.

The disinfectant only gestures toward concealing the smell of feces. Sabrina says you can never fully get rid of it. No matter. I place a clean rubber mat on the floor and over this mat, I lay a towel. The cell is replenished in time to welcome its new inhabitant—a pit bull named Evil. The golden scrambles to her feet and presses her flaring nostrils to the bars. The new neighbors smell each other. Evil's owner, Mike Hanson, also owns Lubbock's best-reviewed tattoo parlor and pays for everything with cash. Sabrina says he once settled a bill for $742 with twenties. "I had to count all those. That was a fun day for me."

Evil's ears are blunted down to her bowling ball of a skull. She licks my hands. She regularly boards at the clinic—like vacationing at a hospital, Mom is known to say. I set a bowl of water, and the pitty sniffs the corners of the run, approves them, circles, and curls into a ball.

"Her name makes no sense," Sabrina says.

Misnomers abound at High Plains Pet Clinic. Sabrina recalls the time Sweet Baby came in: eighty-eight pounds of pissed-off rottweiler. Even the clinic cat, Gandalf, sprang from her path. My mother told the client to get a muzzle, and the client said Sweet Baby never'd bit anybody. Yeah, well. They all say that.

Sabrina pokes a finger between the cage bars to scratch Evil's chin. "You ask me, them two ought to switch names. But no one asks."

Thomas Greener has named each of his consecutive basset hounds Fred. Fred III has been rushed into the clinic on emergency. We hear the dog's cries on the other side of the clinic's glass wall. Dierdre rushes to open the door for Thomas, and he hauls all seventy-five pounds of hound into an exam room. Mom and Dierdre work quickly. Thomas stands back and looks at his dog and blanches. He was managing a controlled burn, and Fred III stepped on simmering brush. The hound tried to move the low gravitational center of his body, but in every direction his feet met with more ember. Thomas had to lift the immobilized Fred III from where he bayed.

Mom and Dierdre carry the dog to the back, and the hound whimpers on the treatment counter. He's rolled onto his side. When he presses his snout into my chest, his hot wet breath beats against my sternum.

"Try to comfort him," Mom says. She peels apart his toes. She says the pads of his feet are nearly burned off. The flesh is pink, and the smell raises every instinct of horror. I tuck my face into the basset's head.

It takes Dierdre and me both to restrain him as Mom dresses the burns. He careens and twists. He runs in place, sweeping the air with his charred paws. Mom is patient. She takes hold of one leg and waits for it to slacken.

"I know this is awful." Her voice is drenched with sympathy. She applies sterilizer to gauze and wipes the exposed skin and Fred III writhes. His cries are reduced to a throaty gasp. Mom retrieves more gauze and spreads an antibiotic gel.

"Can you fetch the lidocaine," she says to no one in particular. The cream is white and guaranteed to sting. Mom spreads it thickly. The basset's groans are wretched. Mom caresses his upper thigh and tells him that this will only hurt for a minute. "It's going to help," she says. Then she wraps each paw. Dierdre and Mom lift Fred III, and the two women sidle with him between them to the back kennel, where they lay him across a dense layer of towels.

Mom explains that she'll need to keep the basset for a few days to monitor him. Infection could be fatal. Thomas is matter-of-fact. How long? he wants to know. How much?

"It's hard to say," Mom says.

"Better to put him down."

"If you can, let's see how Fred does. He's comfortable now. We won't let him suffer."

Thomas ponders his nails, picks at a place with dirt, says he'll call, and wraps his dog's leash around his hand. He guesses he'll square the bill when all this is over. The clinic door chimes, Thomas departs, and Dierdre gives Mom a look.

"He feels guilty," Mom says.

The dog sleeps. Later, his temperature must be checked. Mom stoops with the thermometer. No fever. An intravenous bag hangs from the cage bars. Mom adjusts the slider clamp and closes off the fluids. She culls a brown glass bottle from her pocket, pulls the liquid into a syringe, and injects opioid directly into a rubber port at the IV catheter. The dog lowers his head to the cage floor. Dierdre, standing above us with the record for controlled substances, asks for the amount and logs the number.

For the morphine, Mom says not to charge Mr. Greener. "I'll cover it."

I ask to stay with Fred III. For a while, my hand rides the ridges of his spine. With a deep snore, he relaxes into sleep.

I help to sweep the reception area at closing time, corralling fur from frightened dogs whose last attempt at escape blew off their coats. I neaten a stack of magazines. Jennifer Aniston smiles up from the cover of one. I pick it up. She sports a stacked, shoulder-length bob. My hair has been long my whole life.

"You can take that if you want," Dierdre says.

"I was just interested in the haircut."

"Well. Come here."

Dierdre takes the magazine, glances over her shoulder, and rips off the cover.

"You'd look great with that cut."

Fourth Street passes by. A brick apartment complex, the United grocery store, the bank where we turn south on Quaker; only one more turn before arriving at the house, walking through the front door, and racing past the living room before Dad asks about my day. Mom will treat making dinner like an emergency. Karson, Kendra, James, Mary—each pair of eyes will say: *Can we just go play?*

In the van, Mom turns up the radio, KLOVE 92.7 FM. Rich Mullins is singing "Awesome God." Mom sings along. The door grip is welcome. I wonder at which point on this two-mile drive the veterinarian will give way to my mother. I can't reconcile the two women. How does the one who showed keen, science-informed mercy to the hound square with the one who believes codeine opens my father up to demon possession? This is a question I couldn't articulate at the time, and though I can now, twenty-five years later, it still has no clear answer. How do the two sides of my mother add up to make a whole? Her strong grasp of science at the veterinarian clinic seemed to give way to imitations of science on the drive home. She was an authority at High Plains Pet Clinic.

But that expertise granted her no authority over my father's cancer or the fate of our lives, so she grasped at types of knowledge that claimed to. Most people would think that a background in the sciences would redirect someone from believing in things like demonic possession, but what continues to perplex me about my mother is that she sees her religious belief as an extension of her knowledge of biology and physics.

Even as a child, I find it mysterious.

In contrast, my mother seems to think I bear no mystery. She is the adult who knows more about the complexities of my life than anyone, but she shows no curiosity. Maybe she's afraid of the answer. Maybe the doorway to my turmoil would lead too quickly to Dad's. Maybe she likes it this way: I ponder her, and she doesn't think about me at all. Each instance seems to hold a truth.

The song ends, and Mom turns down the dial.

"Dad says you leave the room whenever he cries." We both keep looking ahead. I wait for her to ask why.

"I think it hurts his feelings," she says.

There's a sound like water in my ears. A wave. It withdraws.

"Thanks for telling me."

We ride the rest of the way in silence. In my pocket, I squeeze the folded magazine cover.

CHAPTER 18

THE EMPTY FAIRGROUNDS FILL WITH tawny headlight beams. We are fifteen minutes from our home—an eyebrow-raising distance across untouchable worlds in Lubbock. Most of the folks here are white working-class. If we'd gone knocking on the doors of people living around the fairgrounds, the faces of most of Lubbock's Black and Latinx families would have answered. The smell of carnival food combs the breeze. There's a portable toilet beside the tent and, God help me, Dad enters it.

I pass between the tent's flap doors and take in the dirt floor, the plywood frame, the drifter's thick fingers wrapped around a microphone, testing, testing. He will test me too, exposing the unworthiness suspending miracle in heaven, Dad in diagnosis.

I plant myself in one of the metal folding chairs, and my siblings sprawl down the row, with Mom as bookend. Dad takes the empty seat beside me. Would that he had not. If the evangelist's calling is true, my reckoning awaits. Dad should be nowhere near it. As for me, I would rather be up in a Ferris wheel than in this tent next to my father. I'm not sure what I dread more: prophesies or Dad's tears. Both could pummel me like a wooden rod.

Wind and sun map the faces of God's flock. Where years have aged the skin, relentless gales and West Texas daylight have deepened the creases. A woman limps to the seat in front of us. A man on crutches swings his legs to the front row.

Dad's feet twitch. Maybe he will be able to run again in the morning. I imagine rising before the city wakes, recording a mile before the traffic rises, and sitting for breakfast as Dad brews coffee before the day's record heat sets in. I'll be happy to be at his side again, and maybe we will both be able to forget how much I loathe our life now. A black fly crawls across my knee, its tall legs bent and soft. I flick it away and feel the fatigue of faith. Prayer for healing is a long haul. We've been at it ten months.

Dad asks me what's wrong. I say that nothing is. He rests his hand on my leg, then takes my hand in his own. The brisk cotton of his polo brushes my arm. He would have found a two-by-four more welcoming. He lets go.

The typhoon chaser I knew sits somewhere inside the man losing weight and shaking in prayer. Cancer quickens in Dad the fearlessness needed to cheat physics. He is caught in a familiar high-stakes bet on his body. Is he not a pilot? A man paid a good salary for doing what human bodies aren't made to do? If only he were aiming for the center of a tropical cyclone. If only he were manning a Boeing plane. Did all those flights train him for a night such as this?

Perhaps what prepared him even more for this trial were the long years as a runner. There is only so much physical training one can do ahead of a marathon. The rest of it is mental. There's a point in every race, he's told me, when your body stops and your mind takes over. All you have to do is breathe.

"All right," the traveling evangelist barks. "Who's God going to touch tonight?" He points to a band and shouts, "Hit it!" and they hit it with vim. "Here we go," the traveler says, aquiver with anticipation. His voice moves quick as an auctioneer's, and he lands great smacks on the chosen. They collapse. The man who entered with a limp throws his crutches to the ground. Someone yelps, *Hallelujah!* The evangelist stalks the aisle, whipping visions before him. At his touch, the woman in front of us dances with him up to the stage. "Make your requests known to God," he shouts. He holds up her arm like she's just won a wrestling match, drops it, palms her forehead, and she passes out.

Amid the tumult, a private silence gathers around a man sitting on the other side of the aisle. His pearl snap shirt is fringed and faded. He steps around the slain in spirit and waits his turn.

"What do you ask of God tonight?" The evangelist aims the microphone at him. The man's voice shakes.

"Money."

"Well." The evangelist's gaze sweeps across the room and he smiles. "You got to give to receive, brother."

The man considers the floor. He works his wallet from a denim pocket and removes a softened dollar bill. He rubs his thumb across it. God asks of us full measure. He passes the tender.

The evangelist shakes the tithe in the air. "Repeat after me." He takes big breaths between each phrase in a call-and-response:

"I believe what I give," he begins. We repeat, "I believe what I give."

"Will return overflowing."

"Will return overflowing."

"Pressed down, shaken together."

"Pressed down, shaken together."

"To make room for more and running over."

"To make room for more and running over."

The man's dollar bill joins the basket already being passed for sinners' bail. He finds his seat and holds his head in his hands.

Mom's eyes are closed in prayer. Dad gnaws his bottom lip. His lips were prone to chapping even when he'd been well. His kisses pressed a slag of Carmex to your face. I used to wait until he wasn't looking to wipe off the smudge. Neither of my parents budge from their seat. The evangelist has noticed.

"I believe everyone here tonight will receive blessing." Wide-framed glasses enlarge the speaker's gaze. If, as the scriptures say, the lamp of the body is the eye, the evangelist's soul is dim, worn ragged with the road, a little red. He squints as though to see into that space enclosed by ribs, spine, and sternum. His focus settles on me. He jabs a finger in the air, pointing toward my spiritual bankruptcy. I know what it means: I am already a tainted woman. I deceived my mother with a razor, and I have been possessed of a demon. Just as Peter had three invitations to prove his belief, I will be given one more opportunity to deny the devil. I picture the bottle of white pills hidden in the high-set cupboard back home.

The evangelist holds his finger steady, lowers the microphone, and walks as if in awe toward us. I grasp the bottom of my seat, lock my elbows, and glare. *Come on,* I think. *Let's get this over with.* Whatever happens next, I am sure of this: I will not cry.

But it's upon Dad that the evangelist lands his reach. He takes a handful of Dad's hair, bucks his head back, and rodeos. "Satan, we command you in the name of Jesus, let go your hold on this man." The evangelist pulls Dad's skull back and forth, as though he might shake him free of cancer. A tremolo of *Yes Lords* floods us. Dad lifts his arms. He looks skyward, where greased fingernails are fluttering over his face. The saints are thatching a canopy of arms over us. My sisters look crazed with excitement and alarm. We reach for each other. This might be it, the thing we've been waiting for. Mom holds Mary Katherine, and her jaw relaxes. She looks at Dad, who has fetched up James, and a secret turns in the corner of her mouth. Faith is what matters. God can work through even the lowest of the low. She takes Dad's hand. I climb to the floor and press my face to Dad's knee. The smell of salt and sweat and body replaces my fear. A sound made of dozens of smaller sounds, voices in throats raised in praise, rush above us. *Make your requests known,* one scripture begins. *And the peace of God, which surpasses all comprehension, will guard your hearts and your minds.* I know it can happen, right now, right here in the sanctuary of fairground and highway. The evangelist gargles worship in the name of Jesus, and a vision fills the thick shadow of bodies. I can see a gray cylindrical tumor loosen and disintegrate. I see the fifteen lesions on my father's liver dissolve. I see the furtive bodies of the men and women above me peel back. I see Dad stand, the word *Hosanna* on his lips. Let it be so.

"Amen!" the evangelist cries, and with one last shove, he releases Dad's head. Light appears in triangles as each arm clears away. A woman springs back and twirls and twirls. Dad blinks as though adjusting to the light, to earthly light, the stained vermillion light of a canvas tabernacle. His sandy hair, usually so straight and softly parted to the side, spikes in a mess of directions. I stand stiffly and return to my seat. Mom bounces Mary on her lap, her mouth pulled back into a tight line, resigned to the whole unpleasant business of being in the tent and now, with the prayer over, resigned to waiting for the end of the service. I look for the man who earlier offered up what little money he had in desperation. He's gone.

"A charlatan," Mom says as we pack back into the van. We pass an old white man plucking a banjo. It's dark, and the late spring air is now damp with the smell of juniper and cow shit.

There are other healers. There is Dumitru Duduman, who wrote a book about the end-time apparitions he beheld, yes Lord, while trapped in a communist prison. In Duduman's vision of the Antichrist, Satan took the form of a blackbird saying, "Power has been given to me to be able to come against the Christians in a short time." Mom listens to his prophesies on cassette tapes that America will burn at the hands of socialists. She joins the supporters of his organization for years, until she learns that she's helped to bankroll Duduman's personal travel and affairs with women. But before the scandal breaks out, Mom writes a letter, asking if the prophet will send a blessing for her sick husband, and encloses a check. A blue-and-purple handkerchief arrives in the mail smelling of incense. We walk into the front yard, where fresh air greets us, and Mom presses the cloth to Dad's forehead and prays for healing under a sky unbroken.

She says, when Dad is healed, he will testify. The whole reason the cancer has invaded his body is to bring glory to God. "We're going to get a bigger van," she says, "and we are going to hit that interstate. Everyone's going to know what the Lord did."

Dad's jaundiced skin, loss of weight, winnowed muscle—all are merely tests of our faith. "How much more miraculous will it be," Mom says, her wet eyes glittering, "when you are healed." The pain of seeing him suffer, the suffering he endures, is made bearable by the dividends we envision every time we seek out another healer.

While praying, my father's face relaxes. His shoulders glide down as though he just dropped a heavy haul. It is in prayer that he appears most like the pilot who returned from trips across the country, most like the runner I ran next to in the mornings. The story he tells himself about his pain seems clearest in supplication: his suffering has meaning, it means miracle, and it will end.

The only other times I've witnessed his relief have been in the hours after he's swallowed the codeine.

The wooden double doors to Grace Church are open. A breeze wafts into the nearly empty sanctuary with only a wheel of people arranged in the middle of it. My parents asked that members gather this evening for a special prayer service for Dad. We're nearing a year since his diagnosis. A handful arrived eager to pray.

The doors have been bolted open so that anyone can enter after the prayers begin without a loud click and whine. But now there are other sounds to contend with: the swoosh of traffic across five lanes, people on their way home, music spilling from windows rolled down to catch a breeze. Light drains from the sky. The sun is level with Thirty-Fourth Street.

Mom has asked that the doors be left open for another reason as well. Tonight they will exorcise the demon of illness from Dad. I'm not so sure the brethren are up for it, but dare they cross her? Mom thanks them and says that of course wooden gates and walls are no contest for demons. Or angels, for that matter. But it's a sign of faith to open the doors and show God that we consider the existence of demons to be real.

Mom holds Mary Katherine, who wriggles free. She is two years old, spry and nimble and curious about the June beetles flying into the church. The prayer begins as they all do: in the Lord's name. Pastor Shawn plants his hand on Dad's shoulder. The police officer Brad, still in uniform, leans across his knees and clasps Dad's hands. Kelly is here with Sally; Jesse is back home. I am also at home, watching Karson, Kendra, and James. I will hear about this night years later, when Mary tells me she can confirm I wasn't there. "If you had been, Mom would have blamed you for what happened."

Beyond the prayer circle, Mary Katherine plays on the floor.

The church floor slopes toward the altar but an intensity slides up it, chilling the gathering; a slip of fear finds the spines of the holy remnant. The group awaits the soft nudging of the Holy Spirit. It requires deep concentration. They must block out all distraction from the outside—the world and its schemes encapsulated in the sounds of traffic and the music pouring out of the open car windows.

Most people call the voice of God a feeling. To me, it sometimes feels like the prickle of nerves coming back online after a limb has fallen numb. The sensation emerges from inside the body, somewhere between the rib cage and sternum. The voice of God can make you cough. The church folks await it. The first to feel it rise will pray. That supplicant is Kelly, the farmer. He finishes and silence falls until Brad the cop prays, saying John is his dear friend and brother in Christ and in Christ's name he will be healed.

The prayer service ends, and Mom's eyes adjust to the bright square of light between the doors where a man stands in silhouette, an evil omen. She blinks again. The stranger is holding Mary Katherine.

"Is this your daughter?"

Mom cries as she runs to the man and tears Mary from him. She trembles, saying this is her daughter, this is her daughter. Dad makes unsteady strides to reach Mom. The passerby regards my parents, then says, chewing his words as he works his jaw, "I found your girl in the middle of Thirty-Fourth Street."

Mom and Dad crack into breathless sobs. With the prayer circle gathered to plead for Dad's life, Mary Katherine, having decided to take her chances in the world, nearly lost her own. A few people from the circle walk over and the man describes what he saw: A baby girl between the yellow stripes of the turning lane, a purple sky rolling above her. Her red hair bright, caught with dusk. The image sure had gotten his attention. At first, he thought his eyes were playing tricks with him. She was so light when he scooped her up.

CHAPTER 19

ONLY TWO THINGS ARE FOR certain these days: God's ways are not ours, and Mom works Thursdays and every other Saturday.

Karson has joined her this afternoon. Dad beckons me, and when I approach, he collapses the footrest and takes hold of my wrists. He describes a pressure in his lower back and an incessant ache that he can't quite locate because he feels it everywhere. He asks me to rub Bengay into his back where fluid has gathered under the skin. I circle the gel into his skin; it feels like massaging a piece of overripe fruit.

An hour passes, and he calls for me again. This time he asks for help standing. I rock with his weight. He steadies himself on the kitchen doorway, then leans across the counter and begins to rummage through the vitamin cabinet. Plastic bottles rustle and click against one another. Electricity pulses in my veins. Dad shifts his weight from one leg to the other. I turn to flee, but his voice claws the air to catch me.

"Kate. Have you seen the codeine?"

I pump my jaw. My eyes feel dry as paper.

"The what?"

He grimaces. It is hard to speak, and harder still to harness the willpower to agree to the terms of our wrestling match. Who knew God would ask us to contest not an angel or a devil, but each other, father and daughter? The terms between us shift now—I might as well call the air elixir, my lie an act of faith, so powerfully do I repurpose language, calling things which are not as though they are.

At last, I think. *This is it.* If I can resist the temptation to tell Dad where the codeine is—to tell the truth—there will be no more tests. The miracle will finally come. On the strength of my faith, Dad will be healed. My heart readies. I presage a future in which I am an adult woman with a living father.

Dad is still shifting from one leg to the other. His eyes shift too. A trembling overcomes him, as though he can no longer switch between sides and must dwell in both. He grips the counter for balance.

Faith demands that Dad call pain a trial, but this afternoon he calls pain pain.

"I need the codeine," he says.

Behind and above Dad, the cabinet coaxes. Dad's eyes train on mine, and he glances over his shoulder. Andy perks up his ears and whines.

"I could call Mom."

"No. Don't call your mom." He whips back around to the vitamin cabinet and digs through the bottles: the algae powder, shark bone, supplements. They clatter onto the counter.

I fly down the hallway. Mary Katherine is sitting in the middle of my room, chewing on a wood block. Saliva dribbles down her chin. I wipe it away with the hem of my shirt, and she winces like she might cry. I say that I'm sorry.

Andy yelps once, then twice more, the pitch high and throaty. Then Dad howls. Andy barks again. Dad shouts someone's name. I pull my face to Mary Katherine's and hold her tightly.

God. He is yelling for God.

I rock Mary. "Shhh," I say. She rests her head on my chest.

Andy is on full alarm: Why will no one come? Above his fearsome barking, I hear my name. Panic cuts through me. *There was nothing*, I tell myself, pretending that I didn't hear my father call for me. Rocking Mary, I quake. Dad's voice thunderclaps.

"Kate! Please!"

Mary looks around the room as if the sound is coming from the walls, the ceiling. There can be no hiding. I cling to Mary and run to the kitchen.

Dad is on his back in the recliner, his legs pumping the air. He throws his head back. His trachea, a knotted bridge, arches as he cries.

I press Mary's head to my shoulder.

"I'm here," I say.

His eyes dart toward me. My breath catches in my throat. Kendra crouches nearby, and I ask her to take Mary. A part of me prays that God will take this task from me too. Kendra vanishes with the baby to James's room.

Dad's eyes blaze, but I don't see a stranger. Nothing evil or alien. I see the same man who woke me to join him on his morning runs, the one who could be short-tempered but whose hand wrote long math proofs as well as thank-you notes, the one who, when he came home with his diagnosis, took my face between his hands and kissed it.

"I can't do this on my own," he says.

He writhes. He shouts at heaven and then at me. I jump.

The air quivers thick and wet. I hear sobs at a distance, like the cries of a wild animal. I realize they are my own.

Dad reaches for me, and with his other hand he lifts the ribbed crew neck of his shirt to wipe his face.

"It's okay when you're in pain to have some relief." His eyes search mine. I break his grip.

"I'll call Mom."

He must know there will be no aid when the screen door slaps behind me. His wails ring through the walls as I dial the clinic. I tell Dierdre it's an emergency.

I believe that when I hear Mom's voice I'll no longer be in this nightmare. The tip of the ponderosa pine makes promises: a crane will appear just as a dove alighted after Jesus returned from days of temptation in the desert. I've done well, and because God is well pleased with me, when I walk back into the house my father will be restored. Peace will wrap around me like a blanket, and for once I will feel and understand it.

The line's hold signal chirps between long intervals of quiet. *Come on*, I think. *Hurry hurry hurry.*

The veterinarian says my name.

Light lurches and ripples across the yard as though everything is once more covered in water back when those things which are were not: lakes instead of dry basins; streams in place of arroyos; the past replacing the present.

I break into wails like echoes of my father's. Grass brightens and blurs around my feet.

"He needs the codeine."

I hear her sigh. Acid bursts in my stomach. I taste bile. Heat rears to kindle. Perhaps I am possessed. But the flame licking up my throat, threatening to blaze, is physical. I haven't betrayed Mom's trust in me; what about mine in her?

"I'll be home in an hour," she says. "I'll deal with it then."

"Mom, he's the same person."

The dial tone hums. A breeze draws sweat from my forehead and neck. The metal chains hanging from the swing set turn and whine and clink. The swings hang like yellow smiles. Dad's cries stop. In the quiet, a truth lurches from storage in my body: whatever trial has just passed, Dad will be no better when I walk into the house.

Dad is still in the living room, and James is building a puzzle at his feet. Mary chews on a plastic ring next to him. Kendra is curled with Dad in his chair. Their faces are puffy. They study the television like they are transfixed on something inside of it. Each of my siblings looks so pale, like a caricature of a child. I set the phone on the receiver and face Dad.

The bookshelf rears behind him. Let it be known that no text there offers grace. Fifteen years will pass before I read these lines about the vast surface of the Llano Estacado in *Lonesome Dove*: "It struck him that he had forgotten emptiness such as existed in the country that stretched around him . . . here there was no sound, not any. The coyotes were silent, the crickets, the locusts, the owls. From him to the stars, in all directions, there was only silence and emptiness."

Dad is beat, the lines in his face worn to deep grooves, as though agony has worn away his veneer. His eyes are closed, supplanting sleep with exhaustion. When he opens them, he looks at me.

Do I still have a choice? The codeine is only a few feet away. Could I just unfold the stepladder and retrieve the pills and place two small white tablets on a tray and set the tray with bread and water and carry it to Dad?

Now that I've started crying again, I can't stop.

"Come here," my father says. "Come in here." I bend awkwardly to hug him and fall into his chest. Kendra rubs my arm in circles. Dad holds the back of my head. The stench of his gore, the burn of analgesic, the familiar trace of his sweat: this is the air I breathe.

CHAPTER 20

ON SUNDAY AFTERNOONS IN THE late spring of 1998, my sisters and I would walk two blocks, then roam the aisles of movie videos at Blockbuster. We could spend hours poring over the shellacked cases, though we knew the inventory by heart. I'd head straight for the image of Harrison Ford's righteous scowl pictured above a rushing plane with "United States of America" scrolled across its wing.

Writing in 1997, Janet Maslin, the film critic for the *New York Times*, claimed that, despite the panache and warmth of Harrison Ford's performance, Wolfgang Peterson's film *Air Force One* was predictable, offering little more than "routine excitement: crazed terrorists, midair dogfights, desperate struggles staged beside an airplane's open door. And dialogue bustling with manful military authority."

The recipe, according to my father, for narrative perfection.

We had rented the movie enough times to own it twice over. A cute guy in requisite Blockbuster blue didn't ask me my age anymore: he'd called my parents many times already for their consent to my renting this R-rated movie. It's a wonder that my home number wasn't on speed dial. The scanner would bleep without the boy giving my choice a second thought.

Dad watches *Air Force One* every night alone in the living room where he sleeps, or tries to sleep.

The red digital numbers of Mom's radio clock display 10:30. I am sure Dad is still awake. Mom's breathing grows deeper and more even. She is asleep. I slide from around my sisters' limbs and lift back the layers of our makeshift sleeping bag.

The ruthless confrontation over the codeine busted the hinges of a gate inside me. It swings open between fear of Dad's pain and a longing to sit at his side. I have only to pass through the doorway. The change I feel brings to mind a dog who springs into the arms of her human on being released at the clinic. I have missed him.

I will never know if my father took the codeine again. I hope that he did, though when I think back, remembering signs of his physical discomfort, I doubt it. The answer is locked within the privacy of my parents' marriage, where I wish the question had stayed from the start. Within an hour of my calling her that wretched afternoon, my mother came home. I remember seeing her stand next to Dad, and I can recall the two of them murmuring together, my father nodding wanly, though who was reassuring whom is unclear. As adults, my sister Karson admitted to me that in her memory Mom once told her that Dad asked her to hide the codeine from him, knowing his temptation would become too great. The two versions don't seem irreconcilable to me.

Twenty years passed before I could put language to that afternoon, my shame has been so great. I was at work on this memoir for a year before I could write about it. I can look back now and see that denying my father relief from his pain was an inevitable consequence of my beliefs at the time—though this recognition offers little comfort to me now. It is ironic, though, that by completing a test of my faith without wavering, I felt the first cracks in my identity as an evangelical Christian, though the fissures were subtle, and the breach would widen slowly over time. When my father was not healed that afternoon, I began to view the reality of my situation with dual vision. Seeing that he was dying allowed me to recognize he was full of life. I should have been filled with fear, but instead I felt, for the first time in a year, the comfort of my father's presence. Though I continued to speak the script of healing as needed, mystery found room next to certainty.

The hallway snakes before me like a dark tunnel. Muffled dialogue builds as I trail down the hall with my fingertips. I pass the door to my bedroom. Blue light flashes across the wall ahead. Harrison

Ford growls on the screen, and in the television's glow I make out my father's chair and the ragged half-moon of his hair. The recliner's shade stretches to the space behind it where I stand. Another step might startle Dad. I fear he may be sleeping. I fear he might not wake.

The arm of the couch is easy to climb. Dad has read Tom Clancy's canon to date, and *Air Force One* is of that milieu—the threatened nation, the specter of communism, a good man fighting against the morally bankrupt for the soul of American democracy. Offscreen Harrison Ford has a pierced ear, solidifying his position as an out-of-touch liberal, but tonight he plays a solid American president.

In the flashings of television light, the landscape of the living room shifts. I wonder how Dad feels in these changing terrains. Is he lonely? Is some part of him absorbed in each landing on-screen, as focused perhaps as he was each time he flew planes himself? When Reese Air Force Base closed, Dad said it was the end of an era and muttered something about Clinton and the order of the new world. He had taught hundreds of pilots to be alone in the sky. The base was shuttered, but its entrails could not be closed off—PFAS coursed from fire-training areas through porous sediment, combs of rock, and waterways. The base had, in a way, taken up permanent residency in Lubbock County and in the bodies of water and people without our knowing.

In our house on Eighteenth Street, I rest in the privacy of my own mind and let in the thoughts that will rise again in adulthood—how my father's life is shaped by flight and flight's fuel and fuel's promise. Each night he revisits the Blackhawk helicopters, F-15s, and the president's private plane—images conjured as much by his memories of flying aircraft above the military bases of his childhood and the American landscape as by the film. Harrison Ford crouches in the cargo area of *Air Force One*, hugging a phone and trying to convince a lackey back at the White House that he is in fact the president and he's calling in an emergency. Light throws mosaics across Dad's face that mask and unmask him.

He doesn't notice me at first. The plot arrives at the point where the vice president realizes that *Air Force One* has indeed been hijacked by terrorists. Obscenity brushes the air. Dad's head turns. I'm not supposed to be here.

"I didn't know you were here," he says. I nod, acknowledging the question between us: Can I stay? He turns back to the television. His arm slides from the chair rest and he reaches for me, palm up. I dash to the floor, perch where light last struck, and fold my hand into his.

CHAPTER 21

DAD WAKES WITH A JOLT. The colonel stands in the entrance to my parents' bedroom. He is dressed in military fatigues. Dad props himself on his elbows, and when the colonel doesn't move, he turns back the covers and rises, stiff from sleep, to go hear what his father has to say. He feels like a boy—he is stripped to his underwear. The same longing he had as a child to please his father tugs at him now, but there is no time to dress. He steps around the sleeping bodies of his children like someone walking in a field in the dark. He sits at the foot of the bed.

The colonel enters the room, turns, and settles next to Dad. The mattress dips. Mom doesn't stir. Dad waits. The two men haven't seen each other since Dad's diagnosis eleven months ago. They sit in the silence of those who share the same secrets. Though slender, the colonel is a man of presence. He makes a quiet sound as he clears his throat and places a hand on the knee of his son. Dad wonders if he has become a young man again, his chest firm, his skin beautiful. But it is not so. He senses his ailing body and the pallid yellow hue of his skin. Below his right rib, his abdomen bloats with malignancy. Fear rushes through him. He is not dreaming. But the colonel's hand keeps a steady hold. There is time yet. Dad waits for his father to speak. Presently he does.

"I am proud of you, son," he says. "I've come to tell you that."

Dad's eyes blink open. He squints into the television light. The last minutes of *Air Force One* play, the soundtrack big and gushy. All around him the room is dark and the doorway to the kitchen gapes. At the back of the house the air is thick with the sleeping breaths of so many children, of his wife. But the dream was too real to be a dream. Dread pitches from his sternum. What if his father has died and appeared to him in the dimension of Christ after death? It is too late to call Universal City. He waits till morning.

Before he dials, he holds a tray with a breakfast of unbuttered toast and green algae powder dissolved in water and Mom listens to his account of the colonel's visit. When he finishes, she says that he wasn't dreaming at all but saw an angel.

Some angel.

Lubbock is separated from Universal City by nearly four hundred miles, but my grandfather's voice sounds farther away than that. He asks my father if there are any updates. Does his son plan to go see a doctor again? It's a wonder that the electricity in my grandfather's voice does not burn up the phone wires stretching across the state.

In his father's voice, Dad detects traces of his grandfather, an Air Force pilot whom he met only once or twice and who was reputed to be harsh and metal of hand. The colonel had distinguished himself from his father. His temperament wasn't brash but easygoing; against his father's dogged opinions, he cultivated equivocation. Perhaps my grandfather is also surprised by the change in his own tone and hastened pulse when he hears Dad say that he is not going to see another doctor.

Dad quenches the tension between them by telling himself that all will be repaired once he is in remission. He believes that no breach is so deep as to sever the bond between child and parent. Grandpa says he and my grandmother plan to drive up.

I wonder if my grandparents will finally warm to our evangelical faith when they arrive, perhaps even begin to share in it. Conversely, maybe they hope that our hearty food and steadfast faith are working; maybe they will see that their son is, as he's said, recovering.

But when the doors to the Lincoln clip shut and his parents catch sight of Dad steadying himself against the bricks of the house as he walks toward them, they freeze. Rather than words, they utter primal sounds I know to be their voices, and I can only look at the ground. They reach past me for my father.

Dad had warned them about his changed appearance, as though anything could. "My skin is the color of carrot juice," he'd said. His parents embrace him and cry. Grandma pulls back and hides her face in her hands. When I look up, I see the red gathering in Grandpa's eyes, the look on his face as much one of sorrow as anger. Mom stands back, faint and restrained. My question about my grandparents' faith is immediately put to rest. They have only one question: What is happening to their son?

My uncle Bobby has made the trip with his parents and is here too. He is thirty-seven, my favorite uncle, a golden retriever of a human. Gravity tugs at his face. He never moved away from Universal City except for a rumored semester at Texas A&M that no one talks about. I am convinced he is the kindest person alive.

As a child, my uncle Bobby was given to sleepwalking. One night he woke, gathered his comic books, and made like a ghost down the street to sell them. I imagine a boy crossing under streetlights and passing into the dark between them. After that, Dad made camp by the front door and slept there. When Bobby was sleepwalking, Dad's eyes would blink open at the sound of his footsteps. He would get up and guide Bobby by the shoulders back to bed. In the morning, Bobby would have no memory of it.

Bobby has traveled to Lubbock with his parents, it is reasoned, to assist them with the driving. But the real cause becomes clear as Bobby stands in a ring with my grandparents and my father. He steadies my grandmother and rests a hand on my grandfather's back. In the family, Bobby plays the role of keeper of the peace. He has become the caretaker, calming their resentment, easing their grief. He stands between his father and brother as both bolster and buffer.

When my grandmother prayed to Mary in the midst of her despair in Colorado Springs nearly forty years ago, uttering the words, *You have to help me*, she believed that God answered her by giving her another son, Bobby. Perhaps only now, as Bobby helps her regain her balance, does she fully understand her prayer and its answer. Her heart broke open when my father entered this world. As surely as some part of her believed when that red car raced past him on the highway that she would never live to see John Blackburn die, another part of her knew that her fate was yoked to his. She would spend the rest of her life recovering from the fact of his existence, and Bobby would comfort her.

Bobby is also here to see his brother. The two embrace. Dad mumbles something in a code they've shared since childhood, and both men laugh. I can't peel their voices apart.

Bobby faces me. "How's it going?" His voice is soft and decomposed as sawdust, like Dad's. I don't feel the automatic impulse to recite how well I am. I have nothing to say.

They stay for two days. In the space where physical details might flesh out a more complete picture of their time with us, I see a sleeve of Oreos tucked back in the shadow of a pantry shelf. Illicit contraband. The identity of the person who put them there will remain a mystery, but when I spot them, I know they are for Dad. Later, the refrain *Beverly didn't even let him have an Oreo* will fuel so much extended Blackburn family lore that it will be impossible to remember whose idea it was to bring the Oreos. Was it Grandma's? A mother's small and tender gift for her son, like a communion wafer, signaling that she accepted his broken body? Or did my grandparents help Dad go to the store to buy them himself? In moments of intense physical pain, he might have reasoned that a treat wasn't a compromise in faith and seen his parents' complicity as a mercy. Could one Oreo stop God? Maybe he confessed to his parents a particular hunger for the chocolate cookie with the smooth white cream and found that, immediately after finishing one Oreo, he had an appetite for another. Perhaps this confession left my grandparents speechless. For them, the cheap cookie would have revealed what they suspected: that doubt was beginning to shake the certainty in Dad's mind, that none of this food and faith project had been his idea.

I flinch when I see the blue packaging and look away, but not before I picture my grandparents convincing themselves by the time they return to Universal City that as Dad's cheekbones sharpen under his eyes and his hair thins, all he really wants is an Oreo. The cookie rising as an unlikely and absurd symbol of Mom depriving their son of medical treatment. There is also something petty about an Oreo. Its ubiquity and modest cost. The hint of cardboard in its flavor. Such a paltry thing to deny a person. They will think of how gaunt Dad has become. *Craving*, they will say. Their son will die craving.

I shake the imagined monologue and close the pantry door.

Grandma watches Mom brew Itzhak tea.

"What can I do to help?"

My eyes beg my grandmother, bless her heart, to not ask Mom one question. My mother has two modes: high-strung and the range only dogs can hear. My grandparents' arrival kicked the latter up to turbo.

Mom keeps her face on the stove and stirs with a steady tempo. "I've got it," she says. "Is it warm enough yet to swim in San Antonio?"

"I wonder, Beverly, if you would let Tom and I take the kids out for Chinese."

I wither, but to my surprise Mom nods. She looks frail. She focuses on the spoon she circles in the tea. "Thank you," she says. I can tell from the tone of her voice she is crying.

Memories of this visit held by Grandma, Grandpa, and Bobby will die with them. First Grandpa, in 2004, when he's eighty-seven, with prostate cancer. Then Grandma, in 2012, when she's ninety-two, with colon cancer. Then, Uncle Bobby, when he's fifty-nine. He'll die of everything: prostate cancer, alcoholism, early-onset late-stage Alzheimer's disease and, according to his psychiatrist, grief.

My aunt Lori, Dad's sister, has survived, by some mercy, breast cancer. By this point in 2023, colonoscopies and mammograms are about as regular a topic as weather in extended Blackburn and

Kennedy family conversations. It is my understanding that among my grandmother Dorothy Kennedy's relatives, there were seven diagnosed cases of colon cancer, though Dad's was the only early-onset case, and the most acute. Karson, Kendra, and I have each had one colonoscopy so far; I had benign polyps removed during my procedure, and my doctor told me that they indicated a genetic predisposition to colon cancer, a fact that I've been warned about by other doctors. It didn't surprise me but echoed a dread of dying that I carry with me. I will soon turn thirty-nine, the age my father was when he died, and as that birthday approaches, part of me has realized I never expected to live past the age of forty. I call this dread the sixth unannounced stage of grief. One of its effects has been an intensified search to understand the causes of my father's cancer.

My aunt Lori and one of her daughters have had genetic profiles completed—Lori now twice—and the results were inconclusive. One major concern has been that we might be carriers for BRCA1 and 2, the breast cancer genetic mutations that are also associated with colorectal cancer. The results, at least for my aunt and cousin, were negative. Both also tested negative for Lynch syndrome, another genetic mutation that one geneticist I spoke with hypothesized may be an issue. The CDC describes Lynch syndrome as the most common cause of hereditary colorectal cancer. The syndrome refers to genetic mutations that affect the ability of DNA to repair mismatches. Normally, human DNA corrects its mistakes, preventing cancer. But a mutation can cause the kinds of malfunctions that are present in cancerous tissue. "However," the CDC report adds, "not everyone with Lynch syndrome will get cancer."

"That's the thing about genetics," the geneticist said to me. "It's a world where almost anything is possible, and nothing is guaranteed." In this way, the study of genetics doesn't sound so different from the study of forever chemicals. Researchers have only recently begun to grasp the consequences of internalizing PFAS over a prolonged period of time. The results of exposure are largely determined by the duration and intensity of that exposure as well as by other environmental factors, preexisting conditions, and genetics.

I spoke recently to Dr. Mark Purdue, a researcher at the National Cancer Institute at the National Institutes of Health (NIH) who focuses on military service people with known exposure to PFAS from firefighting foams. He described the work as an uphill battle: the rate at which PFAS are being released into the environment far outpaces toxicologists' ability to study their consequences for human health. His most recent study was designed to exclude participants who were not active-duty military at the time of their cancer diagnosis, primarily because he was working with a database from military health centers. Thus, most of those excluded were people who had spent at least twenty years in the service or who had retired after less than twenty years but had maintained their military benefits. "Ideally it would be great to study ex-military once they separate from their service, but given the constraints of the data, we couldn't study them very well," Dr. Purdue said. The study was necessarily narrow and excluded personnel like my father, who served only seven years, though he had lived on or near military bases for his entire adolescence—bases that are now included on a map maintained by the Environmental Working Group that shows registered contamination by PFAS at these sites.

One of my father's old high school classmates, a woman named Phyllis, told me that there were two social groups in Universal City—country kids and military kids. She remembered the military boys with their slick crew cuts and inside jokes. They were jocks who wouldn't be around long before the military snatched them off to some other place. My father didn't exactly fit into that category because my grandfather had retired in Universal City. Phyllis remembered that Dad still hung out with the other military youth, though she said he was never too good for anybody.

"When did your dad die?" she asked me. After I told her, she said, "Well, we all lost touch."

Dr. Purdue wasn't aware of any studies that examine the health consequences of PFA exposure for the military brat—children who come of age in the military and spend most of their lives moving with their family all over the place—like my father. There have also not been extensive studies of children of military personnel who may have repeatedly been exposed to drinking water contaminated by PFAS.

Old neighbors in Universal City, hearing about the plague of cancer in the Blackburn family, have said to me, "There's something in the water." As Universal City changed from dirt fields and new development to street upon street of ranch-style homes and ubiquitous outlet malls, some wondered exactly what drained into the water from Randolph Air Force Base. In 2018, it was reported that PFAS sourced back to firefighting foams had been detected in the groundwater at Randolph, and that they had migrated into nearby creeks.

Aunt Lori doesn't think environmental contamination has much to do with the instances of cancer in our family. We're too spread out across the country, and our cousins and uncles with cancer on my grandma's side weren't in the military. She may have a point. During my reading, research, and interviews, I have sometimes wondered if I've wanted too much to see a strong connection between PFAS and my father's diagnosis. Cause and effect can be difficult to trace in environmental stories. I also recognize in myself a strong desire for certainty—perhaps one born of the same trait in my parents, who, when the doctors didn't give them the answers they wanted, went straight to the evangelist's tent. Before my conversation with Dr. Purdue ended, I asked what could be hazardous about concluding too quickly that disease and possible PFA exposure are linked.

"It's rare for a single study to be definitive," he said. "The results that we see in one study may not replicate in another study. It's important to assess the evidence from multiple studies before really drawing conclusions."

So I find myself in a familiar place—pondering the evidence, not yet able to draw a conclusion. There are only a few things I know for sure: PFAS contaminated the water in most of the landscapes where my father lived and worked. I know there are few if any studies examining chronic exposure to forever chemicals among legacy military families, among children of military personnel, or among military service people who may already have been genetically predisposed to develop colorectal cancer. And I know that twenty-five years ago, in 1998, a few hours after my grandparents and uncle arrived in Lubbock, Mom hefted a bag of trash up from the kitchen floor and Bobby asked that she let him do it. She told him no.

"Please," Bobby said. I recognized a note in his voice. It was the sound of total helplessness. I'd heard it when Dad prayed. I sometimes discerned it in the whimper of the sick at healing services. What God could deny such a sound? Tears swelled in Mom's eyes. She let him take the full plastic bag from her hands.

A few years before he died, Bobby wandered from a dinner party in the Texas hill country, finding once more a spectral path in the dark as he had as a child, only now without my father standing alongside and gently stopping him from losing his way, this time with no comic books to sell. No one yet knew he had dementia, or much noticed he was gone, until his cries pierced the air. He was found on the shoulder of an unlit road.

The Chinese buffet might as well be Disneyland. I stack my plate with more egg rolls and orange chicken than I can possibly eat. I decide not to add one vegetable unless it is soaked in thick teriyaki or red sweet-and-sour sauce. At a long table in the back of the restaurant, my grandparents tease us kids into a racket, with jokes ricocheting back and forth. My sisters and I are hyped to the verge of tears. We laugh hysterically, pausing only to stuff our mouths with more food, staying until we can't eat anymore. On the way home, Karson, Kendra, James, and I are crammed into the backseat of the Lincoln, and James says his stomach hurts. Mine is killing me. I've eaten far too much of the kind of food that doesn't sit right with me anymore. I'm not used to fried meats, sugary sauces, and enough salt to float in. My head pounds. It is, I will realize later, the closest I will come to having a hangover before I discover my predilections.

My grandparents are quiet. A toothpick rambles between Grandpa's lips.

"Well, at least we did this," he says.

They leave the next day.

In the evening, the phone rings, and Dad says it is probably Grandpa calling to say they've arrived safely. He holds the phone and speaks and then pinches the skin between his eyes, rubs his finger and thumb across his eyelids, and tugs at the skin again and says goodbye.

Son, his father had said. You're dying. Do something.

CHAPTER 22

THE HAIRSTYLIST HOLDS THE PHOTO of Jennifer Aniston next to my face. I've done the same at home, and it's a tough comparison. Aniston is Aniston, and I'm a thirteen-year-old befriended by oily skin. The hair won't come with the eyebrows, good chin, glint of mystery in the eye. I'll soon learn that the cut doesn't come with skills for styling it either. I will empty my allowance savings buying gel and straighteners, to no avail.

"We can do this," Annette says. My hair trails below the middle of my back. The stylist gathers the coarse tresses into a ponytail, holds up her scissors, snip-snips the air, and asks if I'm ready. My heart races. My mouth is dry with risk. I nod. Mom whimpers.

"I thought you said you didn't care," I say, clipping each consonant.

"It's just hard to watch it fall to the ground," Mom says.

Annette's scissors continue. She directs me to look down, and I find myself in the familiar position of studying my hands. My thumb caresses the cross on my ring. The small green rivers of my veins prove a weak distraction from the weight I feel literally falling from my head with each blond coil that lands on the floor.

I am cutting my hair because I want a change. I've turned thirteen: something besides a piece of jewelry with a false scripture should mark the occasion. I suppose some part of me also wants to feel in control of something, though with Annette's blades whizzing at my temples, that goal feels rather far away. Instead, as I watch my hair gather on the ground, a part of me feels a mounting sorrow. I do not yet recognize grief as grief, nor do I understand that I have asked to cut my hair in part because I am mourning.

One shampoo, shape-up, and blowout later, Annette whirls me around to the mirror, and I sit staring at a teenager, mouth agape. For a minute, my hair is styled perfectly; the layers stacked with volume, the ends tucked at my chin. Someone call Brad Pitt: I even have the zigzag part. Please pause the world. I need to study this young woman who has somehow, despite everything that has happened in the last year, appeared. No, not *despite* the last twelve months, but *because* of them.

I realize, staring at my reflection, that though my family has labeled just about everything from the last year as Satan's attack, each terrifying day has nevertheless aged me. Made me. Gazing back at me from the salon mirror is the teenager I have become. This is the girl who has been hollowed out by desperation to save her father's life, yet knows that he rests at home, still dying. My freckles are dark, my eyes electric blue and harrowing. My jaw is heart-shaped. I look much older than thirteen.

I wish to be completely alone. To rest on my elbows, chin in my hands, and study my jaw, see all the angles. More than any-thing, I don't want to be anywhere near my mother. I don't want her to witness this reveal. I can't bear to look at her for fear I'll see a condescending grin, or worse, more tears. I fear, above all, that she will see the woman I am becoming and—what? Give me more responsibility? Quash me? Take what she sees and try to shape it into something else?

Perhaps my mother has also been taken by surprise. Or maybe to her my coming of age has been gradual and she's observed it with a combination of resistance and welcome. I write this now, from a distance of twenty-five years, and think of her words about my hair—*it's just hard to watch it fall*. To both of us, my long hair signified my childhood. Once, when I was four or five, an elderly woman gathered its gold by the handful and kissed it, and my mother thanked her. My mother brushed my hair at night and braided it in long ropes in the mornings. I had been proud of it too. I hear, in my memory of her words, a release. A mother's bittersweet acknowledgment that her daughter is no longer a child. It is hard to watch. So many things were hard to watch in those days.

Very often in my youth, I felt unseen by my mother. At least, that was the word I used to describe the feeling to myself, but it was more complicated than that. Her observations of me often pained her—as when she grieved at the sight of my white-blond strands piling up on the salon tiles. Or what she saw resulted in more responsibility for me, more training, more discipline. She left me to care for my siblings, took me to the clinic instead of enrolling me in school, and tasked me with praying for miracles because, in each instance, she had concluded that I'd reached a new benchmark. These were the ways in which she acknowledged my young adulthood. In her mind, these were the privileges of maturity. It wasn't that my mother didn't see me. I could feel her eyes, like a harsh light. I just didn't like what she did with what she saw. This was true at the time and has largely remained true.

People sometimes ask me if I talk to my mother about the past. The answer is mostly no. Besides the complicated parts of unpacking deep trauma with a family member, such a conversation would require a transparency from me, a vulnerability that would stand in contrast to the truth I understood when I looked into that salon mirror. My mother is not a person with whom I feel my revelations of self can be left unguarded.

But at the salon that afternoon twenty-five years ago, she did her best. She paid for my haircut and said it looked nice. She asked me what I thought of it, and I said that I liked it.

At home, I approach Dad timidly, afraid his reaction to my haircut will match Mom's, though if it does, his tears won't vex me in the same way.

"Well, look at you," he says. He leans forward from the green La-Z-Boy, takes a few tapered strands between his fingers, and gently rubs them together. Resin from my hair shines on his fingertips. The back of his thumb pauses where it might touch my chin. There is a light in my father's eyes. I brim with pride, and for a moment

I feel confident and assured—not that I can bear what's to come or can even comprehend it. But right now I am the girl I saw in the mirror at the salon, and my father sees her too. Dad smiles and sits back. "I'm sorry we made you grow up so fast."

"Well, you know I've been trying to anyway."

It's a week before Mom's birthday in May 1998, and Dad lifts his keys from the kitchen counter and passes them to me.

"It's time to teach you to drive."

I regard the keys and consider Dad's timing. Still three more years until I turn sixteen. *There's no need for this*, I tell myself.

I drive the van into a curb halfway down the block. Dad throws his hand across the glove box to brace himself. With each jolt, he moans.

"Let's stop," I say. We idle in the middle of a crosswalk.

"You're doing fine," he says.

We drive for twenty more minutes as Dad counsels me to tap the gas and hold my foot there. Then he says to ease up. He is a good teacher, as I'm sure his flight students could attest. He guides me in learning to appreciate the girth of the van and how to shift from accelerator to brake in the time-honored tradition of a father teaching a daughter how to drive.

Roy swings by in his white Cadillac. He grasps Dad's arm to help him stand, and when he does both men stumble. Dad hangs on to Roy's shoulders, and Roy holds Dad's forearms and says, "Okay." The two walk outside. They have been close since they met at Miracles on Thirty-Fourth Street. Dad's got on his maroon Aggie T-shirt, blue cotton shorts, white compression socks, and sneakers, untied. Roy's wearing a business suit and tie. He opens the door to the Cadillac and helps Dad lower himself in.

In Roy and Loretta's living room, the walls are lined with mahogany cases filled with porcelain dolls. Loretta boasts over a hundred in her collection. She refers to each doll as "she," as in, "Isn't she beautiful?" There is one dressed as a bride. Another as Audrey Hepburn at the horse races. From behind their glass doors, the girls stare at Dad. Every time he blinks, another one wins.

"To review last rites with such witnesses," Dad says.

"Don't mind them," Roy says. He opens a leather folder and draws from it a set of documents typed in bold font with lots of dashes between template phrases. Roy calls it legalese. He says that he got in touch with the lawyer, the one they talked about. He pulls out his billfold, flops it open, retrieves a business card, and slides it to Dad. He taps the card, says, "He's a good guy. He'll take care of you."

Dad asks if Roy's got another one of these cards. Roy says that he does and reaches for his billfold again, but Dad holds up a hand.

"That's all right," he says. "If it comes to it, just give the card to Beverly."

When Dad comes home from Roy's, he walks in with a box of Oreos.

You bet it's a Thursday.

Dad grabs up his keys again and says, "I need you to do something for me."

I put on my shoes.

This time he drives. We take Loop 289, the concrete belt that wraps around the city, cross the overpasses to South Plains Mall, turn into the parking lot, and then Dad explains I am to facilitate the purchase of some wind chimes for Mom's birthday. Unspoken between us is the knowledge that he cannot walk far enough to go into the mall and buy the chimes himself. I nod as he says that the chimes are the big ones, long, and coal colored. They'll be hanging in the window of Nature's Gifts. The plan is for me to take Dad's credit card and buy the chimes while he waits in the van. "The get-away van," I say and hop out.

To be alone in the mall is a thrill; to have a mission, even better. I cut a direct path for Nature's Gifts, and if I were at all fluent in profanity, I would say I feel like a badass. Mariah Carey's soaring voice rings above me. I pass Claire's, Hot Topic. The fragrance billowing from the entrance to Abercrombie & Fitch almost knocks me over. I pause at the window display of bras at Victoria's Secret long enough to think of Jesse and get butterflies in my stomach. I carry them away with me. I figure this quest for chimes will be the only time I'm allowed in the mall alone before the age of seventeen. Mom has barred me from both the mall and rock 'n' roll. But I've listened to the sinful music anyway, closing my bedroom door and crouching next to my Sony stereo receiver and tuning to Kool 98 and listening to rock classics from the '60s and '70s. Wasn't everything better back in the bygone? I keep hearing that the world went to crap when Clinton got elected. I like the old stuff: The Ronettes, The Rolling Stones, and Bill Withers. I have a habit of recording long sessions onto cassette tapes so I can memorize the lyrics to songs like "Be My Baby" and "Daydream Believer" and "Stand by Me."

A recording of birdsong and synthesizer plays in Nature's Gifts. I get distracted by the rain sticks and try out several of them, saying to the clerk that they really do sound like rain. The chimes hang in the window as described. They are the second-largest on display. The clerk doesn't hesitate when I pay with Dad's credit card, but I panic when she asks me to sign the receipt. Dad's name is written under the signature line. Do I risk theft or forgery? I scribble something unintelligible. It feels delicious to do so.

I heft the chimes, which are in a large box but light enough, across the parking lot, open the sliding door to the van, settle the box into the seat, close the slider, and open the door to the passenger's seat. Dad is listening to Kool 98. I look at him wide-eyed.

"What?" he says.

"Nothing."

As we drive home, Bill Withers's "Lean on Me" comes on over the radio waves. Dad turns to me. In the moment, I have no idea how perfect a fit the song will appear to me later, but also how saccharine it will seem in retrospect. As I write this now, I hesitate to include this detail. If I were watching some film version of this scene, I'd roll my eyes at such a soundtrack. *We get it!* I'd want to holler at the screen. But at the time the only thing that strikes me is that I like showing off how I know the lyrics. When Dad turns to me, he says, "I didn't know you knew this one."

I like to think this pleases him, seeing evidence of the young woman I am becoming, one with a private life that reveals itself to him only in glimmers. Or maybe he is reminded of our drives to the barber shop on the base years earlier. I imagine some grief gripping the edges of whatever amusement or joy I feel ebb from my father as I shrug and keep on singing. He turns up the volume. All I know for sure in that moment is that the rules don't apply, neither the ones governing what we listen to nor the ones dictating what we believe.

The angels are too busy to pilfer Mom's gift. If she'd hoped for a sign, the only one she receives is a large wrapped box on the kitchen table and a card saying we love her. Dad had directed the proceedings, asking for assurance that each of the children had signed the card. He had requested that the box of chimes, which I hid in my bedroom closet, be brought to the table while Mom readied herself in the bathroom. When she walks into the dining room and sees the box, we each take a tiny breath and hold it.

My mother is one who openly rejects gifts. Her rebukes can be hostile. One time us kids pooled our money to secure the services of a professional photographer. When Mom opened the gift receipt, she scowled. The paper might as well have been a donation receipt from Planned Parenthood. She demanded that we get a refund— she hadn't picked the photographer and did not appreciate the creative license we'd taken in doing so. Another time, Loretta gave Mom a floral comforter. Well. It didn't match anything in Mom's room. She gave the comforter back.

"You should have just thanked her and kept it and then given it away," I said. Her eyes pooled like a cartoon rabbit's.

"You think I should have lied?"

Once, Dad bought her a long, beautiful cotton robe. She demanded to know how much he spent and then told him to return it, and he said he was within his rights to buy something nice for his wife.

Eyeing the unwrapped chimes, I await the fifth degree: How did we procure them? Was I really allowed to enter the mall alone? Were the chimes on sale? I imagine giving her the copy of the receipt and receiving clarification on the lack of integrity required to sign above someone else's name. Though only a few days have passed since our subterfuge, I can see that Dad will not be able to take me to the mall again. He visits the bathroom many times each hour. Mom will have to be the one to return the chimes. I can already hear her insist that I come along; I can feel my stomach knot as I see her chirp her purpose to the clerk in Nature's Gifts.

She pulls apart the gift paper slowly, lifts the lid, whishing away the tissue paper, and beholds the chimes. She lifts them, and low tones fill the room.

"These are exactly the kind I like," she says. She barely finishes the sentence before wrapping her arms around Dad and kissing him, and the two are quiet together. It has been almost exactly a year since Dad's diagnosis. They weep. And though my siblings surround them, they are briefly alone.

The chimes hang from a branch of the red oak out back. Andy looks up, cocks his head, then turns in a circle and sleeps beneath them. Dad calls me from his chair and says, "I need you to do something for me." I am eager for another errand. Dad looks to the front yard, and I follow his gaze. James is making circles on the driveway with his bike, a Cruiser-style fitted with a motorcycle facade and handlebar switches that trigger engine sounds. Dad and I watch as though we are viewing the same stage on which James loops a driveway again and again.

"I want to play with my son," he says.

"Well, you will."

He waves me closer. "If anything happens to me," he says. "Don't turn your back on God."

The chimes are sonorous, and surely God hears them, just as he watches our coming and going. But Dad is talking as though God isn't listening, as if there are spaces in the world where two people can whisper to each other outside the range of God's ear. In this place of something like confession, Dad and I find a reprieve from belief and pledge. An escape from everything but our bodies.

He tugs me nearer, his voice a breath. "And take care of your mom."

Brightness from the kitchen window blinks as Mom waters her hanging plants. How strange it is that I hear my father's wishes without fear. I feel I am speaking to a friend, or to no one, under a night sky, words in the dark, like nothing more than a distant bird call, or sparks flying upward. As incomprehensible and strange as a dream.

CHAPTER 23

WE GIVE HIM A WHITE clip-on book light. He reaches for the
paperback copy of *Christy* and clamps the pages. Though it is afternoon, we can tell that the bulb shines white and harsh and will light
the pages just fine at night. Dad agrees. He clicks it off.

We offer Dad a card that each of us kids have signed, including
Mary, who dashed off a crooked line. It is Father's Day 1998, thirteen months after Dad's diagnosis. This time a year ago I couldn't
believe, looking at Dad's body, that he had cancer. Now I can hardly
remember what he looked like before becoming the enfeebled man
in the living room.

The book light is folded on Dad's breakfast tray. His head is statue-
still as he stares ahead with an intensity that the view through the
window does not warrant. He is pumping his jaw, the tap of his
teeth maniacal, his focus stilled as though he's been hypnotized. I
can't tell what he is eating. A breakfast of undressed toast sits on his
tray undisturbed. Then Dad lifts his napkin to his mouth and tears
a piece from it. My throat tightens.

"What are you doing?"

He flinches and his eyes stay fixed ahead.

"I'm eating." His voice is edged with something sinister. I sprint
from the living room and ram against the kitchen sink, searching
the kitchen window for Mom at her station with the water hose
tending to her hanging petunias and potted geraniums. But only
Andy sits there, in the flecked shade of the red oak, waiting for
anyone to remember how much he loves a tennis ball.

I lurch wildly against chairs and doorways as I tumble through the house. Dad's mind is sliding from the bone. I see the very architecture of our faith crumbling. The light in the hallway bends in strange angles, and the doors fold to polygons, as if I am running through a reflection of the house. It is only when I find my mother that the corners of the room stabilize again.

Above me the blue scripture cards are still taped to the bathroom doorway. Mom is sitting at her vanity mirror. Her face is lit by a ring of lights, and at the sight of her, I beg.

"What's the problem?" Her dismissal splits me in half—one part of me continues to cry to come see Dad *now*. The other part cools to gleaming, smooth rock. I lean into this hardened side, gathering certainty that Mom is right. I am overreacting. Nothing is so wrong. But I am hyperventilating for real this time, chasing breath after breath through the thin tunnel of my throat. I wheeze out that Dad is eating his napkin.

Chin down, she launches to her feet and whisks past me, saying that I need to calm down. I follow her down the hallway, hoping that she'll fix Dad, fix me, fix the whole distorted tilt of the house. Her body narrows and disappears around the corner.

Dad's teeth click.

"Hey, John," Mom says. His eyebrows rise in surprise. His eyes broaden as he looks up at her. His expression makes me feel sorry rather than terrified, a feeling of pity that feels like relief. He looks like he's been caught with a bag full of Oreos. He's worked the chunk of napkin into a golf ball–sized cud that protrudes inside his cheek. Concentrating on Mom, he rolls the bolus from one side of his mouth to the other.

"Oh, hey, Beverly," he mumbles.

"What's in your mouth?"

Dad lowers his gaze. What he'd held in focus is no longer there. He blinks, and his eyes move gently around the room as though he is also trying to figure out what he's eating before tendering his response. Was it not part of the healing diet? My breath slows. Mom settles the moment, as though lifting and smoothing down a rumpled rug. But I am still waiting for what the scriptures promise: the peace that surpasses all understanding. I feel I am in a space beyond comprehension, though I just didn't think such assurance would feel like preparing for tea with the Mad Hatter at the end of the world.

At last Dad shrugs. "I don't know," he says.

"Well, spit it out." Mom means literally, of course. She cups her hand under Dad's chin. He raises himself with his elbows and holds his face forward. Karson grimaces and looks away. I yank Mary Katherine up from the floor and press her to my chest. Kendra and James are like indifferent pale shades playing a game of checkers at the coffee table. Mom's fingers close over the contents in her palm, and she marches out of the room.

I expect her to vanish. I pop my lips at Mary. She jolts and laughs.

"Again!" she says, pressing the sides of my face with her hands; her fingernails cut my skin like the glance of paper. I welcome it. When she throws up on me, sweats on me, drools, leaks, I accept it. My siblings have taught me that our bodies belong to each other.

I lean into her wet kisses and wait for Dad to ask for something—a book, a movie. For my sisters to say they are hungry for lunch, for James to say he is too. Then Mom walks back into the living room and goes to Dad's side and takes his hand.

"Why are you crying?" he says.

"I don't know."

It is raining in Shallowater. Drops pelt the metal roof of the midwife's house. Karson and Ruth and Eden and I are tucked up in the loft. The rain hits so close to my face that I touch my forehead to check for water. It feels like a dare to lie with a sheet of metal between my body and the sky. I have never listened to the rain like this.

"You ever kissed a boy?" Eden says.

"Please."

"Tell me about Jesse."

"He's got nice eyes."

"I figure the first man I kiss will be my husband. We're the only ones like this. I got a cousin in Dallas. He's a year younger than me and already kissing girls."

"That's Dallas for you."

"I'd appreciate it if you'd whisper. My parents are in the room right next to us."

I wonder that anyone can hear us above the roar of rain.

In the morning, Eden and I finish breakfast and roll up our blue jeans. She leads me to the south edge of the field, where stormwater has flooded the irrigation ditch. The hazy morning smells of soil and blood and the memory of rain. The insects are joyous and latch onto my skin despite my insistence that they are not welcome there.

"Wait till you feel this," Eden says. There's a sucking sound as she steps into the mud and sinks up to her knees. I follow suit. The loam swallows my legs. A fog hovers between the city and my view of it, and I imagine the deluge overrunning Lubbock's streets. In fact, early city planners, observing how the gradient of the mesa funneled rainwater to the playas, devised a sewer system of street gutters and underground tunnels that followed nature's design and directed stormwater into the playas in volumes that the desert lakes could not hold. To expand their capacity to a level adequate for the city of Lubbock, the playas were trenched and transformed into containers. The ponds were no longer transient but fixed cesspools filled with runoff from feedlots, military sites, industrial facilities, and wastewater plants.

Mom will tell me later that I am standing in excrement and pesticide. Dumping tertiary effluent into the playas raised the water table, replacing prairie with a new marsh that pillaged the semi-arid savannah. I twist my feet and sink deeper. The sludge is warm and flows east like interest on an impossible debt. Rainfall refills the Ogallala at a rate inadequate for agriculture. No amount can replenish the groundwater pumped away. After the Dust Bowl, the pumping of 200,000 emergency wells continued as the irrigation needs of industrial farming became standardized. In many places scattered across West Texas, the aquifer levels have been diminished by more than hundreds of feet; the dates for when the Ogallala dried completely in some locations are designated as *day zero*.

The runoff is brown as dung. It flexes against my legs, drawn past me as though the land inhales it. But in truth, before the precipitation can recharge the aquifer, it is redirected to the cotton fields and stockyards, and the thirsty earth remains parched.

Back at the house, we hose our legs down and the brown mud parts into tributaries that thin along our legs and puddle at our feet. Eden drinks from the hose and then passes it to me. The well water tastes flat and vegetal. She fills the dog's bowl, and the canine drops her head and drinks.

"You know," Eden says, looking across the field toward Lubbock, which is lost to low hovering clouds so thick that beyond them there might as well be nothing, "I pray for your dad every day."

A crack inside my chest widens, and just as quickly my face breaks into a smile that freezes as I say that he is going to get better real soon.

Mom is increasingly called to water her plants. Never have geraniums enjoyed such attention. She appears in the kitchen long enough to say she needs to make a house call on Janet Price's dog. On the way home, she's going to stop for groceries. She shuts the front door behind her.

Dad's mind is present here but also in other dimensions. His stares have always permitted him to be in two places at once, but now he is stuck between dissonant spaces in time, unable to discern between the *here* of each domain. He speaks like a prophet, as though he knows what is and what will come. After Mom leaves, he leans away from the recliner and beckons me from the kitchen, saying, "Come here." He clasps my hand, then my wrist, and pulls me toward him. He is filled, I can tell, with secret. Jittery. His eyes urgent. I laugh uncomfortably.

"What is it?" I say.

His breath is yeasty and sour. His fingertips chilled from bad circulation. By what grace does some part of me look on him with tenderness where before I would have twisted from his grip and fled? I hold his gaze.

"I am glad," he says.

I wait.

"I never wanted your mom to coddle me. I didn't need a nurse. I wanted to be pushed." He grips me harder. I know he tells me what he cannot say to anyone else—in our refuge of confidence we are not judged—but I don't want to hear what he's saying.

"This is what I wanted. She pushed." He nods decisively. "I would have died without it." He looks away, his grip loosens, and he regards the air in front of him.

"Will you get her for me?" he says.

I tell him I will when she's home.

Our house was supposed to be a refuge, fortified at each doorway against sickness and spiritual attack, but it has become a sick bay caving in on itself, a compression chamber from which we feel we must flee. My siblings are too young to run away. Dad cannot move. Mom leaves in the van, and when I cannot go with her, I watch it disappear down the street. Dad departs by way of his mind, traveling to other realms, practicing his passage from this place to the next. And I begin to escape, as I will in years to come, through memory. I return to the mornings when, in the cool dark, my father woke me. I am lifted from the present and return to the highway flanked by cotton fields where I used to join my father on my bike before anyone else in the world, it seemed, was awake.

I could place this image of riding next to my father almost anywhere in the years between 1991 and 1996. If I could lift the memory from time completely and wear it like a talisman around my neck, I would. But let me try to locate one specific morning with my father in a time and place that feels like the beginning of the story—for that is how those mornings felt to me. Like the beginning of my life, the start of my coming of age, the fields of cotton stretching on in a long promise of prosperity. I would grow up to travel with my father the pilot. I would become a veterinarian like my mother. I would be a follower of Christ. Yes, I believed at the time, this was a beginning, not an ending.

I remember one morning when winds peeled from the sky in blows that took my breath with them. I tired of trying to keep up with Dad's pace. He grabbed the back of my bike seat and I jolted aright. He told me to pedal hard. His step slowed, and we stopped. I unbuckled my helmet and freed my hair. It blew around in the wind, tugging at my scalp. I followed my father as he carried my bike over the irrigation ditch. He paused to make sure I was settled in the dirt. I thrust my thumbs in the air. He said that he would finish the mile and pointed toward the church, the one-mile mark. It was only half a mile away now. "You'll be fine," he said, then raised one hand, turned, and gathered his pace, our dog Andy at his heel. His words echoed. *You'll be fine.* And I believed that I was. I was a child watching her father face into the winds that carved the mesas.

Once he reached the church, Dad turned back. Above him, a plane ascended.

A horn blared. I squinted against the morning sun at a man in a Stetson driving a double-cab pickup. He slowed at the road's shoulder, scowled, pointed ahead, and mouthed the words, *Your dad?* I resented his intrusion and judgment. The entire interaction—the driver's gesture, my frown—occurred within a second before he shook his head and accelerated away at the avenue's speed limit of fifty miles per hour.

A pocket of wind burst in a scattering of sand, and my father, a mirage, came toward me. Or maybe a vision of my father. The memory of my father. No, he was a vortex of dust, a sign of drought. His head moved strangely. His body wavered. When at last he reached me, he was gasping. He once told me that running should feel light. You run with your lungs. The key is to move only as fast as you can breathe. He'd run faster than that. This was the first time I ever saw fear in my father's eyes.

"I'm sorry," he said. "I shouldn't have left you alone."

"I'm fine," I said, just like he said I would be. I won't understand until I'm older how the man in the truck terrified my father, how he realized he could never run fast enough to close the distance. I can only imagine what he saw when he turned in the church parking lot. Maybe it was the plane above him. He once took me to the jet he flew. A shining silver Boeing Super 88 parked on the Lubbock airport's tarmac. We climbed into the cockpit, and he pointed to the white numbered faces on the panel of flight controls: one dial would measure wind speed, another air pressure, another temperature. The seats were warm and smelled of leather and fuel, the way Dad smelled when he came home, the way home smelled when I was seven.

Perhaps when he turned at the church, my father had an aerial view of me looking too small and too far away. For a moment, he must have understood what was meant by the words *semi-arid savanna*: a flatland spread like a patchwork of cultivated fields with playas gleaming like pupils across the plateau. But a semi-arid savanna is not only a terrain. Years later, I will see it is as a fugitive mark, a metered breath. I will remember a daughter sitting on the edge of a field, waiting for her father to return.

"I shouldn't have left you," he says again. He lifted my bike and carried it to the road. "That's never going to happen again."

But I want it to happen again. I want to see my father stop in the distance and turn back toward me. I want to assure both him and myself of his return, at least until God comes for us. At least until I can leave this place with him.

I find Mom roosting at her computer desk. A catalog of supplements fills the computer screen. The mouse clicks and the screen displays blessed oils; the mouse clicks again and the screen shows books on miracle healing.

"Dad needs you," I say.

"I'll be right there."

Viewing her as she faces the monitor, her shoulders rolled aloft, her jaw tightened in a perfect angle under her ear, I feel my back turn to slate. She needs to hear what Dad has to say. A blue flame is sparked in my chest by the realization that there is a need for him to say anything at all.

She turns to me. "I said I'll be right there."

Of all the scriptures hanging in the bathroom entrance, the verse from James is fixed in my psyche. "The prayer of faith shall heal the sick, and the Lord shall raise him up." Only the first line of the scripture appears in bold font on the blue card, but I know the rest of the verse: "And if he has committed sins, they shall be forgiven him. Confess your faults one to another."

Our faults are our failings. They carve through our being like fault lines—the quivers of doubt, the desperate desires, the deepest longings for life that, like water running across stone, wear us down and crack us open.

Blood pours from him and spills onto the white tile floor, a dark waste. He shouts like suffering prey. When Mom opens the bathroom door, I hear his sobs and everything in me prays that I will be spared the sight.

"K.D. and Karson, come here."

The bathroom walls are papered in richly colored fruits: royal grapes, regal pears, a great vine threaded through this Eden. The wallpaper crowds the scene. Stench rises from a soiled adult diaper. Waste covers the floor. Dad gasps as he explains. When he wiped, he could feel the tumor. After pulling on fresh Depends, he cleansed his hands. Then a wet warmth fell down his legs. He braces himself in the doorway. Blood pools at the baseboard. I look away. Mom says that Karson and I will help him walk to her bathroom, and he takes hold of our shoulders and presses as one would upon crutches. The smell is violent and immediately forms a permanent bond with the memory of it.

"Bathe him," Mom says. "And I'll clean up in here."

My hands and my sister's hands leave impressions in Dad's back as we help to lower him. His weight is treacherous. We will not be able to pull him back from a fall. We are scaffolding, nothing more.

In years to come, I will tell Karson that I am writing down my memories of this time. "You do what you have to do," she will say. She will become a professional nurse, the training for which begins here, in my parents' bathroom. She moves with habit as though we have always bathed our father.

He sits in a medical chair in the bath and places a washcloth over his sex. It's hard for me to discern if he cries or is winded. In contrast, Karson and I breathe silently, holding our inhales then gulping down more. We kneel at the tub and Karson turns on the faucet. Water runs forth from well fields to the west and northeast, from a reservoir in the canyons to the southeast, and from the north, where the Lake Meredith reservoir collects water syphoned from the Colorado River. From this scattering of rivers, wells, and reservoirs, Lubbock is to be supplied with water for another hundred years. And it is from these vestiges that we bathe my father.

Karson has an uncanny ability to remember the character of a person's hands, and I wonder if she will remember mine as they twist a washcloth and then run it over Dad's neck. I will remember hers: round palms and short, tapered fingers that massage soap into Dad's shoulders. I have our grandmother's hands, Karson our mother's. Hers lift a plastic gallon container, and Dad bows his head and water rushes down his hair and face and chest. We lather Dad's hair and Karson places a palm to his forehead to protect his eyes as she rinses the soap away. She holds one end of a towel while I hold the other, and Dad stands, reaches for our shoulders, and lets us band the towel to his chest. I try to treat him with respect, mindful of his privacy, though I can imagine nothing more intimate than this.

We settle him on the closed toilet lid. Karson turns to the wash-tub, fills the bucket with water, and rinses the hospital chair. The water turns brown with Dad's blood and drains.

––––––––

Another day. Dad asks me to help him walk to the bathroom. The hallway is a mile-long gallery of portraits of me and my two sisters in our ruffled cotton dresses, grinning, with braces on our teeth. I still have some of the dresses. I pull the bathroom door closed behind Dad and wait. The toilet flushes, and he opens the door. I expect him to direct me to take him back to the living room, but he gestures to his bedroom, just there. Side by side, we can't walk through the doorway. Dad lets go of my shoulder and walks in ahead of me.

His foot catches on the edge of the rug, and his arms spread as he flies forward. His chin smashes the edge of the bed, thrusting his face upward. He lands on the floor with his arms at his side.

Sun streams through the bedroom windows, casting the round shadows of the hanging baskets of petunias onto the carpet. I feel stuck in the doorway as my father falls lightly, at the rate of a feather. I could have lifted a feather at least.

My mother is home, thank God. She is in the garden, and it is easy to quickly find her. She helps me roll Dad onto his back and lift him to his knees, then lift him higher to catch one foot underneath him and then the other. We lead him to the bed. Mom goes back to her garden.

I am crying and have been, I realize, since he fell. Dad says to bring my book. He pats the space in the bed next to him. I leave briefly and return with the novel *Christy*. We enjoy the old feeling of lying on a bed. Before I turn each page of the book, I ask if he's ready.

CHAPTER 24

MOM PICKS UP THE CLINIC office phone, punches the pound key, then the number 1, waits, and apologizes to Dr. Bieri for calling him on his day off. She wants to know if he has a minute to consult on an X-ray.

"I want to make sure I'm reading it right," she says.

Dr. Bieri is a considerable man. His large palms make a brushing sound when he rubs them together. He was raised on a farm, but his dry and calloused hands could match the precision of any embroiderer or tailor, so precise and steady are they with scalpel and gut thread. Mom has told him that should she ever need surgery, she wants him to do it. He's said, with a hint of caution, that's a nice thing to say. His associate could be serious.

In the office now, he breathes ruggedly through his nose as he studies the X-ray. He mumbles his way through the dog's record. Then he speaks.

"Here we go, Dierdre. Can you bring up the Johnston dog?"

Dierdre carries the shih tzu in one hand, his IV bag in the other. She settles the dog on the treatment counter and attaches the bag to a hook strung to the ceiling with bandage tape. Dr. Bieri pinches the dog's skin, pulls back his eyelids, gags him with a finger, turns him hind-end and raises his tail, spins him sideways, and squeezes the dog's abdomen.

"Yeah," he says. He pats the dog on the back and walks back to the X-ray. I find the dog's muzzle and scratch it. His eyes are glazed. Dribble runs from his nose. I stroke his back.

"How you doing, K.D.?" Dr. Bieri asks while studying the film.

"Pretty well."

"That's good." He looks at me. "I ought to hire you officially. But there are those child labor laws."

Mom chuckles. "Doesn't stop me, does it, Kate?" I give the requisite titter. Dr. Bieri is affable. "Well," he says. He palpates the dog again. This time the canine groans.

"I think you're right, Dr. Blackburn," he says. Mom nods. The two exchange analyses. Mom says she'll call the Johnstons.

Dierdre replaces the dog in his cage. Dr. Bieri grabs a Coke from the fridge, opens it, leans back on the treatment counter, and chats up Dierdre about the latest book he's reading on Lincoln. In response to Dad's grim diagnosis, Dr. Bieri has turned tender toward my mother—one of the first blessings, Mom said, to come from Dad's illness. The resentment she felt over Dr. Bieri's allegiance to her former obstetrician has melted away. She washes her hands, says something about writing up records before appointments start.

"I better get going too," Dr. Bieri says.

"Get back to your roses," Mom says.

"Yeah."

"Thanks again."

"Not sure you needed me, but I was happy to."

He finishes his Coke, crunches the can with one hand, and with the other pats the pocket holding his keys. Reaching for the back door, he turns his face to his shoulder but doesn't look over.

"Tell John hello for me, will you? I hope he's doing all right."

I watch Mom for a sign of attrition. As a wife and mother, she can't admit to Dad's worsening state. Could she as a veterinarian? Doctor to doctor?

Mom brightens. There it is: the one note, tight and high. "Thanks, I'll tell him."

Dr. Bieri nods. The back door closes behind him.

I hover outside the office as Mom calls the shih tzu's owners.

"Well, it's not good," she says. In her voice toll bells so soft I have to strain to hear her words.

The last appointment of the day arrives. The exam room door clips shut, and Dierdre comes around with the record. Today's date is written across the top of a pink sheet and next to it, a cat's name—Fiona. Next to the name is the word *euthanasia*.

"You mind if I get back there?" Dierdre steps behind the office chair when Mom scooches it forward, bends to turn a key in a small safe, opens it, and retrieves a brown glass bottle.

The Euthasol is dyed pink. That way, Mom once explained, there aren't any mistakes. The bottle is locked away with other barbiturates and narcotics. Clinics are known to have break-ins and clients who filch the stuff on the sly. There are also stories of those the key doesn't keep out—employees and practitioners who use. Dierdre tracks every dose of controlled substance in a record book, squaring the inventory. If someone was doping, she'd know. If someone was using the Euthasol, she'd know that too. We all would.

"Who is it?" Mom says.

"Lily Patterson's cat." Dierdre passes Mom the record.

"What a way to end the day," Mom says.

At the treatment counter, Mom holds the bottle upside down and draws down the pentobarbital sodium. Neon fuchsia fills the syringe. Mom flicks the barrel.

"Does she want to stay with her?"

"She says so."

"She want us to take care of the body?"

"She's going to bury it."

Mom drops the syringe into her pocket. She asks if I want to come with her and says that the cat is gentle. I don't want to go.

"Yes," I say.

Lily Patterson is seated. She cradles her cat. The two look alike—slender, ivory and gray. Fiona wearies in her owner's lap. Her tail twitches when we walk in.

"I'm so sorry," Mom says.

Lily looks down. Her hand sweeps across Fiona's side and glides to the end of the cat's tail.

"I waited too long," she says.

"You had to go with your timing. She doesn't look like she's been suffering."

"Yeah, well." Lily wipes her eyes.

Mom lifts the syringe from her pocket. She readies hemostats and a rubber band.

"Do you want to know how it works?"

"I do."

"It's basically like a high concentration of anesthetic. She'll feel like she's going to sleep." The dose will stop the cat's heart.

Lily's hand trembles.

"I'd like to hold her."

"That's fine."

I press my back to the doorknob. The two women have forgotten that I'm here. If I open the door, they'll remember.

Mom stoops. With the back of one finger she strokes the cat's nose. The cat's eyes close. She wraps a tourniquet around Fiona's front leg, clamps it, draws the paw forward, and pats the vein. Lily kisses her cat's head. Mom pops the syringe cap, checks for the vein again, hits it, loosens the tourniquet, and pushes the pink liquid through. Fiona's body empties of air. Her jaw freezes slightly open. Her eyelids hold at half-moon. Mom pulls out the needle, covers the intrusion with her finger, waits, lifts her finger, and, seeing no blood, stands.

Lily gasps softly, a loss from the gut, as though she is shocked. When she looks up, her eyes shimmer, welling with tears. I have seen people walk who were crippled, I have seen them rise from the floor of the altar, I have seen their arms lifted in praise—and I have never witnessed in their expressions the glory that crosses Lily Patterson's face.

"Thank you," she says. "Thank you."

A whimper finds its way past Mom's lips. She tells Lily to take as much time as she needs.

Mom returns to the office, and I go to the clinic bathroom, shut the door, and submit to being wrung dry.

CHAPTER 25

THERE IS A HEALER FROM Malaysia who speaks in tongues. He is the cousin of a woman from Mom's Bible study—a woman who has never made off with Mom's tweezers. Stacy says her cousin will be in town for a week. Says he has the gift, and it is real.

The healer knocks on the front door and shakes Mom's hand. He is soft-spoken. Dad is living in the living room, how we define the term now forever changed. His abdomen is so filled with broken liver that, when he walks, he leans forward with the weight of it. He crosses the few feet from his green La-Z-Boy to the couch with a grimace and slumps in the middle. The holy man sits next to him.

"Tell me what God has put on your heart," he says.

Dad holds in his hands something no one can see, as though he can show what words fail to say.

"I've got this cancer—"

"John," Mom says. She's found her piano bench posture. This will be one of my most vivid images of my father: sitting on the couch, flanked by the holy man and my mother.

"Don't say you have cancer," Mom continues. "Say the cancer is in you." Mom reminds us that one can claim a curse, a disease, a destiny, by language alone.

Dad lifts his finger and thumb to the corners of his mouth and pinches his bottom lip. "The cancer is in me."

"Okay, John," the healer says. He lays his hand on the back of Dad's neck. I watch my father's face relax, and I imagine futures that differ from those I envisioned at tent revivals. I picture a much tamer version of healing, one absent high bawdiness and applause.

Air empty of hands. No tours testifying on the road in a big van trailing dust clouds through one Texas town after another. Instead, I believe that, if Dad is made well, my family will go back to being the homeschooled but common enough family we'd been before he was diagnosed, before the weeknight church services. Before the tent revivals. The holy man will leave, and it will all be over.

Twenty-five years later, I do not see my younger siblings in the recollection of the holy man. The moment is spotlit, as though isolated from the very space where it is set—my childhood home on Eighteenth Street in Lubbock. Beyond us sits the emptied Air Force base, its buildings stripped of their labels and repurposed for the study of gun technology. I see derelict brick structures that housed pilots, now claimed by wind and rain, slants of light falling across the floors. I see the topography to the east of the base, so flat you cannot believe it lists.

I look back and remember things I could not have known at the time, in 1998: I see a conflagration of model planes and hear the click of a timer; then thick white lather covers the ground and fields are washed as though they can be redeemed. Sludge filled with PFAS drains into the sewers. In geological time, firefighting foams destroyed groundwater in an instant. Nothing collapses time like toxicity. But no one who prayed for my father thought of those fires—though a few, like my grandparents, simmered with a rage that, searching for a target, had settled on my mother. I am the one who thinks of the fires now—I who can no longer distinguish the story of a body of water from the body of my father.

I'm sure Karson, Kendra, James, and Mary Katherine were all there. Mom liked to bring everyone together for the occasion of miracle, whether in our home or in some other place: an old Baptist church, a tent revival, an empty sanctuary. We believed that, where two or three people spoke the name of Jesus, there the air was transformed with his presence. Hence, the number of churches in Lubbock, Texas, could hardly be counted. But looking back on that afternoon, I see a congregation of only four: Dad, Mom, the healer, and me. I sat at Dad's feet and curled my legs against my chest. He took my hand. Stacy's cousin began to speak a language I'd never heard. In the way that some knowledge becomes embedded through no specific instruction, I understood that Stacy's cousin didn't know what he was saying either. The words emerged from the soul, outside human comprehension. The beauty of the language was in its expression of desires that align with what must be. Just as I'd never been slain in the spirit, never danced holy, I'd never been moved by the strange tongue. The more charismatic evangelicals might have imagined a loss in my lack of such experience: the absence of a dialect that only God and I share. It's not an unbeautiful idea.

I remember the sound of Mom's voice releasing a long "um." I opened my eyes, though we were praying. At first, I thought she couldn't find the words to say. Shock enough. Underneath her eyelids, her eyes shifted wildly. She held her chin aloft. Then she released a melisma of vowels.

There is something unresolvable about being the daughter of Beverly Jacobs Blackburn, and the essence of it lies in hearing the woman rapidly speaking with God in their private language. I heard Mom speak in tongues only this once, and it stunned me. As strange as Dad had become to me in his illness, the woman I opened my praying eyes to watch was even stranger and more unpredictable. I didn't imagine a miracle. I beheld a vision of my life to come with only my mother, a woman who spoke to God in a language I didn't understand. I gripped Dad's hand tighter.

In remembering this part of my life, I thought I would recall some conflict in Dad about choosing faith over chemotherapy. Like my relatives, I've long questioned how influenced he was by my mother. She proudly considers herself an outlier. She adopted Thomas Edison's motto that there are some people who think, some who think they think, and some who would rather die than think, putting herself in the first category. She chose to homeschool in rejection of government institutions, and to homebirth in dismissal of the medical industry, though she was a veterinarian. "Medical practice is embedded with agendas," she said. Pharmaceutical companies. Experimentation. Dad embraced each lifestyle choice, but they were Mom's ideas.

I've often imagined that Dad chose loyalty to Mom as an act of faith—in her, in God. Perhaps, like me, he struggled to distinguish between the two.

But my memory yields a man brimming with belief rather than someone in conflict. I remember how, during the prayer, he grabbed my wrist as though to keep me from falling into despair and doubt. His eyelids were pressed tightly together as the music of tongues went on and on. Dad's forehead was white, tight with determination. He squeezed my arm. My fingers turned purple. When the prayer ended, a red imprint of Dad's hand blossomed below my wrist.

In truth, my memory does not find a daughter so conflicted in her faith as I later came to be. I lived in fear, and my body registered every sign of my father's dying, but such quaking was part of my belief. I was a thirteen-year-old who couldn't comprehend the future—a future that I, now thirty-eight, have lived.

If I could collapse the years between us and appear before my younger self, I'd have a few answers for her. Dad does die, I would tell her, on a summer night at the end of June. Her faith won't be saving anyone's life, not even her own. I'd like to say, "It's not your fault." But the thirteen-year-old would refuse my claims. Evangelicals, when presented with evidence of where their future is headed, reject it. They believe the struggle is against spiritual powers of darkness, not against flesh and blood. As the children of God, their carte blanche is being in the world but not of it. The thirteen-year-old would see thirty-eight-year-old me as a perversion of communism and ignorance, a harbinger of the demonic. A check on her faith, as Satan tested Christ in the desert. The thirteen-year-old is good at tests. I say, "God didn't tell Mom about the razor," and the thirteen-year-old responds, with a rattle of anger, "Who can know the thoughts of God?"

When I remember the holy man who prayed for Dad in 1998, I think of Mom's face held aloft to heaven. I think about the way Dad later studied the red impression of his fingers across my skin. Flesh and blood.

"Whoa," Dad said. He laughed a little. "I didn't realize. I'm sorry."

We might have made good evangelists—my mother's faith one of certainty, my father's one of contradiction, and mine one of fear. Our spirituality matched any wildcat preacher's in Texas. Our house was as thick with visions and prayers as any tent.

I think about how Dad was dying even as the holy man and Mom cried *life* in tongues.

Life had become a foreign word. I think about the bruise that Dad's hand left on my arm.

CHAPTER 26

WHEN DOES FAITH TURN TO grief? Maybe the most West Texas part of me is not knowing the difference.

I lay out quilts on my parents' bedroom floor and join Kendra and Karson and James underneath them. They shudder next to me. Mom drops to her knees beside us. Mary sleeps in her arms.

"Let me lie with you," she says.

I slide Mary Katherine between us. James and Karson stretch out beside Mom, and Kendra hugs me from behind. Mom lifts the quilt, shakes and drops it across all of us. My parents' bed sits neatly made. Mom spreads her arm across us. I look at the bathroom doorway, framed by the blue cards of every scripture we had spoken but the one from James. In the gap, I glimpse a straight line where the corners of the doorframe meet. I look up at the ceiling, and it is no longer there. Above me spreads the sky. Holding us back from the spaces between the stars is only our grip on one another's hands.

Two days earlier, a Tuesday.

Mom calls hospice, whispering into the phone. It had been easier to believe in the unseen force of evil spirits than those things we could see and touch and smell: the blood staining Dad's clothes; the drying paper of his skin; the smell of rot. But the demands of his body have outpaced our belief. He needs a wheelchair and a hospital bed and a nurse to bathe him.

"Just until he gets better," Mom says.

Dad watches Mom hang up the phone and leave with her purse on her shoulder. Then he turns to me and waves, and I scramble to his side and stand on my knees next to his chair. As he had on the night we watched *Air Force One*, he holds his hand out to me. It is cold in mine. For this small gesture, I am rewarded: I have become his confidant and confessor, an accessory and accomplice, though in what exactly I can't say. In a way, I am vanishing like he is, vanishing from the living room and taking up residence on the other side of time where my father will always be alive. I am a shade more than a girl. I lean into the rank air around him and we speak. He strings words together in nonsensical phrases, and we babble and laugh. I am his fool.

"A man," he says.

"An angel?"

"In the kitchen."

"Not again."

"Come here, come here." His chapped lips brush my ear, and my hair falls between his breath and mine.

"God shows me things," he says. I pull back to look at him. His eyes shine with a dazzling clarity so astonishing I gasp. He lifts his eyebrows as though we share the revelation.

"Do you think I should be hospitalized?"

I don't understand.

"The nurses would have taken care of me," he says. "Then it would have been them instead of you and your sisters and your mom."

Dad's face creases with pain. His verb tense changes from present to past in a grammar of longing, as though he is speaking from beyond the grave already.

I whisper into our séance.

"At the hospital, they wouldn't have loved you."

I have lived now twenty-five years since I said this to my father, and since I heard his voice. One thing I do not regret is that I said it.

A hospital bed and wheelchair will arrive today, Wednesday, June 24. And today Dad's sister Lori is due as well. "Long past due," she says, sweeping blond curls behind her ears as she pulls her suitcase up the driveway. When she walks into the house, she breaks. I can only imagine how her memories of Dad clash with the almost unrecognizable man before her. She hears the disembodied voice she'd spoken to every week on the phone occupying the frail and sickened frame of a man who is both her brother and not. She collapses to her knees beside him and runs her fingers through his hair. She takes his hands between her own and kisses them. She kisses his face.

Dad wraps his finger and thumb around one of his biceps and his fingertips touch. It's the kind of gesture an evangelist needs to make his point: God is our only option. Await his mighty touch.

"I want you to accept Christ," he says.

"You know he's always been part of my life." Lori sniffs and strokes his hand. "I've read everything you've sent me."

In a different life, this would have been a scene at a revival, Dad's chair an altar. His arms reach for his sister. But it is she who ministers to him, she who, holding in her body the memory of his as a child, holds him now.

"Don't worry," she says.

By dinnertime, the wheelchair and hospital bed have still not arrived. Mom tells Lori that she attends prayer services on Wednesday nights.

"I try to go on John's behalf," she says.

"You should go, Beverly," Lori says, clearing the table of plates. They clatter in the sink. Neither woman looks at the other. "I'll watch the kids and let hospice in when they arrive. That's why I'm here."

Mom doesn't have the energy to mount annoyance at the suggestion that she needs help, or that anyone should help her, or that anyone could. She is like a scored screw—turned in place so many times it can't advance any further. She thanks Lori and faces me.

"You want to come?"

It isn't a question.

Later, I will wonder what it was like for Dad to see me depart with Mom, if there was some satisfaction for him in it, if he hoped he could die while Mom and I were gone.

Hospice workers show up and assemble a hospital bed in the family room. The joints of metal on metal click together as the staff snap the bed into place. Dad lies in the green chair and observes quietly as one man carries in the pliable white mattress and secures it.

What crosses his mind as my sisters and brother clear their toys away to make room for the new structure? In one vision, I imagine Dad deciding to release his determination to live when he sees the medical bed in his living room, a juxtaposition that tips the scales. Having refused the hospital, the hospital has come to him. There is only one way to resist it now.

In another vision, Dad is relieved. He sees the hospital bed and knows it will be comfortable. And it is the minutes of comfort he is counting when his voice leaves his body.

In yet another imaginative flight, Dad stands up from his recliner, his pain suddenly gone, his stomach flat and firm, his arms thick with round muscle. "Sorry for the trouble," he says to the hospice workers. "I won't be needing that bed after all."

Mom and I walk across the church parking lot after the prayer service. The sun sinks beneath the arches in the expressway. Sparrows dart in the dry blue of twilight. The drive home will take only ten minutes, but it has the feeling of passing into another life—just as roaming preachers once described how they felt traveling to the high plains. I look across the landscape, bereft of trees, the sign you're in the worst place on earth. That's what people believe. "Sorry," outsiders quip whenever I tell them I'm from Lubbock. I've lost count of how many times I've heard that apology; memory has collapsed them all into one line along the flat horizon of the Llano Estacado.

Folks from Lubbock usually beat outsiders to the zinger. We combine superlatives: "You bet it's the flattest place on earth," we say. "And we've got the worst weather. But the nicest people." There you have it. Two truths and a lie.

On into adulthood, I will feel myself stiffening defensively when the subject of Lubbock comes up and someone asks if there are any trees there. I will resist the urge to bite back and say, "There's more to life than trees, you British-estate-fetishizing fop"—a comeback born of my adolescent Jane Austen obsession, my deep desire to leave West Texas, and my guilt for, at last, doing so.

Mom will continue to feel a pure affection for Lubbock, and I'll never meet anyone who delights in the weather more. Admittedly, she could take or leave the wind, but she is a songbird about the occasional eighty-four-degree day in January, a month so desolate it wrings all sentimentality out of most people. She also doesn't mind the flatness. In any place you call home, she says, there will be the chores of living, and Lubbock is just as suited to getting those chores done as anywhere else. No matter where you live, she says, you have to live there.

Mom and I represent two archetypal views of West Texas: hers is a desire for comfort cushioned by a thick layer of denial; mine is an attachment oscillating between love and hate.

"Every time I go home," Mom says as we walk across the church parking lot, "I think this might be it. This may be the day I walk in and find your Dad better. He's just standing there waiting for us." With each one of her exits, Mom has teed God up. Who but her has the nerve?

"Approach the throne of God with confidence," she says, "so that you may receive mercy and find grace for help at the time of your need."

She retrieves her keys from her purse and checks her cell phone. There are six missed calls.

Karson's voice is a muddle.

"Calm down," Mom says. "We're heading home right now." She folds the phone and turns the key in the ignition.

"Your dad can't talk."

"What do you mean?"

"I don't know. Karson just said your dad isn't able to talk."

Tears stream from under Mom's sunglasses. The shades reflect the horizon's burning wire.

Dad blinks as he casts his gaze around the living room. He is lying in the hospital bed and seems to search the air for the words he can no longer say.

"What's happening?" I ask Mom. She looks thin with fear.

"I don't know."

Lori says the hospice workers weren't able to lift Dad into the bed because it was against protocol. So Karson went across the street to get help from a neighbor. Dad had gone quiet as the neighbor hefted him from the green chair to the hospital bed.

"Then everyone just left?" I say, no doubt out of my own guilt for having done the same thing so many times before.

"K.D., please." Mom bends over Dad. "John, can you hear me? Do you understand what's happening?" Dad tilts his face toward her. His eyes flutter, and then his face lolls the other way. Karson and Kendra and James and Mary Katherine stand timidly around the bed. Their young faces glance from mine to one another's to Dad's.

I do the only thing I know to do. "I'm going to call some people," I say.

I call Pastor Shawn. I call Kelly and Jesse and the cop Brad. Then I call Roy. When I hear his voice, I start crying.

"I'm coming now," he says.

When, in years to come, my grandmother lifts her finger to point above her sickbed and asks if I can see the Air Force insignia spread like wings above her, I will remember standing at Dad's side on the last night of his life.

Roy walks in and drapes his arms across my father and weeps. And then the same men who thirteen months earlier walked down the long hallway to pray down the first healing surround my father to pray down the last.

Reflecting upon this years later, Roy's wife Loretta will say, "We tried to keep him alive. We did, K.D. But every single one of us has an appointment to keep."

Jesse crosses the living room and pulls me to his chest. He is bony and too strongly cologned. I do not find warmth there, but a racing heartbeat and trembling muscle. I pull away and turn to my father. His mouth is a dark pit in his face. He has turned gray.

There is a howl like I have never heard. I look around the living room. The shriek comes from elsewhere. I find Andy, wretched and almost rabid. I let him out to the backyard, and he runs in circles under the oak tree and yelps. Jesse follows me onto the porch. Andy charges him, throws his paws up, and nails Jesse in the chest.

Back in the kitchen light I see that Andy ripped Jesse's shirt and broke the skin.

"That dog's only ever liked us," I say.

Dad gasps for breath. His mouth opens for air with surprise. Between the prayers, in the silence after each exhale, the men cry *breathe*.

The white book light we gave Dad for Father's Day rests on the table next to him. Mom picks up the light, clicks it on, and holds it to Dad's gaping mouth. She chokes. Dad closes his arm over his eyes. "There's blood," she says. I ask what it means. No one answers.

I run to find the words adhered to the bathroom doorframe and snatch the scripture from James and sprint back down the hall. Shouldering through the circle, I force my way to Dad's side and hold up the scripture.

"Is any sick among you?" I say. He lifts his chin and meets my eye, and I tremble. A knot thickens in my throat. "Let him call for the elders of the church," I say. "And let them pray over him, anointing him with oil in the name of the Lord, and the prayer of faith shall save the sick." Around the scripture, I close my fist. "It says you'll be healed. Dad, it says you will."

Someone pulls me away, and one of the men moves into the space where I stood.

Then Lori kneels beside Dad as she did when she arrived. She leans under the men's arms and runs her fingers through his hair. Beneath the strings of prayer, she speaks to Dad.

"Johnny," she says. "You're running." She smooths his hair back from his forehead. "This is wind."

Near midnight, almost four hours after Dad stopped speaking, Mom stands back from the prayer group and says that her eyes are burning. She bends over Dad and touches his hand.

"John, I have to go change my contacts. I'll be right back." Then she disappears to the back of the house.

We all chant *breathe, breathe.* The wings of Dad's rib cage flutter open, then fold, then flutter and hold open. Above him pleads everyone but my mother. Later she will say he snuck off while she was away.

I race the length of the hallway. Mom stands in front of her mirror, putting her glasses on. How simple it looks. Putting on glasses.

"He's not breathing," I say.

Mom lets out an unbearable cry. She runs ahead of me.

I am alone in the hallway when I realize my father's gone. I hear him leave. It is a sound like voices rising that with relief bursts.

EPILOGUE

PART I

Spring 2017. Dad has been gone almost nineteen years. I am living in a village on the western edge of Chicago's city limits. Mine is the second-to-last stop on the Chicago Transit Authority's blue line. Forest Park is a small country of dads: dads barbecuing, dads pushing lawn mowers and baby strollers. I saw one the other day in Oak Park, the posh village next door. He was carrying his kid and his kid's stroller, and he walked right into a Frank Lloyd Wright house. He appeared to live there. A plaque told me it was the Hills-Decaro house, its roofs pitched like a Japanese temple. The dad was wearing shorts and a ball cap and tennis shoes. He was probably a generic millionaire, but he appeared to be a generic dad, living in a Frank Lloyd Wright house.

My husband and I moved to Forest Park to be near the train, which carries me quickly to the university where I'm completing graduate work in English. We live in a brown bungalow next to a car wash called Crystal Car Wash. In front of our house stands a sickly maple that nevertheless prevails, blossoming in violent pink buds that are downright phallic. We have one couch, fully occupied by our two dogs and our cat. We chose Forest Park because here we could afford a place with a yard for our dogs, who in return have made of the garden a dirt patch. From a Forest Park bridge arching above the Eisenhower freeway, I can see downtown Chicago. Beyond it, I picture the shores of Lake Michigan, a body of water so vast that I feel its waves surge west to greet me.

A few days before Easter, I receive a package in the mail from Mom. Her neat writing appears in the left-hand corner of the label, above the address for the white brick ranch-style on Eighteenth

Street. Actually, that's not quite right. She's had the house painted. It's gray now. She lives there with her husband and their son, my baby brother, who was born when I was twenty-two and Mom was forty-seven. She's still the kind of woman who likes particular kinds of risks. Can't resist them.

Inside the package is a basket filled with glossy plastic grass. Artificial pastel eggs peek through the fake turf. They are filled with speckled-robin malted milk balls. More candy hides near the bottom of the basket: Reese's peanut butter eggs and bite-sized Butterfingers, my favorite. Her card says, "Happy Resurrection Day!" She doesn't say *Easter* because of something she read about Ishtar being the Mesopotamian goddess of fertility. Given her own efforts to bear children, you'd think Mom might have made an exception for Ishtar/Easter. If you didn't know her, you'd think that.

As with most of Mom's beliefs, part of her position is steeped in fact. Under the Roman empire, Christianity appropriated the pagan rituals of places and peoples colonized by the Romans. Some researchers claim the empire's aim was to convert the unconverted by allowing them to retain their former traditions as the reborn.

But only part of Ishtar's symbolism is connected to fertility. She was worshiped as the goddess of sex and war, as well as fate and storms. Her followers practiced sacred prostitution: women having sex with strangers in exchange for divine blessing. These days we just call it ethical nonmonogamy. Contrary to what the near-homonyms Ishtar and Easter would suggest, the word *easter* comes from the German *Eostre*. But this derivation doesn't get us out of the god paradigm either: *Eostre* is the goddess of the dawn, the bringer of light.

As for the fertile egg, some say the ancient Egyptians told a story of creation in which a cosmic goose gives birth to the sun. It is said that from this sun emerged the phoenix, a glorious red and gold bird. Which brings us back to resurrection. In the basket, Mom has included a thumb drive. Her card explains that she has had all the family home videos converted to a digital format.

I'm surprised by this gift. The last two decades have been a long diminuendo into silence about my father. No one in my family really speaks of the years before he died, as though any joy remembered there would only amplify the trauma and shame we experienced in his illness, the grief in his absence. I haven't seen most of the footage. After Dad died, I couldn't bring myself to look at old photos, much less watch the recordings of what seemed to me a past so distant it didn't appear to be mine at all. I put the thumb drive in a dresser drawer and shut it.

The last time I saw my father was in 1998, technically June 25, though he had been hours in his dying, and I think he must have drawn his last breath some minutes before midnight. The recorded time of his death reflects our delay in understanding that he had died. Strange how cancer takes one part of the body at a time. First it was Dad's colon, then his liver, then his voice. He was catatonic during the last five hours of his life, and during the final month he couldn't walk. For the previous year, my family had believed he would live, and this faith circumscribed the ever-present threat of death. Who can locate in time the moment when a person dies if their demise is so accumulative?

Over the years, Dad's face has made some appearances. At my great-aunt Gayle's eightieth birthday party, Dad's face emerged in the features of Gayle's nephew Tommy, my father's second cousin. I wasn't at the event, but Aunt Lori told me that her second cousin walked and talked and laughed like Dad. As one can imagine, the resemblance got all the Blackburns stirred up. Great-aunt Gayle's birthday devolved into a bunch of white people crying out in celebration: "It's John! It's John!" I imagine some of the Blackburns felt like their Johnny had returned to them, if briefly, from an exile that began when he married my mother. "Aren't genetics the darndest thing?" Aunt Lori said.

When Dad was alive, his taut face was clearly of sound Irish origin. He looked like the story of his life: captain of the football team, commercial pilot, carpenter, husband, father. But once, a few years ago, I caught a glimpse of Dad's face in Uncle Bobby's face, and it had changed. All his features were sliding down, especially at the eyes, which had almost always held a long gaze. This isn't to say that

Dad's face was conspicuous in Bobby's; he was a courteous resident. I had to stare from some distance, focusing hard, like you do when you're looking into one of those stereogram 3-D images and a shape emerges from behind the surface, or so it seems. I gazed steadily, then let my focus shift, as though looking at my own reflection. Then Bobby said, "How's that?"

I also once caught Bobby calling on my dad in my face. We were at a taco place in Universal City that smelled like salsa and Pine-Sol and sounded like tortilla chips crunching in the mouths of all my relatives. I felt a cool airstream and looked up. Bobby's eyes were like words or hands, knocking at my face door. He didn't see me looking back at him, or he would have dodged. No, he was looking at his brother. I saw the deep love and also something like pleading, a word like *stay* that couldn't form and then dissipated across Bobby's expression as he looked away.

Since Bobby's death, I've stopped looking for Dad's face, even with all these dads everywhere. One of them just walked by. A balding dad in khaki shorts, pulling his little girl in a red silicone wagon. She was pointing at something behind her, and he was singing to her to the tune of "The Wheels on the Bus Go Round and Round." He sang, "You just saw your shadow, your shadow, your shadow."

Down from our bungalow in Forest Park lives a woman with a neon sign in her window that says PSYCHIC. We had lived in Forest Park three days before I went to see her. All I had was a twenty. She said it was enough. Bent over a spread of Tarot cards, she said a man follows me.

"Do you know who it is?" she asked.

"My dad."

She lifted a card with the image of a heart and three swords and told me I would have three children. At the end, she said, "You are destined to live by water," which I took as an easy guess as I had just moved into Lake Michigan's watershed. But I didn't realize, while sitting in the psychic's living room, that I always had.

Water is, of course, part of most creation stories, including contemporary ones. A woman I met while traveling up the shores of Lake Michigan told me that when she was pregnant doctors warned her that the baby would come too early to survive. So she stood in the waters of the lake, and they helped her carry her baby. She said she could feel healing in the currents.

And there is my own creation story. A story of water that begins with fire.

In June of 2017, the nineteenth anniversary of Dad's death passes, and I retrieve the thumb drive that Mom sent for Resurrection Day. I tell myself that nineteen years is long enough. I imagine I can view whatever images are stored in this small device from a safe distance. I don't expect the past to erupt; it has lain latent for almost two decades. We lie to ourselves to approach the truth.

The footage begins with Dad sitting in the center of the frame. The walls surrounding him are built of cinder block, made to withstand Pacific typhoons. It is 1984. He and Mom are living on Guam, an island no wider than twelve miles at its widest point. The United States acquired the island in 1898 as part of the treaty ending the Spanish-American War. Before that, Spanish imperialists had occupied the island since 1521. But the island belongs to the Chamorro, whose creation story holds that humans originated from their ancient ancestor Fu'una, a woman who gave up her body for the creation of mankind because she was lonely. Fu'una walked into the ocean and hardened into rock, the legend goes. As the tide pulled across her, she dissolved into particles of sand that bore her spirit. These grains of earth emerged as people, who either stayed on Guam or spread across the world. The first Spanish imperialists led by Ferdinand Magellan appeared on the Pacific horizon in 1521, just twenty years before Francisco Vásquez de Coronado traversed Apache land in what is now considered West Texas and called it an ocean of prairie grass. At the sight of Magellan's crew, the Chamorro, thinking their brothers and sisters had at last returned from an impossible diaspora, rushed out in canoes to greet their murderers.

Dad looks at the camera and greets his parents, "Hey, Mom and

Dad." The sound of his voice shoots through me. He is twenty-five, with the alto voice of a man younger than I am now. Something inside me splits open. A Christmas tree glistens next to Dad, and he holds an infant not a month old. He introduces her. "This is Kathleen Dorothy. We're calling her by her initials, K.D. Of course, you try to explain this to people, but when I went back to the office, they had a cake and big banner that said, 'Welcome, K-A-T-I-E.' I told them it was the letters, 'K period, D period.' But it was a nice party and everything." I laugh. Dad has just described in full the experience I have had all my life trying to explain my name. And despite all the explanations, while he lived, Dad called me Kate.

In 1984, Aunt Lori was the first to get the news that my parents' baby was a girl. She phoned Grandma. "You know what they named her, don't you?" she asked. Grandma didn't. "They named her after you." Lori says Grandma wept.

Dad points around the living room, says it's real nice. He gestures to the corners of a wicker coffee table. The dogs have chewed the table's edges down to nubs. The military set my parents up with the furniture and are expecting its return when Dad is restationed. "We're going to have to convince them it came like this," Dad says.

As Dad continues his video letter, there is the sound of cabinets clapping shut. Dad pauses and looks over his shoulder. "Beverly, come say hi."

Mom's voice is muffled. I hear a sound like "what." Dad waves her in. "Come on. Come say hi." The cabinets go silent, and Mom appears. She always said that she never much cared for Guam. The narrow island made her feel claustrophobic. Part of me sympathizes. Exists there a person more outsized than Beverly Jacobs? Not for me. But in the video she looks slight and human and very young. She wears high-waisted shorts and glasses with enormous frames. Dad does all the talking. Mom doesn't look at the camera. She gazes at the fat, bald baby in Dad's arms. My head slouches to the side, and Dad cups it with his hand. "She's a good one," he says. "She's strong."

Watching Dad's video letter, I go quiet. For a month afterward,

I can only talk to my husband, when I speak at all. We pack up the dogs, and Michael drives us north to Michigan, where we stay in a small room with wood paneling at an old inn that I swear smells just like my grandmother's house in Universal City, though I haven't been there in five years. I sleep very little. It's maudlin to admit this, but I spend most of our trip crying. Standing on the shores of Lake Michigan, I feel this twenty-year period without my father collapsing in on itself—an infinitesimal amount of time when one considers how glaciers carved the bed of the Great Lakes. I speak in heavy metaphors, saying every memory is erupting in a flood I can't control. I remember things I've told no one: a traveling evangelist; my mother speaking in tongues; the verses in the doorway; Dad begging for codeine; my grandmother sobbing into his chest; Dad's hand between my own. Stories my family and I have never shared, even with one another. I speak in ghost tales, telling Michael I feel Dad next to me. I say that I am having a nervous breakdown.

PART 2

Summer 2023. Six years ago, Mom sent the thumb drive with the videos to each one of her adult children, a generous gesture, and a surprising one, as none of us talk together about the past. It was a rare acknowledgment of a shared and painful history. Mary Katherine, who is now twenty-seven, is the only sibling who has talked to me about watching the footage. We have even viewed some of it together, holding hands tightly at the sight of an infant Mary learning to walk within a diamond formed by the outstretched arms of our father and me. Mary and I often try to piece together our childhoods. Because we are eleven years apart, at opposing ends of a time line, it feels a bit like corresponding with each other from opposite coasts of the same country.

I've had brief, spontaneous conversations with Karson and Kendra about moments from when our father was sick, some of which have been included in this memoir. Those exchanges have felt simultaneously numbing and startlingly brutal; the wounds our words touch feel very live. My brother James and I, to my recollection, have never once talked about my father's illness.

Following my father's death, it took a great deal of energy, much of it semiconscious, to manage the shame and grief of those thirteen months when he was sick. When I watched the video footage, I felt the two decades of that effort come undone in about three and a half seconds. It was an astonishing physiological experience, to say nothing of being reduced to a sobbing heap. My brain turned to fizz. So when I say I understand why my siblings may not want to talk about the past—or may have found their own ways of doing so that do not involve me—I cannot overstate my respect for their boundaries. Karson is thirty-six, with two sons. Kendra is thirty-three and a two-stepping queen. James, at thirty-one, is ex-Air Force and a surfer. They lead enormous lives that are deeply complex and private. As a rule, they do not often read my writing.

I have sometimes wondered if we avoid discussions about the past because we may realize we have different versions of what happened. We bonded deeply as children. I even fall into using the first-person plural *we* when I recall it now. I did not think of myself as a separate individual when I was a child, except perhaps those times when I thought of myself as their mother, to my sister Karson's great chagrin. My experience might feel like a violence or a betrayal to my siblings if it differs from their own experience.

But when I told my sister Karson that I was writing a memoir, she told me something that caused me to consider the exact opposite. She said, "If anything you write is true, I won't be able to bear it." After hearing this, I began to think that my siblings and I avoid talking about the past, not because we share different versions of the truth, but because of the sheer force of a shared truth. The power of it. But why is it so unbearable? Maybe my sisters and brother would say, like my grandmother, *What's the point of talking about it? We know what happened.* But do we know what it means?

My sister Mary Katherine read this book in manuscript form. Before she read it, she told me she was nervous. She didn't know what was so terrible. Why all the silence? I promised her I wrote everything I remembered. She read the pages in two days, and then she called me. Her critique extended beyond the family. She said the silence in our family was representative of the problem with whiteness in general. We are too committed to the myth of our innocence. We refuse to face ourselves. "But there is nothing here that can't be talked about," she said.

Dad's next video letter opens with two sleek greyhound mixes running after a tennis ball. They are Jake and Kelly, my parents' first dogs. They dash across a plain of such shimmering brilliance that the grass looks like a river. I don't hear Dad's voice, but I see a ball launched from behind the camera and I realize I am seeing what Dad wants to show us. We are watching through his storyteller's eye. The recording cuts to the windshield of a car through which I see a curving road wind through Guam's forests.

I once used to think that Guam emerged from the ocean as a volcano. This is easy to imagine as Dad aims the camera at mighty bluffs overlooking the rowdy waves of the Pacific. "I love running by these cliffs," he says. "And it's too bad the governor here hasn't run over one of them."

Mom drives the car. She says, "It's getting dark," and I hear the voice of the woman who raised me. Michael watches the footage too and laughs. "So she's always been like that," he says.

During the Eocene, the earth's floor slipped, and the Pacific plate slid beneath the Philippine plate—such a simple way to describe an earthquake. The plates trenched, and the magma that resulted from the collision sprang up into a string of volcanoes. And it was refuse from these underwater mountains of fire that gathered on the western side of the trench to form Guam.

For so long I was haunted by my father's face, but because I considered water, especially in West Texas, to be invisible, I couldn't see the water in him or in my family's story. Too often, I thought of water as a glass sheen on the earth's surface. To me, living in West

Texas, water was something far away, cresting beaches I had never seen. I knew there was an aquifer underground, but the dry dust and red clay of Lubbock's terrain suggested that water, however alive, was deeply buried. Only by learning of legacy chemicals can I now see everywhere in the story of my family the water that shaped it. I hear water in my father's voice. I smell water in his blood, ancient water transformed by a process that began with touching flame to jet fuel so as to demonstrate the power of a chemical to extinguish the deadliest fire. Such power has come at the cost of over seven hundred groundwater sources at military sites that are considered compromised. One of those sites is Colorado Springs, where Dad was born. Another is Universal City, where he was raised. Another is Lubbock, where he is buried.

The Environmental Working Group (EWG), a nonprofit activist organization, maintains a digital map of known and suspected discharges of PFAS from military bases that displays a staggering number of clusters of orange and purple dots across the United States: purple for confirmed contamination, orange for suspected. The map brings to mind CT-scan images showing how many cancerous lesions are scattered across a body.

The consequences of PFA exposure can be devastating. Stillborns, varying kinds of cancer, ulcerative colitis, liver failure, and kidney failure are among the most commonly identified effects of PFAS. Forever chemicals are now found ubiquitously across species. A sketch of the chemical's molecular anatomy looks like a centipede, each leg a bond of carbon and fluoride that crawls through all of us, as all oil-based products require oil-resistant counteractive products to cope with them. Anyone who has used a nonstick pan or owned a couch is a hybrid of chemical and water. But toxicity is a matter of amount and duration of exposure. The groundwater surrounding some Air Force sites abounds with PFA amounts that are three thousand times higher than the federal health limit. It is possible that Dad drank carcinogenic water for most of his life.

The environmental violence of PFAS, like that of radiation and PCBs, can be difficult to demonstrate. The impacts of PFAS are diffuse across geographies and across time. In a world where we think of cause and effect as something like a gun and a bullet, the slower, less instant forms of destruction often hide in plain sight, in bodies of water and land and people.

In 1997, the year of Dad's diagnosis, 3M stock rose to a high of $52.75 per share. In 1999, an environmental specialist, Richard Purdy, resigned his position at 3M, citing the company's inaction despite his claim that PFOS, a type of polyfluoroalkyl used in fire-fighting foams, were the most insidious pollutants to enter the environment since the manufacturing of polychlorinated byphenals—a carcinogenic chemical that was banned in 1979. In his resignation letter, Purdy referenced the gag order placed on scientists hired by 3M to analyze the impacts of fluorochemicals and reported their findings that PFOS in animal DNA indicate a widespread transfer. These findings, he wrote, were shelved, and the company put off performing ecological risk assessment for over twenty years. "I am told the company is concerned," his letter stated. "But their actions speak to different concerns than mine. For me it is unethical to be concerned with markets, legal defensibility and image over environmental safety."

Purdy's letter became public as part of a lawsuit filed by the state of Minnesota against 3M in 2010 after more than thirty years of industry use and waste of perfluorochemicals. The company's net worth reached an all-time high of over $149 billion with a price per share of $259.77 in 2018, the same year it paid $850 million to the state of Minnesota to settle the lawsuit.

To date, the companies that manufacture PFAS—DuPont, 3M, Chemours, and Corteva—have paid over $11.5 billion in damages for contamination. They have consistently denied before Congress having any responsibility for the toxicity draining from their manufacturing facilities. The vice president of 3M, Denise Rutherford, claims that the chemicals pose no threats to public health. She has gone on record saying there have been no victims of PFA contamination.

The EWG map does not show contamination at US military

sites abroad, but in 2018 the Office of the Attorney General of Guam filed a lawsuit to make the designers, manufacturers, marketers, and sellers of aqueous film-forming foam (AFFF) pay for the damage done to Guam's environment. Guam's attorney general released the "Guam PFAS Fact Sheet," which includes a time line showing that, in the 1940s, 3M first produced a chemical that prior to World War II didn't exist on the planet at all but now invades every organic body on the planet. The time line marks 1960 as the year the Pentagon purchased AFFFS exclusively from 3M. In 1975, 3M found that PFOAs were universally present in samples from people living across the United States.

Robert Bilott is an environmental attorney known for bringing hallmark lawsuits against DuPont that recovered $753 million in individual damages caused by exposure to forever chemicals. Currently leading lawsuits against DuPont, Bilott describes PFAS as ubiquitous, affecting not only isolated communities, but spreading throughout global waters and the blood of most species as manufacturing industries profit and fight those injured by these chemicals.

In March 2023, the Environmental Protection Agency took some unprecedented steps toward addressing forever chemicals. The agency established new standards, called maximum contaminant levels (MCLs), that target six notorious PFAS—including those often associated with historic firefighting foams—and set the highest level allowed in drinking water at four parts per trillion, the lowest threshold to date. These are the first federally proposed drinking water limits for PFAS, and according to EWG vice president Scott Faber, they mark historic progress for the EPA. "The EPA's proposed limits also serve," Faber adds, "as a stark reminder of just how toxic these chemicals are to human health at very low levels."

In Dad's last video letter, he flies into a typhoon. The footage opens with the ramp to a C-130 cargo plane and Dad's voice announcing that he is going to take his parents up into the storm. In the next shot, Dad fills the frame. A crew member holds the camera as Dad swivels in his pilot's seat, cocking one eyebrow as the plane rattles with the turbulence. He smirks a little with each jolt. Not a hint of caution troubles his expression.

Dad is holding the camera again for the final shot, which opens with a view of the clearing above the storm, and it is this, I think, that he wanted us to see. The plane glides in gold light. On the horizon, the sun radiates a deep, violent red. The color shocks me. I wonder if Dad will pan away from it to show more of the sky's landscape, the peak of cumulus clouds like the tops of mountains. The east drawing its purple curtain. But Dad zooms in on the red light as though he himself were drawing nearer to it. He is fixated. The lustrous crimson expands to fill the frame, as deep and reverberating as a wound.

Surely stored on the very plane Dad and his crew flew above the typhoon was an extinguisher filled with firefighting foam.

But Dad leads me closer to the edge of sky where something like fire burns. A hemorrhaging light on the horizon, as it was at creation. The atmosphere erupting in glorious bursts of sun and blood. What he beholds there he beholds with astonishment. Red is the last color we see. Then Dad lowers the camera and the aircraft descends into the rain.

ACKNOWLEDGMENTS

I WROTE THIS BOOK OVER the course of six years and spent several years prior becoming the writer who could accomplish it. There are many people I am eager to thank.

Casey Kittrell, thank you for taking this book all the way with me. It was a sheer, reckless joy to work with an editor I trusted so completely. Your brilliant sensitivity to language and story made this memoir better, and I too am better for it. To everyone at the University of Texas Press, especially Danni Bens, Robert Kimzey, Gianna LaMorte, Cameron Ludwick, Bailey Morrison, Joel Pinckney, Christina Vargas, Elizabeth Winkler—the best damn band in the land—thank you for believing in this memoir and ensuring it will reach readers.

To Cynthia Buck, my humble and endless gratitude for your precision and talent in fine-tuning the music herein.

Sarah Schulte, that this story of bombastic tent revivals and high plains desperation should meet with the surreal dreamscape of your artistic brilliance leaves me in awe. Thank you for engaging with the fine art of Jack Spencer to design such an arresting cover.

To my agent, Jennifer Lyons, thank you for taking a chance on me and for your tireless advocacy.

There are many paths to publication, and mine was lit by the lightning thrower Luis Alberto Urrea, whose literary genius is matched only by his generosity and humor. Luis, thank you for helping me to resurrect this story and find its way home.

For his tenacity and resourcefulness, I am grateful to my research assistant Finn Hartnett. I am also thankful to Sophia Kang for her sophisticated and scrupulous fact-checking.

For editorial feedback on early chapters that were accepted for publication, which helped to bolster my confidence in the project and to shape the rest of the book, my thanks to CMarie Fuhrman, Joshua Gottlieb-Miller, Jonathan Bohr Heinen, and Toni Jensen.

What successes in craft this book might boast are largely owed to the opportunities offered by the creative writing programs at Texas Tech University, the MFA program at Ohio State University, and the Program for Writers at the University of Illinois at Chicago and to the feedback and generosity of their students and faculty. I am especially grateful to Jill Patterson for bringing me on board at *Iron Horse Literary Review* and holding on to me ever since; to Lee K. Abbott and Andrew Hudgins for teaching me to commit to the sentiment; to Lee Martin for endlessly believing in me as a writer; and to Erin McGraw for LOBE.

Dennis Covington was the first writer to take me on as a student. Dennis, whatever I accomplish in my career is a tribute to you, my friend, my heart.

This book owes its heritage to Kim Barnes's *In The Wilderness*, which Dennis Covington placed in my hands twenty years ago. How stunned I would have been then to know that she would help me shepherd my own story into the world. My thanks to you, Kim, for the feedback and conversations that pointed me in the right direction.

I completed the research for this book and many drafts during my doctoral studies at the University of Illinois at Chicago, and I am deeply grateful to the following people: every member of Bad Larry and the Shartlettes, Daniel Borzutzky, Victoria Bolf, Margaux Brown, Peter Coviello, Rachel Havrelock and the team at the Freshwater Lab, Carrie McGath, Ann-Marie McManaman, and Alonzo Rico.

I had the good fortune of working with wonderful students at the University of Illinois at Chicago and at the University of Chicago while writing this memoir. A special shout-out to the "Stories of Water" class at the University of Chicago in the spring of 2021 for their experimentation and insights, which helped me to reimagine what an environmental narrative could be.

To the wonderful faculty and staff in the Creative Writing Program at the University of Chicago, thank you for your support, friendship, and inspiration.

For reading my work, talking me through my soul's dark nights, and saying the right thing at the right time: Carla Barger-Haddad and Jessie Haddad, Cristina Garcia, Lindsay Gerano, JBH, Sarah Kuntz Jones, Christopher Kellerman, the LPG (Nancy Dinan, Kate Simonian, Jess Smith, Sarah Viren, and Kelsy Yates), Dave Lucas, Kim O'Neil, Allison-You're-My-Only-Spikes, Evan Steuber, the Thai McGuckin Family, Cecilia Villarruel, and Nick White.

For being the reader who keeps my voice true, Mary Katherine Lucas.

To my friends in Secrets Burst, my first writing group—Anthony, Ashley, Bonnie, Emerson, Eric, Meghan, and Taryn—thank you for reading the worst first lines I ever wrote. The final chapter's last line is an homage to you all.

To Alan, thank you for being in my corner. I miss you.

Now for the deep cut: Katy Gillan, Kristen-my-soul-sister-Lewis, Grace Park, Carrie Wiley, and Lora Williams—may I live a long life with such friends as you.

I am very grateful to the friends who spoke with me during my research for this book. Especially to Sonia Evans, Becky Johnson, and Wren Manners; and to my family members Thomas Blackburn IV, Richard Kennedy, and Susan Malaska, for their willingness to share memories and to answer questions about our family history. A champion in this category was my aunt Lori, who spoke to me for countless hours over the last six years, comparing notes, filling in gaps, and tracing the absences of what will remain unknown. I don't think writing memoir is cathartic, but good lord, those conversations with you, Lori, were some of the greatest gifts of healing to come from this process. Thank you for being there twenty-five years ago, and for being here now.

To my uncle Bobby, my grandfather, and my tiny Irish blue fire of a grandmother, thank you for the stories. I'm glad we're not done with each other yet.

To my three sisters, my brother, my mother, and my father, the six people whom I have hoped to honor in each sentence of this book: Each one of you lived some version of this story along with me. I have tried to leave room for the truth of your experiences. Much has changed since I was a child, but in writing this book, I was reminded that I once believed that the greatest blessing of my life was being a daughter and sister in our family. That remains unchanged.

For all the ways you've showed up, Marc, I'm grateful.

Ian, life is so much fuller and more fun with you in it.

DJ Lucas, you have given of your talent, humor, and support so generously; thank you.

Kody, Kaiden, and Lincoln: I love you three wildly.

To the Palmers—Kaye, Bruce, River, Amanda, Matt, Chelsea, Lydia, Afton, Atticus, and Cora—thank you for loving me as one of your own.

To my son, whose name means *young at heart*: if this book looks to the past, you draw me back to this joyous present.

On a road trip between Nebraska and Austin in 2014, I told my husband some of this story. It was the first time I ever spoke any of it aloud. And he was the first person to tell me I had a story. Michael, for reading the earliest draft and the last and every attempt in between, for picking my body up from a sobbing heap and setting it back at the desk, for your editor's eye, for your artist's ear, for your writer's understanding of every practical need, for your belief in me, for your conviction reflected in these pages: all my life, all my love.

A coda for my dad: Since he's been gone, my father has felt closer in the last six years as I wrote than in the nineteen years prior. Dad, thank you for imparting to me a love of story that would lead me back to you. Thank you for your poetry and for a story so beautiful I could not keep it to myself. Stay near. I can still hear you.

SOURCES FOR PFAS RESEARCH

Over the course of six years, I wrote five versions of this book. With each revision came a new possibility of what kind of book it might be. There were times when it appeared to be a work of investigative nonfiction. Other times, it seemed it could be entirely narrative, with no need for extensive research.

The book you hold in your hands, like most books of its kind, is informed by each revision that came before it. The process over the years was paradoxical: the more research I completed and the more I wrote, the more mystery and contradiction the story revealed. Ultimately, we—the publishers and I—agreed that this is a *memoir*, a genre with a strong relationship to uncertainty. The research for *Loose of Earth* helps to illuminate parts of the narrative, but these cracks of light throw long shadows.

Uncertainty is also a big player in our current understanding of the environmental and health impacts of PFAS. Recently, the August 16, 2023, issue of the *New York Times Magazine* centered the headline of Kim Tingley's article, "'Forever Chemicals' Are Everywhere. What Are They Doing to Us?" *Forever chemicals* refers to the carbon-fluorine bonds that refuse to degrade in nature, but I've also come to think of the term as a metaphor for persisting beyond one's full grasp.

Firefighting foams were once called *light water*. The beauty of those words stumps me. So-called light water should have been something fleeting, the stuff of magic, capable of snuffing out the deadliest fire in an instant and then vanishing. The term was used by industry. Manufacturers built the myth of light water to conceal the destruction wrought by PFAS.

Meanwhile, instead of disappearing, light water simply went underground and became permanent, contaminating our pervasive sources of life—water, soil, blood. Scientists, journalists, activists, attorneys, policy experts, and people living in changed ecosystems have committed to the exhaustive work of understanding the molecules that were supposed to disintegrate but didn't even as the elements of our world that could have lasted are disappearing all too quickly. Separating the myth of light water from the reality of PFAS has been, as one researcher told me, an uphill battle.

In what follows, I acknowledge my debt to those who have fought that uphill battle and continue to do the extraordinary heavy lifting of investigation that helped me understand more of my own story. My research on per- and polyfluoroalkyl chemicals was based on many sources. The summary here is a selection featuring those that most directly shaped the memoir and that also, I hope, might offer the interested person a starting point for further reading.

Rob Nixon's 2011 book *Slow Violence and the Environmentalism of the Poor* has been essential to my understanding of the diffuse, delayed, deliberately obfuscated, and unequally distributed consequences of ecological harm like those of PFAS pollution and exposure. I write in my epilogue that the environmental violence of PFAS is often not perceived as violence, and this insight owes its wisdom to Nixon.

No list of starting points for key texts on PFAS would be complete without the following books:

Bilot, Rob. *Exposure: Poisoned Water, Corporate Greed, and One Lawyer's Twenty-Year Battle against DuPont.* New York: Simon & Schuster, 2019.

Lyons, Callie. *Stain-Resistant, Nonstick, Waterproof, and Lethal: The Hidden Dangers of C8.* Westport, CT: Praeger, 2007.

Magner, Mike. *A Trust Betrayed: The Untold Story of Camp Lejeune and the Poisoning of Generations of Marines and Their Families.* New York: Da Capo Press, 2014.

The Interstate Technology and Regulatory Council (ITRC) maintains "Technical Resources for Addressing Environmental Releases of Per- and Polyfluoroalkyl Substances (PFAS)," an impressive and fairly comprehensive online source that includes PFAS fact sheets, regulatory guidelines, and deep dives into AFFF information, water treatment, and toxicological reports (https://pfas-1.itrcweb.org/).

The Environmental Working Group is another comprehensive online resource. EWG maintains a digital interactive map, entitled "PFAS Contamination in the US," that documents PFAS pollution in public and private water systems. The map was crucial in helping me identify the military sites with confirmed PFAS contamination where my father lived and worked (https://www.ewg.org/interactive-maps/pfas_contamination).

I found some of the most compelling details about the USS *Forrestal* fire in the photographs and historical accounts of the digital historical collections of the Naval History and Heritage Command, specifically files H-008-6 and CVA-59 (https://www.history.navy.mil/about-us/leadership /director/directors-corner/h-grams/h-gram-008/h-008-6.html#:~: text=On%2029%20July%201967%2C%20Forrestal,ship%20since %20World%20War%20II; https://www.history.navy.mil/browse-by-topic /ships/aircraft-carriers/forrestal.html). Additional sources that amplified my discussion in chapter 6 of the *Forrestal* fire and the widespread adoption by the Department of Defense of AFFFs include:

American Cancer Society. "Perfluorooctanoic Acid (PFOA), Perfluorooctane Sulfonate (PFOS), and Related Chemicals." March 21, 2023.
https://www.cancer.org/cancer/risk-prevention/chemicals/teflon-and-
perfluorooctanoic-acid-pfoa.html.
Back, Gerard G., Edward Hawthorne, and Casey Grant. *Firefighting
Foams: Fire Service Roadmap.* Quincy, MA: National Fire Protection
Association, May 2022. https://www.nfpa.org/-/media/Files/News-
and-Research/Fire-statistics-and-reports/Emergency-responders/RFFir
efightingFoamsFireServiceRoadmap.pdf.
Lerner, Sharon. "The US Military Is Spending Millions to Replace
Toxic Firefighting Foam with Toxic Firefighting Foam." *The Intercept*,
February 10, 2018. https://theintercept.com/2018/02/10/firefighting-
foam-afff-pfos-pfoa-epa/.
Lim, Xiao Zhi. "The Fluorine Detectives." *Scientific American*, February
13, 2019. https://www.scientificamerican.com/article/the-fluorine
-detectives/.
Roman, Jesse. "The PFAS Problem." *National Fire Protection Asso-
ciation Journal*, July 22, 2022. https://www.nfpa.org/News-and-
Research/Publications -and-media/NFPA-Journal/2022/Fall -2022
/Features/Foam/Foam-Sidebar.

The Environmental Working Group also maintains a digital archive of primary source documents, including memos, studies, and reports, that help to make transparent the historical points at which companies and government agencies knew that PFAS were toxic to humans and the environment. I am grateful especially to Scott Faber and Jared Hayes for their work on two of the EWG's time lines: "For Decades, the Department of Defense Knew Firefighting Foams with 'Forever Chemicals' Were Dangerous but Continued Their Use," March 6, 2022 (https:// www.ewg.org/research/decades-department-defense-knew-firefighting -foams-forever-chemicals-were-dangerous), and "For Decades, Polluters Knew PFAS Chemicals Were Dangerous but Hid Risks from Public,"

August 29, 2019 (https://www.ewg.org/research/decades-polluters-knew-pfas-chemicals-were-dangerous-hid-risks-public). These sources gave me access to military reports, industry memos and correspondence, and studies that helped to recontextualize my father's biography.

The following selections were especially crucial in chapters 7 and 8:

Crawford, G. H., to L. C. Krogh, J. D. Lazerte, R. A. Newmark, and J. A. Pendergrass. "Record of a Telephone Call—August 14, 1975." August 20, 1975. https://static.ewg.org/reports/2019/pfa-timeline/1975_Dr-Guy.pdf?_gl=1*7irgyd*_gcl_au*OTAxOTg4OTkwLjE2ODk5NzQwODE.*_ga*MjQ4Njg1MTguMTY4OTk3NDA4MQ..*_ga_CS21GC49KT*MTY4OTk3NDA4MS4xLjEuMTY4OTk3NTYyNy44w LjAuMA..&_ga=2.199613806.1130290523.1689974081-24868518.1689974081.

Kroop, Ronald H., and Joseph E. Martin. "Treatability of Aqueous Film-Forming Foams Used for Fire Fighting." Technical Report AFWL-TR-73-279. Greene County, OH: Air Force Weapons Laboratory, November 23, 1973. https://static.ewg.org/reports/2019/pfas-dod-timeline/1973_Kroop-Report.pdf?_gl=1*1v9e8lo*_gcl_aw*R0NMLjE2OTIyMjMwNzQuRUFJYUlRb2JDaE1JcHBuQ3RKT GlnQU1WOGZLVUNSMjZfUV9QRUFBWUFTQUJFZ0t5Y3Z3 EX0J 3RQ..*_gcl_au*MTY0NjMyODUuMTY4ODQwNDUwMA..*_ga*NzAzMTY4MTYyLjE2ODg0MDQ1MDA.*_ga_CS21GC49KT*MTY5MjU1NTE2My4xMy4wLjE2O TI1NTUxNjMuMC4wLjA.&_ga=2.72516115.1663409824.1692549430-703168162.1688404500&_gac=1.44894992.1692223076.EAIaIQobChMIppnCtJLigAMV8fKUCR26_Q_PEAAYASABEgKycvD_BwE.

Lefebvre, Edward L., and Roger C. Inman. "Biodegradability and Toxicity of Light Water® FC206, Aqueous Film Forming Foam." Subject Report EHL(K) 74-26. Kelly, TX: US Air Force Environmental Health Laboratory, November 1974. https://static.ewg.org/reports/2019/pfas-dod-timeline/1974_Biodegradability-and-Toxicity-of-ANSUL-K74-100-Aqueous-Film-Forming-Foam.pdf?_ga=2.71326171.959248329.1648422523-2123137255.1639662520.

Mandel, Jack S., to Larry R. Zobel. April 6, 1989. https://static.ewg.org/reports/2019/pfa-timeline/1989_Cancer-Rates.pdf?_gl=1*1052wrj*_gcl_au*OTAxOTg4OTkwLjE2ODk5Nz QwODE.*_ga*MjQ4Njg1MTguMTY4OTk3NDA4MQ..*_ga_CS2

1GC49KT*MTY4OTk3NDA4MS4xLjEuMTY4OTk3NTY2N
S4wLjAuMA..&_ga=2.199094511.1130290523.1689974081-
24868518.1689974081.

Salazar, S. M. "Toxicity of Aqueous Filmforming Foams to Marine
Organisms: Literature Review and Biological Assessment." Technical
Document 825. Environmental Sciences Division, Naval Facilities
Engineering Command (Code 032), Marine Environmental Quality Assessment Program. San Diego, CA: Naval Ocean Systems
Center, July 1985. https://static.ewg.org/reports/2019/pfas-dod-
timeline/1985_Navy-Study.pdf?_gl=1*4gblso*_gcl_aw*R0NML
jE2OTIyMjMwNzQuRUFJYUlRb2JDaE1JcHBuQ3RKTGlnQ
U1WOGZLVUNSMjZfUV9QRUFBWUFTQUJFZ0t5Y3ZE
X0J 3RQ..*_gcl_au*MTY0NjMyODUuMTY4ODQwNDUwMA
..*_ga*NzAzMTY4MTYyLjE2ODg0MDQ1MDA
.*_ga_CS21GC49KT*MTY5MjU0OTQzMC4xMi4xLjE2O
TI1NTE2ODAuMC4wLjA.&_ga=2.132350350.1663409824
.1692549430-703168162.1688404500&_gac=1.142336646
.1692223076.EAIaIQobChMIppnCtJLigAMV8fKUCR26
_Q_PEAAYASABEgKycvD_BwE.

Schoenig, Gerald. "Report to Minnesota Mining and Man-
ufacturing Company: Acute Oral Toxicity Studies on
Two Materials." ABT A4414. Northbrook, IL: Industrial Bio-Test Laboratories, September 21, 1966. https://
static.ewg.org/reports/2019/pfa-timeline/1966_Acute-OralTox
.pdf?_gl=1*16jtvkr*_gcl_au*OTAxOTg4OTkwLjE2ODk5NzQwODE
.*_ga*MjQ4Njg1MTguMTY4OTk3NDA4MQ..*_ga_CS21GC49KT
*MTY4OTk3NDA4MS4xLjEuMTY4OTk3NTM4My4wLjA
uMA..&_ga=2.27597436.1130290523.1689974081-24868518
.1689974081.

Taylor, David W. "Candidate Environmental Impact Statement: Dis-
charging Aqueous Film Forming Foam (AFFF) to Harbor Waters
during Tests of Machinery Space Fire-Fighting Foam Systems aboard
US Navy Ships." Bethesda, MD: Naval Ship Research and Development, January 1978. https://static.ewg.org/reports/2019/pfas-dod-
timeline/1978_Navy-Study.pdf?_gl=1*cxht1v*_gcl_aw*R0NMLj
E2OTIyMjMwNzQuRUFJYUlRb2JDaE1JcHBuQ3RKTGlnQU
1WOGZLVUNSMjZfUV9QRUFBWUFTQUJFZ0t5Y3ZEX0J
3RQ..*_gcl_au*MTY0NjMyODUuMTY4ODQwNDUwMA..*_ga*
NzAzMTY4MTYyLjE2ODg0MDQ1MDA.*_ga_CS21GC49KT
*MTY5MjU1NTE2My4xMy4xLjE2OTI1NTU3MDcuMC4w
LjA.&_ga=2.101728513.1663409824.1692549430-703168162

.1688404500&_gac =1.238889652.1692223076.EAIaIQobChMIpp
nCtJLigAMV8fKUCR26_Q_PEAAYASABEgKycvD_BwE.
Zagursky, Gregory, William H. Jefferson III, and Robert D. Binovi.
"Biological Analysis of Three Ponds at Peterson AFB, Colorado
Springs CO: Final Report." Brooks Air Force Base, TX: Air Force
Occupational and Environmental Health Laboratory, Human Systems
Division, November 1989. https://static.ewg.org/reports/2019/pfas-
dod-timeline/1989_Airforce-Study.pdf?_gl=1*1ejbjc2*_gcl_aw*R0N
MLjE2OTIyMjMwNzQuRUFJYUlRb2JDaE1JcHBuQ3RKTGlnQ
U1WOGZLVUNSMjZfUV9QRUFBWUFTQUJFZ0t5Y3ZEX0J
3RQ..*_gcl_au*MTY0NjMyODUuMTY4ODQwNDUwMA..*_ga*
NzAzMTY4MTYyLjE2ODg0MDQ1MDA.*_ga_CS21GC49KT
*MTY5MjU1NTE2My4xMy4xLjE2OTI1NTY1MTEuM
C4wLjA.&_ga=2.107621890.1663409824.1692549430-
703168162.1688404500&_gac=1.254027324.1692223076
.EAIaIQobChMIppnCtJLigAMV8fKUCR26
_Q_PEAAYASABEgKycvD_BwE.

The reportage of the investigative journalist Sharon Lerner at *The Intercept* played a fundamental role in guiding me through the history of industrial pollution from PFAS in the last ten years; in particular, I found myself returning to her "Bad Chemistry" series and selected readings: "3M Knew about PFOA and PFOS Decades Ago, Internal Documents Show"; "Did the White House Stop the EPA from Regulating PFAS?"; "Lawsuits Charge That 3M Knew about the Dangers of Its Chemicals"; and "People Exposed to PFAS Criticize EPA Action Plan as Too Little, Too Late" (https://theintercept.com/series/bad-chemistry/).

Additional key sources include Patricia Kime's 2020 articles for *Military Times*, specifically "Dozens More Military Bases Have Suspected 'Forever Chemical' Contamination" (April 3) (https://www.military.com/daily-news/2020/04/03/dozens-more-military-bases-have-suspected-forever-chemical-contamination.html) and "Military Firefighters Say DoD Isn't Moving Fast Enough to Protect Them from Toxic Chemicals" (July 2) (https://www.military.com/daily-news/2020/07/02/military-firefighters-say-dod-isnt-moving-fast-enough-protect-them-toxic-chemicals.html); Jessica A. Knoblauch's coverage for Earth Justice in her November 18, 2019 piece "Toxic Taps" (https://earthjustice.org/feature/pfas-toxic-taps); and Annie Sneed's *Scientific American* article published January 22, 2021, "Forever Chemicals Are Widespread in US Drinking Water" (https://www.scientificamerican.com/article/forever-chemicals-are-widespread-in-u-s-drinking-water/).

As discussed in chapter 13, a pivotal point in my understanding of PFAS exposure in Texas and its broader troubling political context was reading the June 19, 2019, *Texas Observer* article by Christopher Collins, "Nearly 500,000 Texans Live in Communities with Contaminated Groundwater. Lawmakers Aren't Doing Much about It" (https://www.texasobserver.org/nearly-500000-texans-live-in-communities-with-contaminated-groundwater-their-lawmakers-arent-doing-much-about-it/). Chapter 13 was further informed by Annie Snider's *Politico* article of May 14, 2018, "White House, EPA Headed Off Chemical Pollution Study" (https://www.politico.com/story/2018/05/14/emails-white-house-interfered-with-science-study-536950); the article by Abrahm Lustgarten, Lisa Song, and Talia Buford published June 20, 2018, by *ProPublica*, "Suppressed Study: The EPA Underestimated Dangers of Widespread Chemicals" (https://www.propublica.org/article/suppressed-study-the-epa-underestimated-dangers-of-widespread-chemicals); and Kase Wilbanks's local coverage of contamination monitoring in Lubbock for KCBD, "EPA Actions on PFAS Chemicals Could Impact Cleanup of Reese Area Contamination," October 20, 2021 (https://www.kcbd.com/2021/10/20/epa-actions-pfas-chemicals-could-impact-cleanup-reese-area-contamination/).

Though their work did not directly speak to specific chapters, I would be remiss were I not to acknowledge the tremendous influence on this book of the environmental journalist Amal Ahmed, who has covered PFAS and fracking in Texas and who generously pointed me toward the investigative reportage of Ev Crunden, who has expertly reported on PFAS for years.

Key reports, studies, and resources that familiarized me with the health impacts of PFAS include:

Agency for Toxic Substances and Disease Registry. "PFAS: An Overview of the Science and Guidance for Clinicians on Per- and Polyfluoroalkyl Substances (PFAS)." Centers for Disease Control and Prevention, 2019. https://www.atsdr.cdc.gov/pfas/docs/clinical-guidance-12-20-2019.pdf.

Backe, Will J., Thomas C. Day, and Jennifer A. Field. "Zwitterionic, Cationic, and Anionic Fluorinated Chemicals in Aqueous Film Forming Foam Formulations and Groundwater from US Military Bases by Nonaqueous Large-Volume Injection HPLC-MS/MS." *Environmental Science and Technology* 47 (10, 2013): 5226–5234. https://doi.org/10.1021/es3034999.

Barzen-Hanson, Krista A., Simon C. Roberts, Sarah Choyke, Karl Oetjen, Alan McAlees, Nicole Riddell, et al. "Discovery of 40

Classes of Per- and Polyfluoroalkyl Substances in Historical Aqueous Film-Forming Foams (AFFFs) and AFFF-Impacted Groundwater." *Environmental Science and Technology* 51 (4, 2017): 2047–2057. DOI: 10.1021/acs.est.6b05843.

Blum, Arlene, Simona A. Balan, Martin Scheringer, Xenia Trier, Gretta Goldenman, et al. "The Madrid Statement on Poly- and Perfluoroalkyl Substances (PFASs)." *Environmental Health Perspectives* 123 (5, 2015): A107–A111. DOI: 10.1289/ehp.1509934.

National Institute of Environmental Health Sciences. "Perfluoroalkyl and Polyfluoroalkyl Substances (PFAS)." Last reviewed August 17, 2023. https://www.niehs.nih.gov/health/topics/agents/pfc/index.cfm.

Olsen, Geary W., Jean M. Burris, David J. Ehresman, John W. Froehlich, Andrew M. Seacat, John L. Butenhoff, and Larry R. Zobel. "Half-Life of Serum Elimination of Perfluorooctanesulfonate, Perfluorohexanesulfonate, and Perfluorooctanoate in Retired Fluorochemical Production Workers." *Environmental Health Perspectives* 115 (9, 2007): 1298–1305. DOI: 10.1289/ehp.10009.

Rhee, Jongeun, Kathryn H. Barry, Wen-Yi Huang, Joshua N. Sampson, Jonathan N. Hofmann, Debra T. Silverman, et al. "A Prospective Nested Case-Control Study of Serum Concentrations of Per- and Polyfluoroalkyl Substances and Aggressive Prostate Cancer Risk." *Environmental Research* 228 (July 2023). DOI: 10.1016/j.envres.2023.115718.

US Environmental Protection Agency. "PFAS Explained." Last updated October 25, 2023. https://www.epa.gov/pfas/pfas-explained.

Significant reports that informed my understanding of monitoring for PFAS contamination in Lubbock, Texas (see chapter 19) include:

Agency for Toxic Substances and Disease Registry. "Lubbock County, Texas: Per- and Polyfluoroalkyl Substances (PFAS) Exposure Assessment: Report." Agency for Toxic Substances and Disease Registry, Centers for Disease Control and Prevention, May 2022. https://www.atsdr.cdc.gov/pfas/docs/Lubbock-County-Report-508.pdf.

Agency for Toxic Substances and Disease Registry. "Lubbock County, Texas: PFAS Exposure Assessment Community Summary: Report." Centers for Disease Control and Prevention, May 2022. https://www.atsdr.cdc.gov/pfas/docs/PFAS-EA-Lubbock-County-Community-Summary-H.pdf.

Agency for Toxic Substances and Disease Registry. "Lubbock County, Texas: CDC/ATSDR PFAS Exposure Assessment Community Level

Results: Report." Centers for Disease Control and Prevention, May 2022. https://www.atsdr.cdc.gov/pfas/docs/factsheet/E-Community-Level-Results-Lubbock-County-Texas-H.pdf.

Sources referenced in the epilogue include:

Environmental Working Group. "EPA Proposes Bold New Limits for Attacking 'Forever Chemicals' in Drinking Water." March 14, 2023. https://www.ewg.org/news-insights/news-release/2023/03/epa-proposes-bold-new-limits-tackling-forever-chemicals-drinking?gad=1&gclid=CjwKCAjwloynBhBbEiwAGY25dMFy-UukwJ2ObqRNpUMfN_jpJ_ZhnSbD5plVVFZAbm8887s2Ar3NohoCwpwQAvD_BwE.
Kluger, Jeffrey. "'Forever Chemical' Lawsuit Could Ultimately Eclipse the Big Tobacco Settlement." *Time*, July 2023. https://time.com/6292482/legal-liability-pfas-chemicals-lawsuit.
Minnesota Attorney General's Office. Rich Purdy to 3M, March 28, 1999. https://www.ag.state.mn.us/Office/Cases/3M/docs/PTX/PTX1001.pdf.
Office of the Attorney General of Guam. "Guam PFAS Fact Sheet." No date. https://oagguam.org/wp-content/uploads/2019/09/PFAS-Fact-Sheet-1.pdf.
Rich, Nathaniel. "The Lawyer Who Became DuPont's Worst Nightmare." *New York Times*, January 6, 2016. https://www.nytimes.com/2016/01/10/magazine/the-lawyer-who-became-duponts-worst-nightmare.html.
Tangel, Andrew. "3M Agrees to Pay $850 Million to Settle Minnesota Water Contamination Lawsuit." *Wall Street Journal*, February 20, 2018. https://www.wsj.com/articles/3m-agrees-to-pay-850-million-to-settle-minnesota-water-contamination-lawsuit-1519167944.

As I relate in chapter 13, my requests for interviews with and information from the Air Force officers who were involved with monitoring PFAS contamination and who might have had knowledge of the historical use of AFFFs in Lubbock were denied or ignored. I was directed by CDC agents working for region 6 (the CDC/ATSDR-designated region for Lubbock) to contact Air Force representatives when I reached out with questions about the likelihood that military personnel on active duty in the 1980s were exposed at Reese Air Force Base.

But there were individuals who did agree to interviews. Dr. Mark

Purdue, a senior investigator in the Occupational and Environmental Epidemiology Branch of the National Cancer Institute for the National Institutes of Health, contributed to the recent study "A Prospective Nested Case-Control Study . . .," cited earlier. He also made a crucial intervention by helping me lean into some of the most difficult questions I had yet to ask in my research, questions that remain unanswered. I am indebted to Dr. Purdue for his time and expertise in allowing me to explore the questions that appear in chapter 21. They helped to make some of the book's most important implications explicit.

In that same chapter (21), I reference the person who was the first to direct me to PFAS. I contacted her early in the drafting process, when I was reaching out to former classmates of my father's to interview them about what he was like in high school. She didn't know he had died, but as I told her about the number of people in my family who had since been diagnosed with cancer, she said that I had to look into the water. Then she described what she knew of PFAS through, unfortunately, her own experiences. There is no overstating the impact of our conversations and relationship on my life and work. She is involved in her own actions for environmental justice, and I am protecting her anonymity here. But she knows that I am grateful, and I am in her corner.

Many of my own personal doctors have walked through my family's complicated medical history with me, including a handful of geneticists, and I have thanked them personally along the way. Though I expressed my gratitude to my Aunt Lori in my acknowledgments, I won't shy from thanking her again here, especially for forwarding me her genetic reports, and by extension thanking the medical professionals who have attempted to help us Blackburns figure out where the porous, nearly nonexistent line falls between our genes and our environs.